The WoodenBoat Series

10 Wooden Boats You Can Build

10

Wooden Boats You Can Build

FOR SAIL, MOTOR, PADDLE AND OAR

Series Editor, Peter H. Spectre

Text design by Richard Gorski and Nina Kennedy; cover design
by Richard Gorski; cover photograph by Chris Kulczycki

Published by WoodenBoat Publications
P.O. Box 78, Naskeag Road
Brooklin, ME 04616-0078

Introduction

The desire to build a boat ... begins as a little cloud on a serene horizon. It ends by covering the whole sky so that you can think of nothing else.

— Arthur Ransome

Who with an interest in things nautical hasn't been gripped by the monomaniacal passion to build a boat? As my friend George Putz used to say, those who haven't are either psycho-emotionally wrecks or their nautical interest isn't as serious as they thought it was. (There are those — usually cynical, non-nautically inclined spouses — who see the mania to build a boat as itself an indication of psycho-emotional wreckage, but we won't get into that....)

Some people with a desire to build a boat fight off the notion. They convince themselves that they don't have the skills to do the work properly, or lack the necessary building space, or don't have the tools or the money, or can't find the plans for the boat of their dreams. Others surrender to the imperative and get on with the job. They know full well that given the desire the skills can be learned; the building space can be found; so, too, the tools, the money, and the plans.

The truth of the matter is that anyone with a reasonable facility with their hands can build a boat. This is because all wooden boats are built in pieces. If you can make one piece, you can make another. If you can make another, you can make yet another. If you take the project step by step, concentrating on one piece at a time and paying attention to how each piece relates to the others, you will eventually have a seemingly complex whole constructed of several simple parts.

The keys to the building of a proper wooden boat are a carefully considered construction plan, good materials, and good workmanship. These are manifest in this book, which describes the building of ten boats: the plans to follow, the materials to use, and the skills and methods necessary to make each project a success.

The boats herein range from the most elementary to the more advanced, which means there is something for everyone in this book. The less skilled or the less financially flush can concentrate on a simple boat. Those with a higher level of skill and more money can move along to something more complex. The truly ambitious can start from the beginning and go to the end, and gain two essentials from the experience: They will have a variety of boat types to enjoy, and will have gained practical knowledge of the major methods of building wooden boats today.

How broad is the selection? Here is what we have, from the simple to the complex:

The Caddo Lake bateau, a basic flat-bottom paddling pirogue that uses the most elementary construction method and does away with complex plans — a boat that can be built for minimal cost in a couple of days.

A Norwegian lapstrake pram that can be built in two variations and offers great latitude for those who prefer to adjust the design by eye as they go along.

A flat-bottomed skiff that is elegant, practical, and lightweight, and offers what amounts to a crash course in traditional construction as practiced by builders from an earlier age.

The Cartopper, a lightweight rowing-sailing skiff constructed without a building jig — cut out the plywood parts, stitch them together with temporary wires, join the seams with fiberglass tape set in epoxy or polyester putty, and you're in business.

The Cape Charles sea kayak, also stitch-and-tape construction, a boat that has everything you would expect in a factory version and then some; a kayak that is easy to build and one you will be proud to say you built.

The Wee Lassie double-paddle canoe, strip-planked on a building jig, as light as they come, as handsome as a small boat has ever been, as versatile as anything like it can be.

The Gull, a round-bottom rowboat that is built with the almost magical Constant Camber method — custom make your own curved plywood panels using a form and a vacuum bag, saw the panels to shape, join them along the keel, fit gunwales and seats, and go rowing.

The sailing-paddling canoe Piccolo, traditional lapstrake construction, finely fitted, stylishly finished, rigged like a thoroughbred, a challenge in every shape and form — the boat that will make you the talk of the town.

The Biscayne Bay 14, plywood married with traditional construction methods; speedy, maneuverable, agile — the feel of a sports car on the water.

The Downeaster 18, an outboard-powered runabout designed for speed and seaworthiness in coastal waters, a project for the builder who wants to test his abilities in the workshop and then explore the waterways in a handsome, classic craft with substance.

The beauty of these boats is that the construction bugs have been worked out of them. Every one was built before the plans and instructions were published. Every one has been built by people with all levels of skill, from rank amateurs working in their basements to professionals working in the finest boatshops. Many, like the Cartopper, the Cape Charles, and the Wee Lassie, have been built by the hundreds and have tasted the waters all over the world.

This is a book for doers, not dreamers. Select a boat, get your tools and materials in order, find a building space, follow the step-by-step instructions, and keep in mind the immortal words of R.D. "Pete" Culler:

"Any man who wants to can produce a good boat. It takes some study, some practice, and, of course, experience. The experience starts coming the minute you begin, and not one jot before."

— Peter H. Spectre
Camden, Maine

About the Authors

ROBERT H. BAKER, noted for the refined simplicity of his work, designed, built, and restored boats in Westport, Massachusetts. He passed away in 1983.

MAYNARD BRAY, former shipyard supervisor at Mystic Seaport Museum, is the author of numerous articles and books on wooden boat building and repair. He lives in Brooklin, Maine.

JIM BROWN is a designer and long-distance sailor of cruising multihulls. He has a boatshop in North, Virginia.

ARNE EMIL CHRISTENSEN, JR., is one of Norway's foremost maritime historians and an expert on Scandinavian boat design and construction. He lives in Oslo.

JIM CONRAD is the director of Oral History, East Texas State University Library, Commerce, Texas.

CHRIS KULCZYCKI designs, builds, and paddles kayaks; he has a professional boatshop and kit manufacturing facility in Arlington, Virginia.

ERIC DOW, who has taught boatbuilding and model making for several years, has his own professional boatshop in Brooklin, Maine.

GRAHAM ERO taught at the Sound School, New Haven, Connecticut, and now has his own professional boatshop in Still Pond, Maryland.

HENRY "MAC" MCCARTHY has been a paddler for most of his life and a teacher of boatbuilding for the last five years. He has his own professional boatshop in Sarasota, Florida.

JOHN MARPLES, who has made several ocean passages, operates a yacht design company in Port Orchard, Washington.

RICHARD NEWICK, known for his record-breaking multihulls, designs yachts in Kittery Point, Maine.

HAROLD H. "DYNAMITE" PAYSON, author, boatbuilder, and model-maker, has his own boatshop in South Thomaston, Maine.

THAD SITTON is an oral historian in Austin, Texas.

Table of Contents

The Caddo Lake Bateau

—————— by James H. Conrad and Thad Sitton ——————

All my life, I've fiddled with boats. I expect I've built 180 to 200, all wood boats. I like wood. A wood boat is much better for one's health than a metal one. The vibration of a metal boat has a very adverse effect on a person's central nervous system — it causes headaches and high blood pressure. Mother lived to be over 90 years old, and she rode only in wood boats. A wood boat absorbs vibration and soothes one's nerves. Why, an outboard will last two or three times longer on a wood boat than on a metal one. In hot weather, the shade under a wood boat is cool. A metal boat is hot and drives away fish. Besides, if a metal boat fills with water, it sinks. A wood boat floats.

But boatbuilding is not like piling up some brush. If you don't do it right, you wind up with something crooked.

-Wyatt A. Moore

On Taylor Island, Texas, at nine o'clock Saturday morning, June 28, 1983, Mr. Wyatt A. Moore and Mr. Paul Ray Martin started with two shaped mulberry stems, four 16-foot cypress boards, assorted pieces of cypress planking, a sack full of nails, some silicone caulking compound, and a crude plan sketched on a scrap of plywood. By three o'clock that afternoon the boat was more or less completed, except for some minor finishing work, sanding, and painting. The following day, at about noon, after a special treatment to seal and waterproof the hull, Moore officially launched and successfully tested the craft on the waters of Caddo Lake.

As Moore summed up the construction process,

We started on it one Saturday morning and rode in it on Sunday. We built the boat from scratch—there was nothing but lumber, just lumber lying out there. Wasn't anything but lumber sawed up.

The boat design is that of Mr. Moore, then 83, of Karnack, Texas, who throughout his long life had built wooden boats for use on Caddo Lake, mostly types referred to locally as "paddle skiffs" and "bateaux." These types are usually called "esquifs" and "planked pirogues" in Acadian Louisiana. Moore learned his boatbuilding techniques from Frank Galbraith, a near-legendary Caddo Lake boatbuilder. Perhaps the last living builder of this type of boat in the Caddo Lake area, Moore was ably assisted in the construction by Paul Ray Martin, a skilled carpenter and builder of fiberglass kayaks.

In its heyday, the Caddo Lake bateau was noted for speed, maneuverability, and seaworthiness. The functional, canoe-like craft was widely used by fishermen, hunters, fishing guides, and bootleggers before the introduction of aluminum and fiberglass motorboats after World War II.

Moore recalls using his bateaux for a variety of activities, legal and illegal:

Once, nearly everybody felt that one of those little fishing boats was a necessity, not a luxury. You couldn't go out there and do a hard day's fishing in a big, old hard-to-paddle boat, and get up in here, there, and yonder, and cover lots of territory, and keep the fish alive. The old-time fishing boat was a tool of the trade, and was designed to serve that purpose. There was a couple here [on Taylor Island] who each had a bateau. They fished until they died.

I used to use one of 'em a good deal in the fall of the year. I would take a Buelspinner on a cane pole and troll the edge of the timber, hunt the squirrels out over the water; I'd fish in combination with it, and maybe kill a duck. I'd come in with ducks, squirrels, and a few fish, every day. One day, I hauled a full-grown deer from up the creek in one of my bateaux. And during the seven or eight years I almost exclusively made whiskey, I had a bateau I had carried 800 pounds of whiskey in. I knew they couldn't outpaddle me in a bateau, and I could go places where they couldn't go. Here, our method was mostly to put a platform out over the water in Caddo Lake in thickets where only a small canoe-like boat could get into, and run five or six barrels of mash. I never did plow one of Jim Ferguson's mules, but some of my friends told me that they thought I would finally make it. But I didn't quite.

Origins of the Bateau

In many ways this particular "folk boat" seems unique to the Caddo Lake area, perhaps evolving from the planked pirogue [pronounced "peer-oh"] of southern Louisiana.

William B. Knipmeyer, in his classic study, *Folk Boats of Eastern French Louisiana*, identified six kinds of Acadian folk boats. These were: dugout pirogue, planked pirogue, chaland, esquif, flatboat, and bateau. The Acadian "bateau," a large, flat-bottomed rowing boat with blunt bow and stern, is a very different craft from Moore's creation. Instead, his boat seems a special Caddo Lake variant of the planked pirogue, perhaps most closely resembling the planked pirogues of the Atchafalaya Basin. Describing the latter craft, Knipmeyer noted, "In the

Atchafalaya Basin, plank pirogues are smallest and have the most sheer. Generally they have a coaming about 2 inches wide at the waist, which diminishes to nothing toward the bow and stern. Often they are equipped with fish wells, which are made by placing two boards about 2 feet apart across the waist of the boat. Holes are bored in the bottom of the boat and closed with pegs." As will be shown, the perforated fish box/bait well is a striking feature of Moore's Caddo Lake bateau.

The planked pirogue, perhaps the direct ancestor of the Caddo bateau, had developed around 1900 in southeast Louisiana from the modern dugout pirogue, which was hewn from a single cypress log. As Knipmeyer observed, "The remarkable similarity between the dugout and the plank pirogue in form, size, use, and associated equipment makes it clear that the former was the inspiration for the latter. The time of the plank pirogue's arrival coincides with the expansion of cypress lumbering activities, which created new uses and a greater need for pirogues. It seems certain that these new interests did not invent the plank pirogue, but were undoubtedly responsible for making it more possible and spreading its use."

The modern form of the Acadian dugout pirogue, the immediate ancestor of the planked pirogue, had itself evolved from an earlier and larger variety of Acadian dugout. This large pirogue had been in wide use all across the southeastern United States, and derived in turn from aboriginal forms of the dugout. Native Americans used the bark canoe in the North, bull boats in the West, dugouts on the West Coast, and the ancestral pirogue dugout in the Southeast.

So, in both form and function, the Caddo bateau that Wyatt Moore and Paul Ray Martin assembled in the spring of 1983 seems a lineal descendant of the ancient Indian dugouts described by early French and British explorers in the Southeast. The intervening stages of "larger 19th-century dugout pirogue" and "modern dugout pirogue" may or may not have been present at Caddo Lake, but they were certainly present in Acadian Louisiana. Moore's boat springs from a long tradition.

The pattern for this particular form of the Caddo Lake version of the planked pirogue was taken from a surviving boat built by master builder Frank Galbraith. Galbraith lived with Moore for several years in the 1920s and strongly influenced Moore's boat designs and construction techniques. Galbraith, according to Moore, was "the Cadillac of the industry":

Galbraith's tombstone has written on it, "A builder of

fine boats." He was a marvelous man with tools. If he wanted to make something to do something with, he'd just whittle it out and make it. He could almost look at a place he wanted to put a piece of timber and saw it to fit. He'd saw it a little bit long to start with, and then he'd put it down in there and scribe it, mark on either side of it, and then he'd saw it out. He said he never used a rule much; he could guess it better. But he could twist that wood around, and do a marvelous job of working! He was a very conscientious worker who wouldn't put a piece of poor material in a boat. He said there was no use in wasting that much labor with poor material. He wouldn't use anything but the best red-heart cypress lumber.

Knipmeyer mentions that the terms "two-plank pirogue," referring to the number of planks in the bottom, were in general use in Acadian Louisiana at the time of his 1950 study. These terms were both descriptive and expressive of value. A two-plank pirogue has two planks in its bottom, a three-plank pirogue has three; and the fewer seams, the better. The fewer seams in the bottom, the fewer places there were to leak. All other things being equal, a two-plank pirogue was more trouble-free and more valuable than a three-plank model. Moore doesn't use these terms, though he clearly shares the opinion that the fewer planks in the bottom, the better the boat.

Using the Bateau

Moore recommends a fairly short paddle, about 4 feet 8 inches in length, for the Caddo Lake bateau. In a technique very different from the Cajun pirogue-men studied by Knipmeyer, who used longer paddles and J-strokes from one side only, Moore paddles on both sides of the boat, changing hands with great speed and dexterity to keep the boat tracking in a straight line, or to execute a turn. While fishing, Moore sculls one-handed with the paddle, thus freeing the other hand to control the fishing rod. When jump-shooting (or "bushwhacking") ducks, he devised a special two-paddle strategy. One paddle would be in hand, another carried in the boat. Upon jumping a duck, he drops the paddle-in-hand, usually into the water. Then, after grabbing his gun and shooting the duck, he uses the second paddle to retrieve both the downed duck and the first paddle. For the business of jump-shooting ducks in heavy timber, Moore contends that the split second saved by instantly dropping the paddle makes a significant difference.

The live box and minnow well, which are located just aft of amidships, have holes bored in their bottoms or sides so that they exchange water with lake or river to keep the fish alive. The weight of water in these areas is designed to balance with the weight of the paddler, who sits in an unusual position just forward of amidships. However, when the bateau is "dry," ballast must be added to the stern to trim the craft. As Moore tells it:

If you don't carry water in the live box, or some sort of ballast, the boat's stern will stick out of the water and will not be balanced properly in the water. If you move back toward the rear of the boat to balance it, you will be too far back to paddle good. I usually carry a good deal of ballast and put my seat forward so that I can paddle good.

As late as the 1950s, fishermen and hunters still used the bateaux, but their habit was to tow the bateau to the fishing or hunting grounds behind a motorboat, then anchor the motorboat and hunt or fish from the bateau. Today, Caddo Lake is mostly traveled by motor boats — some remarkably large, considering the maze-like nature of the Texas end of the lake, with its labyrinth of channels, numerous cypress "islands," and endless meadows of lily pads. The motorboats roar along the narrow and well-marked boat trails, or make short excursions into the nearby swamp, leaving vast portions of the area untraveled by man — unless the man should have a bateau!

The Caddo Lake bateau originally evolved to meet these special circumstances, and as a swamp boat it seems almost without parallel. With its narrow waterline, it paddles easily and with good speed. The boat's flat bottom and the paddler's low center of gravity ensure stability, and the rockered bottom means that the boat can be spun around almost as easily as a whitewater kayak. The shallow hull slides easily over water vegetation — a trait that can be fully appreciated only by someone who has actually tried to navigate in the frustrating world of the swamp, where the natural boundaries between land and water seem often to disappear, being replaced by a third element that has the characteristics of neither. On the occasional stretches of extensive open water that are also typical of Caddo Lake (the "lakes" within the lake), the upswept ends of the bateau allow it to ride over big waves instead of plunging wetly through them, and the flared sides repel waves coming in from abeam, making the boat remarkably seaworthy.

Moore and his bateau are still capable of venturing where few others could go. As he says, "The old-time fishing boat was a tool of the trade, and was designed to fit that purpose." For exploring the watery resources of the Caddo Lake swamplands, Moore's bateau works as well today as it ever did.

The Building Process

1

The first step in building the Caddo Lake bateau is to prepare the mulberry stems — the bow and stern pieces. Moore splits a short length of mulberry log into wedge-shaped sections with an axe and a sledgehammer. He uses a hatchet for roughing out and trimming, and a hand plane, bevel, and square for finishing and dressing off.

2

Martin and Moore consult the "blueprint" board, a piece of plywood with the basic dimensions of the boat on it. The bevels are also marked on the board for the bow and stern angles and for the bulkhead flare.

3

Moore considers selection of the two 16-foot cypress sideboards, the most crucial step in the building process. (He uses only good red-cypress heartwood from Louisiana.) He carefully inspects all four planks for size, shape, location of knotholes, and flexibility. The two chosen for sideboards should be about matched in flexibility; Moore bends the boards repeatedly to determine this.

3a

After cutting the bow and stern angles, picked up from the "blueprint," Moore does some fine-tuning of the sideboard's shape. (He works on the smaller of the two selected boards first, and will later use it as a pattern for the other sideboard.) "What you do is to take a little at both ends at the top, because the boards at the top are going to stick up and the sides are going to lean down, and if you don't take some off, the ends will stick up too high in proportion to the bottom. Sometimes you cut some out of the bottom, a little strip from the bottom, if the boards don't have a little swoop to them."

4

Moore and Martin nail the two sideboards to one of the stems, then bring the other ends of the sideboards together while their middles are held apart by a 3-foot divider board, placed there temporarily until the bulkhead is installed. The first bulkhead will largely determine the shape and curve of the board, and the decision about its dimensions is the second most critical point. The wider it is, the greater the carrying capacity of the boat. Likewise, the side angles of the bulkhead determine the flare of the boat's sides, once the flexible sideboards are pulled into conformity with it.

5 & 5a

For springing the sideboards so they fit the bulk-head, Moore clamps 4-foot planks to each sideboard near where the bulkhead will be, holding them in position with a rope. Nails are then driven into the sides to secure the bulkhead in place — cement-covered nails for the bulkheads and stems, because they are less likely to pull out under stress.

6

Placed bottom-up on leveled sawhorses, the boat has a string stretched down its center from one end to the other to check for symmetry. If things look okay, the most treacherous stages of bateau construction have been completed.

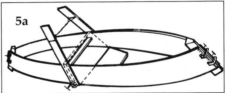

7
The middle bulkhead — the one between the minnow well and the live box — goes in next, followed by the second bulkhead, which forms the outer wall of the minnow well, and the third (shown here), which is the other wall of the live box.

8
Now for the remaining stem fastenings. "Nail the hell out of it," says Moore. He claims that only dense mulberry wood can take this many nails without splitting.

9
Leftover cypress from the bulkheads is used to make the 3-inch-wide cross supports or "knees" for the bottom. Their spacing is about 15 inches, and Moore advises, "Build the longer ones first. This way, if you botch up one, you can use it for a shorter crosspiece."

10

Moore has modified an old bread scraper for working down the sides so they'll be even with the rest of the bottom. A drawknife will not work, because one's knuckles would hit the cross supports.

11

All must be absolutely flush with the sideboards before the bottom can be put on the boat. It's quite an operation, and both Moore and Martin are at work here with hand planes.

12

Following a tradition established by legendary boatbuilder Frank Galbraith, Moore places the two bottom boards at a slight angle to the true center of the boat, assuring that the ends of the seam, because they'll be back from the stems, will always be in the water, and therefore will stay swelled up and watertight.

13

One bottom board is nailed in place, from the center outward, before the other board is cut. Although silicone sealant is used along the seams in this bateau, heavy green paint (along with the usual good fit) kept the water out in the old days — at least in some of the boats. Other builders used cotton twine for caulking, or would "pooch" (compress with a blunt tool) one side of the mating edge, then plane the remaining wood down to it. The bruised or "pooched" wood would swell abnormally and keep the seam from leaking. When Moore is ready to nail on the second and final bottom plank, he'll draw it tightly against the first plank with furniture clamps.

14

Turned right-side up for the first time, the boat is ready for finishing work — dressing down the sideboards and bulkheads, installation of decking, and paint, which is always dark green over the entire boat.

15

There is also a skeg, which Moore almost always puts on his boats so they'll keep running straight under the paddle. Skegs were put on rowing skiffs as well, but, according to Moore, "When we got to running motors on the skiffs, we quit putting skegs on the boats."

16

Moore likes to deck over the bow and stern and the outboard sides of the live box and minnow well. A latticework cover goes over the central part of the box and well to keep the fish from jumping out, and, of course, there are holes bored through the boat's bottom to let water flow into these compartments.

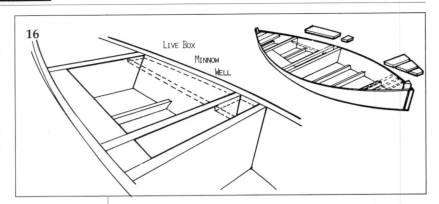

17

Stem guards — outer stems — of mulberry are added at each end of the boat for a finished appearance, and a hole is bored through the top of each stem for attaching a rope painter.

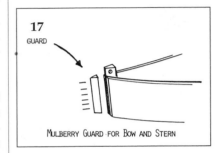

18

The optional seat, like the rest of the boat, is made from cypress boards. It is jam-fitted between the bulkhead and the cross-support and left unnailed so it can be moved to another location, if desired. "We would turn around and paddle backwards with the live box in front — just for traveling purposes — and then turn around and fish. We'd probably not paddle it back home backwards with the live box full of fish, because it wouldn't be practical."

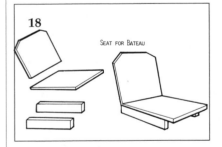

19

Wyatt Moore tries out his not-quite-finished Caddo Lake bateau. Bow and stern decking, stem guards, painting, and a latticework cover for the live box and minnow well will complete the boat.

A Norwegian Pram

by Arne Emil Christensen, Jr.
Photographs by Terje Olsen and drawings by Samuel F. Manning

Norwegian boatbuilding is best known for its sharp double-ended keel boats claiming a Viking ship ancestry. In fact, this tradition is so strong that all other types of boats are somewhat frowned upon by Norwegian maritime purists. In the days of sail and oar, nothing but keel boats were accepted in western and northern Norway, yet on the south coast, and in the Oslo Fjord area, where the double-enders were rather heavy and better suited to sailing than rowing, another type was in use. Here the pram was the favorite boat for small-scale fishing and all kinds of errands on the water.

Prams come in many shapes and sizes, though a pram of less than 8 feet in overall length tends to become inelegant, since its nose must be made large to give it enough lift forward. An ordinary pram gets unwieldy over 18 feet, but the shape has been used for small lighters and I have seen them over 30 feet long.

A pram may be built on a flat bottom, but on most of the Norwegian coast, prams are round-bottomed boats, built on a bottom plank instead of a keel. Prams have a large transom aft, and a smaller one, usually called the "nose," forward. On the coast, the most well-known types are the Holmsbupram and the Arendalspram, each named after important pram-building districts.

A pram is generally regarded as a pure rowboat, but they are occasionally rigged for sail. Before outboard motors became common, the transom usually had a semicircular cutout for a sculling oar. Like all transom-sterned boats, prams will take a small outboard motor if the owner is too lazy to row.

The pram has several advantages over other boats. It is easy to build, for professional and amateur alike; it is cheap; and its shape makes it an excellent yacht tender, as it tows well.

Traditional Norwegian boatbuilding does not require building plans at all. (The lines included with this chapter were taken off existing boats that were built without plans.) Norwegian boatbuilders usually build by hand and eye, and it might be a rewarding experience for you to try to do the same, just using these lines as inspiration and guidance. If you prefer, you can make a set of molds and build according to standard American lapstrake methods, but building by hand and eye is very fast, once mastered. No time is lost in lofting or spiling. On the other hand, the Norwegian method works best for building one type of boat only, as it takes time to train your eye properly to see the best run of a line in a particular type of boat.

Getting Started

To begin construction, make a building bed from a piece of scrap lumber, 4 inches by 4 inches or heavier, about 2 feet longer than the pram you intend to build. Raise it on sleepers about 1 foot from the floor for easy access to the bottom of the boat, and fasten it securely. For keelboat building, Norwegian boatbuilders usually use an overhead "shore-beam" set parallel to the building bed and just high enough to clear their heads. This is not necessary for pram building, but it can come in

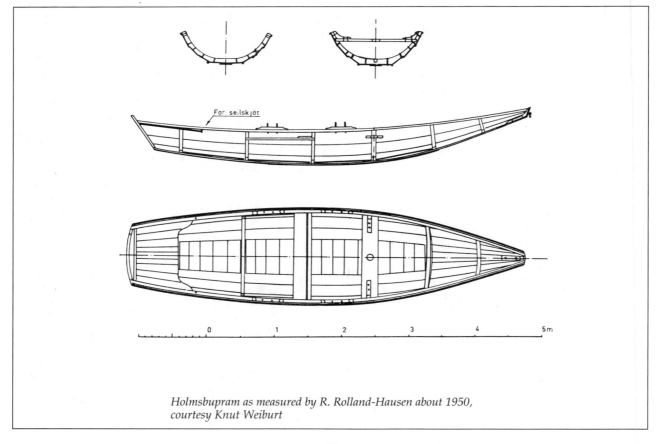

For seilskjöt

0   1   2   3   4   5m

Holmsbupram as measured by R. Rolland-Hausen about 1950, courtesy Knut Weiburt

handy if you have a means of rigging it up without too much work. Another possible setup is to use three sturdy blocks, one under the lowest part of the bottom board, and the other two at the ends.

Plane your planking stock to ½ inch thick for softwood or 7/16 inch for oak. Your stock should be flitch sawn (live edge) and fairly wide. Because of a pram's shape, planking stock may taper quite a lot, but it should be long enough for unscarfed use.

Select a good piece for the bottom board, stretch a chalkline or sooted string down the middle of the board, and snap in a centerline.

Now we face the small structural difference between Arendal and Holmsbu prams; this will govern your next step. As can be seen from the lines drawing, an Arendalspram is built in standard clinker or lapstrake fashion, with the garboard tucked under the bottom plank and the bottom plank beveled to give the garboard some deadrise. In a Holmsbupram, the garboards have no deadrise and are above the bottom plank, with a small filler piece added between the garboards under the transom and nose.

If you have decided on an Arendalspram, pick up the widths across the bottom plank at the nose, the transom, and the widest point, and lay them out on your plank. For a Holmsbupram, remember to add for a 1-inch overlap along both edges. When the plank is marked, spring a batten through the points, look closely at the curve for fairness, and adjust the batten if the curve looks bad. Tack or clamp the batten, and run in the line with a pencil or your knife point. Repeat on the other side.

Forget about the bandsaw. Now is the time to start practising axe work. Place the plank on a low bench or on a pair of stools, and hew as closely to the line as you dare, then plane to the line the rest of the way.

I remember with great pleasure the amazement of one of Lance Lee's apprentices at the Apprenticeshop in Bath, Maine, as he first tried his hand at pram building. With shining eyes he exclaimed, "I can get closer to the line with an axe than with the bandsaw!" When using an axe, study the run of the grain as you go to avoid splitting the wood. It might be a good idea to make a couple of trial runs on scrap lumber before starting on your real planking stock.

If you are building an Arendalspram, now is the time to mark and cut the bevel. Make yourself a drawing gauge like the one shown, and set out the lap width on the underside of the bottom plank.

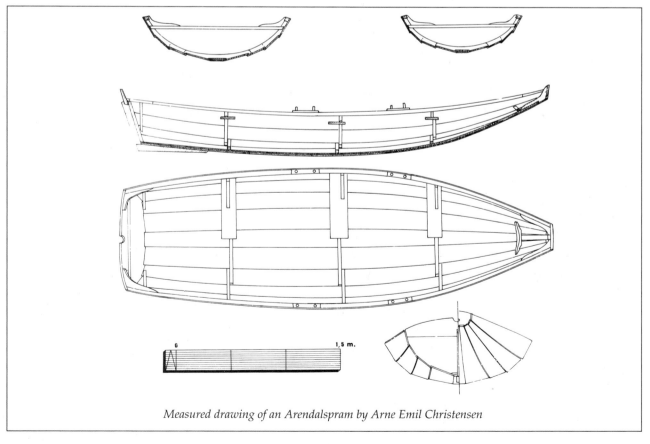

Measured drawing of an Arendalspram by Arne Emil Christensen

The bevel on the bottom plank is shaped with a drawknife.

The roughed-out bevel is finished with a hand plane

The planed plank is checked with a sliding bevel set to the appropriate mark on the bevel board.

Pick the correct bevel from the bevel board with the help of an adjustable bevel, then cut the bevel with an axe and a plane. The safest way to go about this is to cut a few short but correct notches, then fair to them with the plane. The bevel gets just a little steeper towards the nose; this is faired in by eye.

Now fit blocks to the building bed, corresponding to the height from the baseline to the underside of the bottom board, fore and aft, as shown in the drawing. The blocks must be sturdy and well fastened. Do not cut the bottom board to the right length yet; leave it somewhat longer at both ends. Spring the bottom board by nailing it to the building bed and the blocks, or by shoring it from the strongback in the middle and tacking it to the blocks.

If you're building a Holmsbupram, shape the garboards by tracing one edge from the bottom board, then lift a few measurements from the drawing and use the batten and axe again. Spring the garboards into place, then clamp and rivet. The bevel for the next strake can be cut at the bench before you spring the three-board bottom, or you can cut it on the boat after riveting the garboards. Again, the bevel is lifted from the bevel board.

The remainder of the building process does not differ much between the two types of prams. There are some minor details, but I'll describe them as we go along.

For the next strakes take a piece of planking stock and clamp it onto the bottom board (Arendalspram) or garboard (Holmsbupram) with as little overlap as you can get away with. All planking stock should be used with the side which was toward the heart of the log facing inward. When the piece is clamped, mark or score it by running a pencil or knife along the inside top edge of the strake already in place. Unclamp the plank, and cut it to the line with axe and plane. Run in a score with the marking gauge to show the lap width, reclamp the plank lower than the first time by the width of the lap, drill, and rivet. Repeat this process on the other side of the boat.

Both strakes, left long as with the bottom board, should now be firmly riveted in place, with their upper bark edges looking rather untidy. Now go back to the drawing and study the curve of that particular strake. With the help of measured plank widths taken from the drawing in a few places, and a batten, try to establish the right sheer on the top edge of one of the strakes. Clamp the batten, alternating on the inside and outside of the strake, and use your eye from various sighting points until you are happy with the run of the line. Strike the line and work down to it with axe, drawknife, spokeshave, and plane. Duplicate this on the other side; a few measurements will keep the boat from becoming lopsided. Then mark and cut the bevel on the strake for the next strake and go on like this strake after strake. As your routine gets better, it may be possible to forget about the batten and measurements and run in the top edge curves of the planks by eye.

The riveting sequence is this: drill, drive the rivet until the point is just through, place the rove (which is a force-fit on the rivet shank), drive the rivet home with a dolly, cut the point, and peen or rivet the cut-off end with your axe head held loosely to back up the rivet head. Correctly placed, the axe head will "answer" the hammer blows. Good riveting has a slight calypso rhythm. Many light blows make a better fastening than a few heavy ones. Keep an eye on your clamps as you rivet and tighten them up if they start to work loose.

With good planking stock, the easy lines of a pram require little shoring, but it may be necessary to shore unwilling strakes from the floor and, very rarely, from an overhead shore beam. If you have had to put in many shores, it is a good idea to stabilize the shell with a few floors before the planking is finished, otherwise you can finish planking before you start on the internal framing.

When you are ready to start framing, begin with a close inspection of the planked shell; make sure it is symmetrical and not lopsided or twisted, and correct all small defects you see by shoring to a better shape. Start framing in the middle of the boat and work toward the ends. If you can find natural crooks that will give you one-piece frames, wonderful. Otherwise, use two futtocks fitted to a center floor timber.

Before fitting the transom and nose, it is common to smooth the notches formed by the plank laps in order to avoid the small "triangles" of cross-grained wood that would otherwise have been necessary for a close fit. The transom of a Holmsbupram is flush, usually made from two planks closely butted and fastened together with nails driven obliquely, while the Arendalspram has a small "sternpiece" fitted to the outside of its

Above: The bottom board, garboards, and first side planks are in place.

Below: The hull is planked and the framing is underway. Here, a floor timber is being drilled before it is riveted.

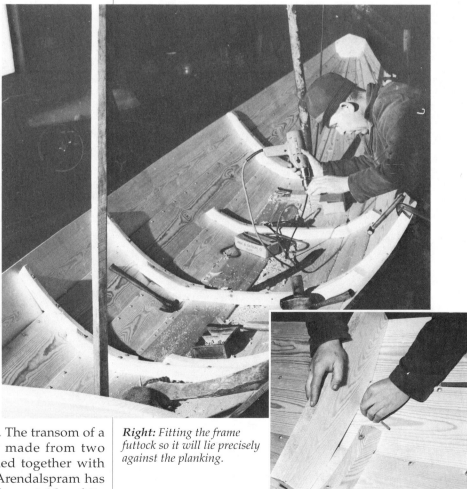

Right: Fitting the frame futtock so it will lie precisely against the planking.

lapped two-piece transom. When the nose and transom are in place, and fastened at the correct angle, cut off the excess planking projecting beyond and plane it flush.

Now the time has come to fit the inwales — steamed if necessary — and the knees and thwarts. Most prams have five knees: a rather substantial one securing the nose to the bottom, and a smaller one in each quarter against the inwale and transom or nose. Some prams, in addition, may have a knee between the transom and bottom board.

On most Arendalsprams, the space between the garboards is closed by a filler strake on the outside, and a small skeg is added aft. Holmsbuprams do not have this protective skeg, but they generally have laths tacked on the bottom for the protection of the laps.

In order to strengthen the transom, two futtocks are usually set obliquely against it. The aft seat is supported by these and the aft frame. Many prams have a bulkhead of thin boards on this frame so the space under the stern seat can be used for fishing gear, the coffeepot, etc.

Some boatbuilders leave the top of the sheerstrake rather rough and finish the sheer after the inwale is in place. Fit hardwood pads for the oars and bore through them for the tholepins with a tapering auger, if you can find one. Cut out the sculling notch, add a workboat finish to your fancy, launch, and row.

For downwind sailing, you can fit a small block of wood with a hole in it for a mast step under a suitable hole in the forward thwart, fit a small lugsail, and steer with an oar in the sculling notch. For more serious sailing, you can fit a more permanent fin keel or build a centerboard case.

The futtock is shaped with an axe.

Riveting the futtock. Note the limbers just above each strake.

With the inwales, rubrails, thole pins, painter ring, and thwarts fitted, the pram is ready for her finish coats.

Tools and Materials

A small broadaxe is a good and necessary tool, if you can find one; for Norwegian clinker work, you do not need an adze. A couple of planes, one of them preferably a short smoothing one, are necessary, and a spokeshave is a good tool for the curved insides of the frames. If you are hesitant about developing your axemanship, a drawknife should be included.

A good crosscut handsaw is an absolute must. Access to a bandsaw will make things easier, but you can survive without one. For riveting you

Sheath knife

need a drill; any type will do providing its bit suits your size of rivet. A light riveting hammer is necessary, and you should have a strong pair of nippers to cut rivet points. If you do not have a dolly for driving roves, make one out of hardwood, perhaps ash or black locust. Whittle out a good hefty piece that looks like a plain chisel handle, then drill a hole into the end grain that is large and long enough to house the rivet points. I first saw this tool in use in the boat shed of Ingvald Sande in western Norway, and he told me that it worked just as well as an iron dolly, was more comfortable to hold in a cold shed in

winter, and when it was worn out it could be replaced inexpensively.

Norwegian boatbuilders generally carry a sheath knife as an all-purpose tool. Due to the marketing genius of our neighbors the Swedes, this kind of knife is known in the United States as a Swedish whittling knife. The Swedish factory-made knives are good, so I will grudgingly approve them.

The right shape of knife is shown in the drawing. The blade should be 3 inches to 4 inches long, and the handle should be shaped to fit the hand. If you cannot find such a knife, a fair substitute can be made by annealing an old file to a purple color, grinding it to shape, and fitting a handle to your fancy. Once you have learned to use such a knife, you will find it next to indispensable. Thin, stiff leather is best for the sheath.

Some pram builders use a couple of special, homemade measuring tools. The drawing shows a control level used to keep the boat from becoming lopsided. The tool is placed on one side of the boat, as shown, a pencil mark is made, and the

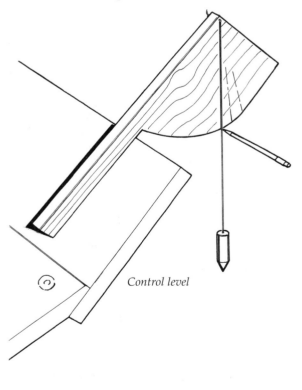

Control level

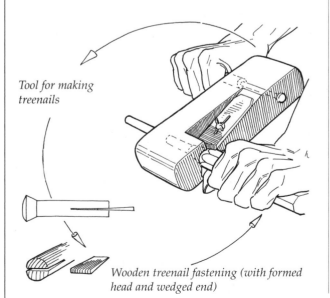

Tool for making treenails

Wooden treenail fastening (with formed head and wedged end)

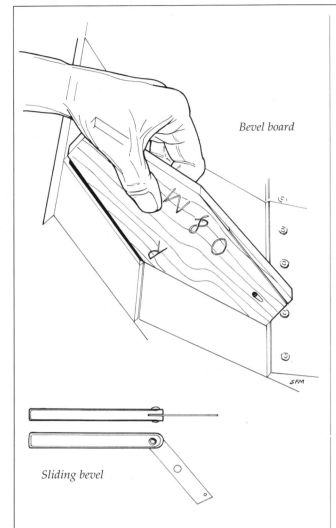

Bevel board

Sliding bevel

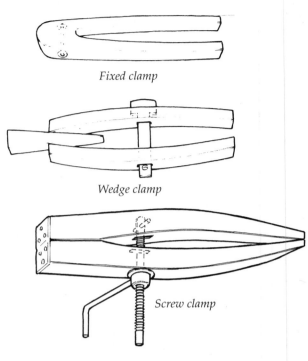

Fixed clamp

Wedge clamp

Screw clamp

corresponding station on the other side of the boat is checked. If the plumb line does not hit the pencil mark, it is time for alterations. From time to time you can clean off the old pencil marks with sandpaper.

The other tool, the bevel board, is also home-made. I have seen it in a couple of variations. The idea behind the tool is to record the plank bevels for future use in building other boats. In other words, this is another way of taking the lines off a successful boat, without paper. For picking up and transferring the plank bevels to the strakes, a sliding bevel is necessary.

You will need an ordinary rule, either foot or metric, for marking your timber, as well as a chalkline or sooted string, and some battens.

You will need at least eight clamps, easily made from scrap hardwood. Norwegian clamps come in three main varieties: fixed, wedge, and screw. An amateur setting up for one boat will be

helped considerably by fixed clamps. Make them long enough to go well across your widest planking stock, "bite" where the lap is located, and hold the joint tightly together. Use a small counter wedge in the opening if the clamp is too wide. Screw clamps are hinged with a piece of leather, and wedged clamps should be made with the crosspiece rather loose fitting.

Norwegian prams are generally built of pine (*Pinus silvestris*), with oak for a few pieces like knees and thole pins. In places where winter ice is a problem, the lower strakes are sometimes made of oak. The European oak (*Quercus robur*) is somewhere between red and white American oak in rot resistance and working properties. My knowledge of American boatbuilding lumber is

Copper rivet and rove (Norwegian style)

limited, but on the New England coast I would suggest cedar or white pine planking and hackmatack crooks. The best idea probably is to use the standard workboat lumber of your own district.

In Norway a century ago, treenails would have been used for fastenings in both the strakes and the frames, with juniper (*Juniperus communis*) or selected pine as the preferred treenail material. The job of cutting a few hundred treenails would probably scare most people today, but old boatbuilders tell how this was their first job in the shop, guided by Father or Granddad, and how all the men and boys in a family might sit in the evening and cut enough treenails to last for the next day's work on a boat.

Treenail size differs with the size of the boat. For small, open boats, frame treenails are generally about $5/8$ inch to $3/4$ inch in diameter, while strake treenails are about $1/2$ inch in diameter. All treenails have a tapering head and are driven from the outside of the boat and wedged on the inside. Whether they are cut by hand or turned, the shape is as shown in the drawing.

A special auger is used to bore for countersinking the head of the treenail, since it is important that the heads fit well. If they are too loose, the joints will leak. If too tight, a treenail will easily split a strake or a frame.

If you decide to use treenails, first get yourself drills or augers of the sizes you want to use, with countersinks to match. If you will be whittling treenails by hand, drill and countersink a test hole or die in a heavy block of hardwood, preferably with interlocking grain so that it will not split. Drive all finished treenails into the hole and out again in order to size them.

Alternatively, make a tool like the one shown in the drawing. Again, the hole should be bored and countersunk with the tools that will be used for boatbuilding. Anneal an old plane iron, bend it to shape, then re-harden, temper, and sharpen it. When in use, the handle and unfinished treenail are used together as a crank to turn the nails.

If you use metal fastenings, they should be galvanized iron or copper rivets with roves. Clenched nails are considered very unprofessional by Norwegian boatbuilders. If you use galvanized iron, the same rivets can be used as nails to fasten in the nose and transom. If copper rivets are used, bronze screws or bronze ring nails, such as the "Anchorfast" type, must be used for the nose and transom.

A Flat-Bottomed Skiff

Text and photographs by WoodenBoat
Drawings by Spencer Lincoln

This flat-bottomed skiff is based on a boat built by the score by Asa Thomson of New Bedford, Massachusetts, from the years near the turn of the century until the mid-1930s. The modified design came from consultations among Maynard Bray, Spencer Lincoln, Joel White, and Jonathan Wilson; the prototype was built in 1979 by the Brooklin Boat Yard, Brooklin, Maine. Since then hundreds have been built to these plans.

Light, strong, handsome, and tight because of her double-planked bottom, this skiff will serve well as an all-purpose waterfront rowboat and, because she tows well, will make an excellent tender to a larger craft.

Here's how to build her.

Anne Bray, having just sculled around Deer Isle, will now row to Machias... ah, youth!

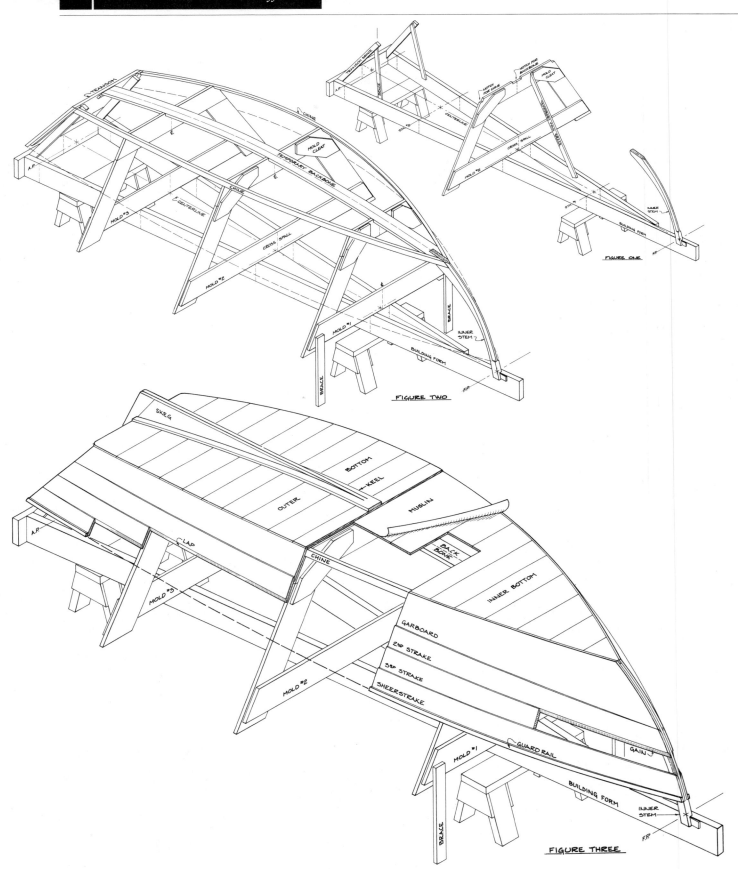

FIGURE ONE

FIGURE TWO

FIGURE THREE

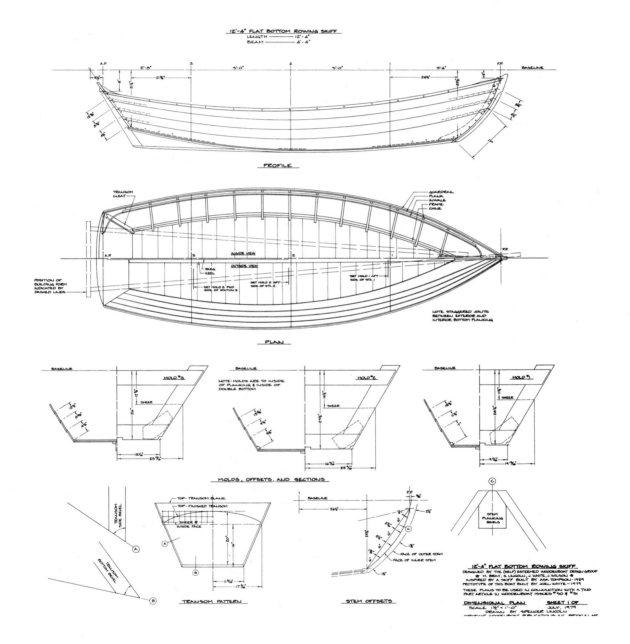

12'-4" FLAT BOTTOM ROWING SKIFF
LENGTH ——— 12'-4"
BEAM ——— 4'-4"

PROFILE

PLAN

MOLDS, OFFSETS, AND SECTIONS

TRANSOM PATTERN

STEM OFFSETS

12'-4" FLAT BOTTOM ROWING SKIFF

DIMENSIONAL PLAN   SHEET 1 OF
SCALE: 1½" = 1'-0"   JULY, 1979
DRAWN BY SPENCER LINCOLN

1

Using measurements given on the drawing, the three stations plus the stem are laid down full size on a convenient flat surface — heavy building paper in this instance. A complete lofting, with the fore-and-aft lines and all, is not really necessary for a boat as simple as this one. Except for the stem, all the lines that have to be "picked up" from the lay-down are straight ones, so the molds can be built directly on them. To make this easier, both the port and starboard sides of each station are drawn out directly on the building paper. Picking up the shape of the curved stem is best done by cutting with scissors around its outline, as laid down on the building paper, and using this piece as a pattern.

The three station molds are made of rough pine boards cleated together at their lower corners (just clear of where the chine will eventually be) and tied together with cross spalls at their upper ends. The cross spalls are located on a common base line, so the molds will be at the right height when set up on a level building form. As each mold is made, its vertical centerline is marked as an aid to setting it up and aligning it with the others. Locations of the plank laps are also indicated on each mold.

The pieces that will make up the transom are splined together and glued. After the glue has dried, the expanded transom is laid out and sawn to shape, with care that the correct bevels are left on the bottom and sides. The drawing clearly shows all this. At this point, the oak corner cleats are gotten out, beveled the same as the transom sides, and fastened in place.

The stem is built in two pieces, dory fashion. Making the inner stem requires sawing it out to the shape traced from the paper pattern, smoothing it up with plane, spokeshave, or sander, then beveling it by cutting away the wood between the bearding line and the face. The angle of the bevel is given on the drawing.

2

The boat is built upside down on a V-shaped building form that is mounted on blocking to a convenient working height and leveled in both directions. While each builder has his own way of setting up a boat, it would be hard to imagine a more direct or simpler method than the one Joel White at the Brooklin Boat Yard used here. A couple of 2 by 6s and scrap boards and blocking are all that is needed; the way it goes together is shown in the drawing.

With the building form complete, the molds are set up on their stations and centered by means of a centerline string. After leveling, the molds are made plumb and held that way by diagonal braces as

shown. A couple of angled brace boards, set to the proper rake, provide a landing for the transom. The stem head is held in position near the floor by a bracket as shown, braced to the building form.

3

Tying the molds, transom, and stem together, and adding greatly to the overall strength of the setup, is a strongback that ultimately is let into the molds and notched around the stem to hold the stem heel in position. The after end is held down flush with the underside of the transom with a small oak cleat that is temporarily fastened to the transom. To center the strongback, a fore-and-aft centerline is marked on the underside of the strongback; this is aligned with the centerline mark on each mold.

4

The corner of each mold is also notched out for the chines. Although the chines were sawn out to a spiled shape for this boat and bent in place cold, Joel recommends the use of steam to make them more flexible. If steamed, spiling is unnecessary; they can be sawn out as straight pieces on a table saw. Spiled or steamed, the chines must be beveled top and bottom as shown on the plan. Once landed and nailed temporarily in place to each mold and fastened permanently to the stem, they are accurately trimmed down so the bottom planking will land fairly against them. A straightedge, shown here, is used to check for fairness. Note also that the strongback has been let into the molds, where it will help support the thin cross planking of the bottom.

5

With everything planed fair, the bottom planking is begun. The bottom is planked in two layers. The first layer comes just flush with the outside edge of the chines so the garboard plank overlaps it. The second runs out over the lower edge of the garboard. Double planking like this is not caulked along the seams; rather, it is made watertight with a sheet of muslin sandwiched between the inner and outer layers.

6

The joint between the bottom planking and the chine is made watertight with a strand of cotton wicking laid in place as the bottom is planked. This first layer of planking is fastened to the chines with short bronze Anchorfast nails.

7

The first layer of bottom planking is planed flush with the chine on each side, so the garboard will lay nicely against it. The temporary fastenings holding the chines to the molds should be pulled at this point, so the molds can be easily removed when the boat is righted later on.

8

The correct shape of the garboard plank can be obtained directly from the boat itself. Simply trace the shape of the bottom onto the board from which the garboard will be made and transfer the marks from each mold indicating where this plank's upper edge should fall. Similar marks for cutting should be made at the stem and at the transom.

9

So the laps will lie flush at their forward and after ends, a so-called gain is planed into this part of the garboard by means of a rabbet plane and a short guide batten. (See sketch in construction plans.)

10

The gain at the forward end of the garboard shows clearly in this photo...

11

...and at the after end in this one. (There will be a bevel planed along the entire edge of the garboard between the fore-and-aft gains in way of the lap, but this will be done after the plank is hung.) Along the stem, as with the bottom planking, cotton wicking is laid in place before the plank is landed. But at the transom the seam is easily caulked afterwards.

12

With the lower edge of the garboards planed flush with the first layer of bottom planking, the second bottom layer is gotten out and dry-fitted. The seams are aligned so they land more or less in the middle of the planks in the first layer beneath. Dry-fitting the second layer at this stage is best, because the seams of the first haven't yet been hidden by the muslin. It is also easier to complete the bottom now before the rest of the topside planking is hung, as the builder can stand closer to the work.

13

Muslin is laid over the first layer of bottom planking in bedding compound cut to a good working consistency with linseed oil. Before this is troweled on, the planks are primed with straight linseed oil so the wood won't absorb the vehicle from the oil-based compound. The objective is to allow the planking to shrink and swell without splitting; a somewhat flexible, but watertight, bond between layers is the key.

14

The muslin is pulled wrinkle-free and rolled firmly in order to squeeze the bedding compound into its weave.

MATERIALS & FASTENINGS

PLANKING —⅜" WHITE PINE/CEDAR, 4 STRAKES (LAPPED) PER SIDE
   LAPS FASTENED W/ ⅞" COPPER CLENCH LINES 2" O.C.
   FASTENED TO STEM W/ 1" #10 F.H. BZE. SCREWS
   FASTENED TO TRANSOM CLEAT W/ 1¼" #10 F.H. BZE. SCREWS
   FASTENED TO CHINES W/ 1" #10 F.H. BZE. SCR. 5" O.C.

INNER BOTTOM —⅜" WHITE PINE/CEDAR, CROSS PLANKED, RANDOM WIDTHS O.C. (6" MAX)
   FASTEN TO CHINES W/ 1" ANCHOR FAST NAILS

LAYER OF MUSLIN SET IN BEDDING COMPOUND BETWEEN INNER & OUTER BOTTOMS

OUTER BOTTOM —⅜" WHITE PINE/CEDAR, CROSS PLANKED, STAGGER SEAMS W/ INNER BOTTOM BY 1½" MIN.
   FASTEN TO INNER BOTT. W/ ⅝" COPPER CLENCH NAILS 4" O.C.
   FASTEN TO CHINES W/ 1¼" #10 F.H. BZE. SCREWS
   FASTEN TO TRANSOM W/ 1½" #10 F.H. BZE. SCREWS

INNER STEM — OAK, SIDED 1⅛", SHAPE AS SHOWN

TRANSOM —⅞" WHITE PINE/CEDAR/MAHOG., 6" PLANKS GLUED & SPILINED TO FORM BLANK FROM WHICH TO CUT TRANSOM SHAPE AS SHOWN

TRANSOM CLEAT —⅞" x 1⅛" OAK
   FASTEN TO TRANSOM W/ 1¼" #10 F.H. BZE. SCREWS

CHINES — OAK, SIZED & BEVELED AS SHOWN, STEAM BENT IF NECESSARY, TEMPORARY FASTENED TO MOLDS W/ SCREWS
   FASTEN TO STEM W/ 1" #10 F.H. BZE. SCREWS
   FASTEN TO TRANSOM CLEAT W/ 1" #10 F.H. BZE. SCREWS

SECTION THRU TRANSOM
SCALE 3"=1'-0"

CONSTRUCTION SECTION
SCALE 3"=1'-0"

SECTION THRU STEM
SCALE 3"=1'-0"

Labels: SCULLING HOLE, QUARTER KNEE, SECTION @ SIDE, TRANSOM CLEAT, CHINE, INNER BOTTOM, OUTER BOTTOM, KEEL (SPLIT), SKEG, KEEL, BREASTHOOK, HOLE FOR PAINTER, INNER STEM, OUTER STEM, CHINE, INNER BOTTOM, OUTER BOTTOM, KEEL

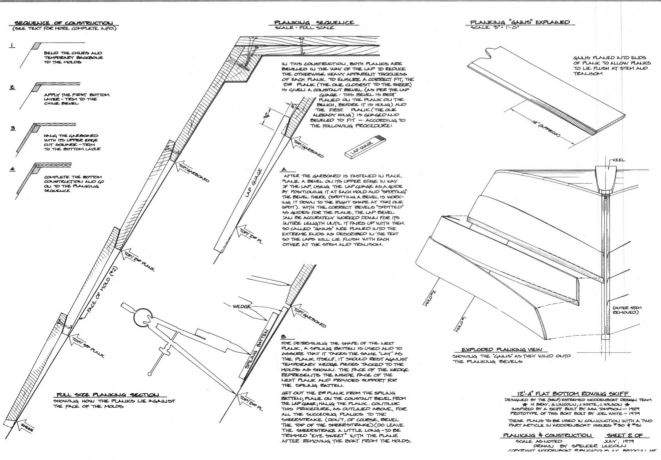

SEQUENCE OF CONSTRUCTION
(SEE TEXT FOR MORE COMPLETE INFO.)

1. BEND THE CHINES AND TEMPORARY BACKBONE TO THE MOLDS

2. APPLY THE FIRST BOTTOM LAYER — TRIM TO THE CHINE BEVEL

3. HANG THE GARBOARD WITH ITS UPPER EDGE CUT SQUARE — TRIM TO THE BOTTOM LAYER

4. COMPLETE THE BOTTOM CONSTRUCTION AND GO ON TO THE PLANKING SEQUENCE

PLANKING SEQUENCE
SCALE : FULL SCALE

IN THIS CONSTRUCTION, BOTH PLANKS ARE BEVELLED IN THE WAY OF THE LAP TO REDUCE THE OTHERWISE HEAVY APPARENT THICKNESS OF EACH PLANK. TO ENSURE A CORRECT FIT, THE 2ND PLANK (THE ONE CLOSEST TO THE SHEER) IS GIVEN A CONSTANT BEVEL (AS PER THE LAP GAUGE) — THIS BEVEL IS BEST PLANED ON THE PLANK ON THE BENCH, BEFORE IT IS HUNG) AND THE FIRST PLANK (THE ONE ALREADY HUNG) IS GAUGED AND BEVELED TO FIT — ACCORDING TO THE FOLLOWING PROCEDURE:

A
AFTER THE GARBOARD IS FASTENED IN PLACE, PLANE A BEVEL ON ITS UPPER EDGE IN WAY OF THE LAP, USING THE LAP GAUGE AS A GUIDE BY POSITIONING IT AT EACH MOLD AND "SPOTTING" THE BEVEL THERE. (SPOTTING A BEVEL IS WORKING IT DOWN TO THE RIGHT SHAPE AT THAT ONE SPOT). WITH THE CORRECT BEVELS "SPOTTED" AS GUIDES FOR THE PLANE, THE LAP BEVEL CAN BE ACCURATELY WORKED DOWN FOR ITS ENTIRE LENGTH UNTIL IT FAIRS UP WITH THEM. SO CALLED "GAINS" ARE PLANED INTO THE EXTREME ENDS AS DESCRIBED IN THE TEXT SO THE LAPS WILL LIE FLUSH WITH EACH OTHER AT THE STEM AND TRANSOM.

B
FOR DETERMINING THE SHAPE OF THE NEXT PLANK, A SPILING BATTEN IS USED AND TO ASSURE THAT IT TAKES THE SAME "LAY" AS THE PLANK ITSELF, IT SHOULD REST AGAINST TEMPORARY WEDGE PIECES TACKED TO THE MOLDS AS SHOWN. THE FACE OF THE WEDGE REPRESENTS THE INSIDE FACE OF THE NEXT PLANK AND PROVIDES SUPPORT FOR THE SPILING BATTEN.

GET OUT THE 2ND PLANK FROM THE SPILING BATTEN; PLANE ON THE CONSTANT BEVEL FROM THE LAP GAUGE; HANG THE PLANK. CONTINUE THIS PROCEDURE, AS OUTLINED ABOVE, FOR ALL THE SUCCEEDING PLANKS TO THE SHEERSTRAKE. (DON'T, OF COURSE, BEVEL THE TOP OF THE SHEERSTRAKE) (DO LEAVE THE SHEERSTRAKE A LITTLE LONG - TO BE TRIMMED "EYE SWEET" WITH THE PLANE AFTER REMOVING THE BOAT FROM THE MOLDS.

Labels: TOP/GARBOARD, LAP GAUGE, TOP/2ND PL., FACE OF MOLD (×2), TOP/2ND PLANK, WEDGE, TOP/GARBOARD, SPILING BATTEN, TOP/3RD PLANK, TOP/2ND PL., SHEER

FULL SIZE PLANKING SECTION
SHOWING HOW THE PLANKS LIE AGAINST THE FACE OF THE MOLDS

PLANKING "GAINS" EXPLAINED
SCALE 3"=1'-0"

GAINS PLANED INTO ENDS OF PLANK TO ALLOW PLANKS TO LIE FLUSH AT STEM AND TRANSOM

Labels: 18 (GARBOARD), KEEL, MOLD 2, MOLD 1, (OUTER STEM REMOVED)

EXPLODED PLANKING VIEW
SHOWING THE "GAINS" AS THEY WIND ONTO THE PLANKING BEVELS

12'-4" FLAT BOTTOM ROWING SKIFF
DESIGNED BY THE (BELF) ESTEEMED WOODENBOAT DESIGN TEAM
★ H. BRAY, S. LINCOLN, J. WHITE, J. WILSON ★
INSPIRED BY A SKIFF BUILT BY ASA THOMPSON — 1929
PROTOTYPE OF THIS BOAT BUILT BY JOEL WHITE — 1979
THESE PLANS TO BE USED IN CONJUNCTION WITH A TWO PART ARTICLE IN WOODENBOAT ISSUES #50 & #51

PLANKING & CONSTRUCTION   SHEET 2 OF
SCALE AS NOTED
DRAWN BY SPENCER LINCOLN
JULY, 1979
COPYRIGHT WOODENBOAT PUBLICATION

15

As each plank of the second layer is fastened in place, additional bedding compound is spread over the muslin to land it in. Fastenings are somewhat longer Anchorfast nails than used for the first layer, bored for ahead of time. Note that the muslin has been rough-trimmed, and that tacks are temporarily holding it in position until the second, or outer, layer of bottom planking is completed. Rows of copper clout nails hold the two layers of bottom planking together, the rows placed so that none is more than an inch from either side of any seam. Boring for these clout nails prevents the chipping of the plank as the nail emerges from it.

16

With the outer planking of the bottom laid, fastened and trimmed, the planking of the sides can resume. For a lighter and more delicate appearance, the full thickness of the planking isn't allowed to show at the laps; rather, the edge of the overlapping plank is beveled a bit all along its length, leaving an apparent thickness of about ¼ inch. And of course, due to the gains that were planed into the forward and after ends of the plank being overlapped, this ¼ inch dies out completely at the stem and at the transom. Details are shown in the sketch in the construction plans.

A spiling is taken on each of the planks above the garboard to determine their shape. The spiling batten lies along wedge pieces that have been tacked to each mold as shown in the sketch. Once cut out and planed down fair to that line, each plank is beveled by the method shown in the sketch and fastened into place on the boat. Laps made in this manner are generally laid up dry, with no caulking or sealant of any kind in them; to be watertight, however, the bevels must be carefully laid out and planed fair and smooth.

Copper clench nails were used for lap fastenings in this boat, but rivets can also be used, though they will involve more time. The disadvantage of rivets is that they will protrude along the inside of the laps, making sanding and painting in that area more time consuming. Rivets are stronger than clench nails, but experience has shown that clench nails are perfectly adequate for the laps of small boats like this one.

17

An even spacing of lap nails is ensured with a pencil compass. If the boat were to be finished bright, with each fastening showing up plainly, the builder might want to take the extra time to spot in evenly the fastenings for the side framing, to be installed later.

18

This boat has four strakes on each side. Fitting and fastening are about the same for each successive strake except for the top or sheerstrake. The latter is not beveled on its upper edge. The width of each strake is indicated on the drawings. For good looks the planks should be fair and evenly tapered without bunches, and should generally follow the widths given. Each plank should be sanded on each side before it is hung. That way the task can be done right on the workbench, which is a lot easier than on the boat after it is finished.

Once the side planking is hung, and before the boat is turned right-side up, the fore-and-aft ends of the strakes are planed down flush with the stem and the transom.

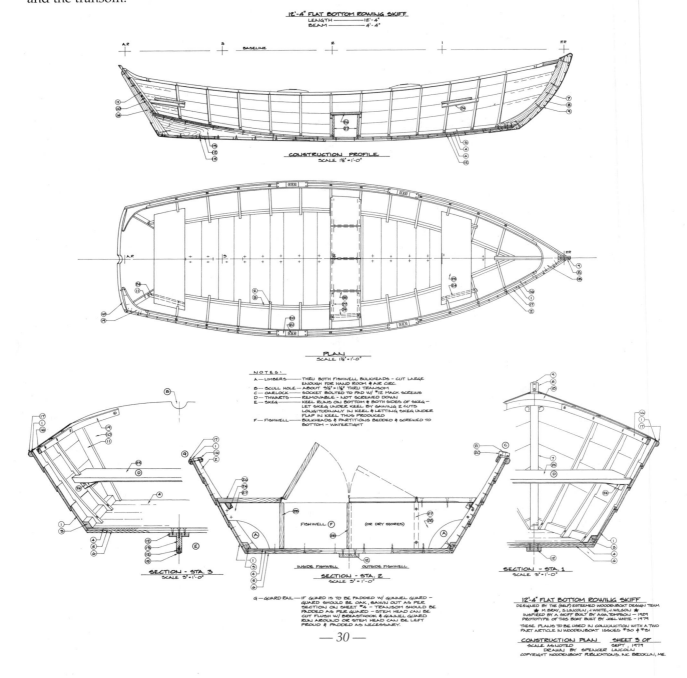

19

With the sides planked and the transom caulked around the edges with a strand of cotton worked in with a putty knife, the hull is pulled off the building form and turned right-side up. Here she is resting on a couple of sawhorses, which bring her to a convenient working height.

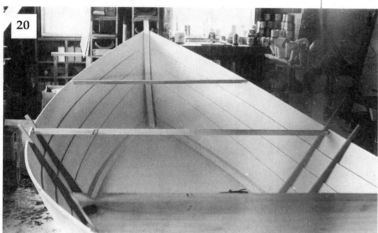

20

She is little more than a shell at this point, free of most of her internal structure — an ideal time to smooth her up and prime and paint her interior. This is also a time when she needs help in holding her proper shape: A couple of cross spalls at the sheer act as spreaders to keep her sides the right distance apart. Before going on to the next steps, make sure she is sitting without twist on the sawhorses.

21

The oak side frames are gotten out next. They should be planed down to the correct thickness but left with enough extra width and length for scribing down to the sides and bottom of the boat. Their positions are shown on the drawing; mark these positions in the boat before actually fitting the frames.

The frames are fitted by scribing with a pencil compass as shown; the first step is to mark and cut the bottom or heel.

22

With the compass held horizontally and its legs spread to span a bit more than the largest gap (just above the chine in this case), the frame is marked for fitting. The top of the chine and the location of each plank lap must also be indicated by projecting them horizontally onto the frame. There is no need to fuss with a precise fit at the laps; the frames are intentionally notched to clear the laps by about ¼ inch so rainwater can't be trapped there. The inboard edge of the frame is marked for cutting with a pattern positioned as shown on the plans.

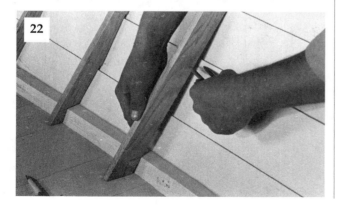

The frames are fastened at their lower ends with a single screw driven into the chine, and are held firmly against the planking with screws driven in through the planking from the outside. Screw sizes are shown on the plans.

23

The outer stem is of oak, with its width and after edge sized and shaped to fit the forward end of the boat. For good looks you'll want to bevel it to a rather narrow width of face over most of its length, leaving the upper part square. The bevel is started with a drawknife; after it has been pretty well roughed out you can work it accurately down to the line with a spokeshave. Keep an eye on the run of the grain during both of these operations to avoid raising a chip that will run below the marked line.

24

The outer stem is smeared with bedding compound or sealant and fastened with screws from the outside. Leave plenty of extra length both top and bottom, to be dressed off later after the keel and breasthook have been installed.

25

Now is the time to batten off the final sheerline and to dress the planking and frames down to it. The top of the transom is trimmed down at the same time; the shape is shown on the drawing. This skiff is a jaunty little boat, and to complement her jauntiness we gave her a high-crowned transom

The quarter knees go in next and are angled upward considerably to strengthen the transom along its top edge.

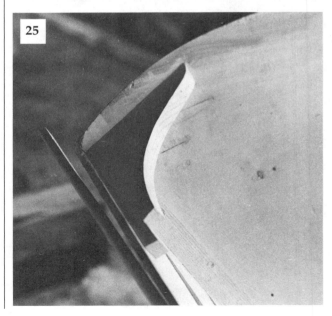

26

The breasthook is made in two pieces so the grain will run parallel to each rail. The pieces are fitted together to form a ridge or high point where they join, instead of in a single plane. This ensures there will be necessary crown to the top and bottom surfaces without having to remove much wood. The underside is smoothed up before installation, but the top surface is best done after the breasthook is fastened in place. By fitting the roughed-out breasthook ¼ inch or so high all around, you'll have extra wood with which to fair its surface into the rails and sheer.

The guardrail is fitted next after the breasthook and quarter knees. It is of white pine and will be left unpainted. A heftier rail of harder wood, such as oak, would be better if you are planning to attach a rope or rubber fender to it.

27

With the inwales lying in the boat ready to go in, Joel is dressing down a frame head that stands too far away from the planking. For good appearance, it is important that all frame heads are of uniform depth so the opening between the sheerstrake and the inwale will be a constant width. The frames have added sufficient stiffness to the hull; only a single cross spall is now needed. It has been pushed lower than the top of the sheerstrake so the inwale can clear it.

28

The inwales for this skiff have a beveled top edge as indicated on the plans. The plans also show the procedure for setting the inwales to the right height relative to the sheerstrake, which Joel is doing here. With some experience, setting the inwale can be done largely by eye, but if this is your first boat, you'll probably want to fuss a bit more — particularly at the ends where the inwales must fair into the breasthook and the quarter knees.

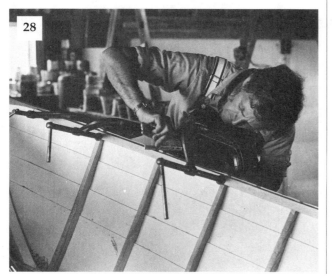

29

Rivets hold the inwale in place against the frames and provide additional fastening for the guardrails. A rivet is located at each frame, with its head counter bored into the guard-rail and its burr left standing proud on the inside face of the inwale. Getting good, fair "eye-sweet" lines is much of what boatbuilding is about; when putting on the rails, great care should be taken to ensure they are free from "yanks, bunches, and swoops."

30

The after end of the inwale needn't be fitted to the quarter knee until the riveting is within a few frames of it. At that point (assuming you have left it long enough) the inwale may be cut off to the right length for a good fit. Notice that some extra "shaping wood" has been left on the quarter knee to be faired into the inwale once it has been installed.

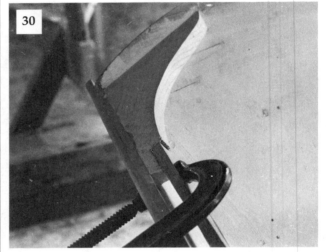

31

It's the builder's choice as to whether the rails, stem head, etc., are given their final shaping before or after the remaining outside work is done. It makes little difference, really, and needs no description other than what the drawings themselves provide. So let's get on with the rest of the structural work on the boat's exterior.

The pieces making up the keel/skeg assembly are shown here. They consist of the keel itself — kerfed in way of the skeg as shown in both the drawing and this photo — and the skeg and stern-post. The first step in putting all these pieces together on the boat is to scribe down the skeg for a good fit against the bottom of the boat, and to cut off its after end to the correct angle (a continuation of the transom). The projecting edge of the bottom planking is notched for the sternpost, and pilot holes are bored in from the outside for both the skeg and the sternpost. Using the pilot holes as guides, and with the pieces to be fastened held in place, holes of the proper size can be bored back out from inside the boat. All that then remains is to slather the faying surfaces with bedding compound and fasten the skeg and sternpost permanently in place.

32

The keel is the last member to be installed. Installation is begun by making a good fit at the keel's forward end, where it fays against the projecting end of the outer stem. The method of fastening is the same as that used for the skeg and sternpost.

33

Working aft, the keel is fastened progressively, with screws driven up through the bottom, until the forward end of the skeg is reached. Here the saw kerfs will allow the center portion of the keel to run along the skeg while the two others run close along either side of it — a neat and easy way of putting it all together.

34

Not certain just where the rowing stations should be and eager for a chance to try her out, Joel White and Tim Horton, who, under Joel's guidance, did most of the building, clamp oarlocks temporarily in place. With a nail carton for a seat, they will test-row the boat. Afterwards they will adjust the oarlock and seat positions for correct trim — that is, so the boat will be level and the transom will ride clear of the water under a wide range of loads. The best location for the painted waterline will also be established.

MATERIALS

1—PLANKING—3/8" CEDAR/WH. PINE
2—FRAMES—5/8" OAK, SAWN
3—CHINES—7/8" × 1¼" OAK, STEAMED
4—INNER BOTTOM—3/8" CEDAR/WH. PINE
5—MUSLIN—
6—OUTER BOTTOM—3/8" CEDAR/WH. PINE
7—INNER STEM—1¼" OAK, SAWN
8—OUTER STEM—1¼" OAK, SAWN
9—STEM BAND—½" BRASS HALF OVAL
10—TRANSOM—¾" CEDAR/WH. PINE/MAHOG.
11—TRANSOM CLEAT—5/8" × 1¼" OAK
12—KEEL—5/8" × 3¼" OAK, TAPERED
13—SKEG—7/8" OAK
14—STERN POST—7/8" OAK
15—SKEG BAND—¾" BRASS HALF OVAL
16—INWALE—½" × 7/8" OAK/MAHOG.
17—GUARD RAIL—½" × 7/8" WH. PINE+
18—BREASTHOOK—1⅛" OAK/MAHOG.
19—QUARTER KNEES—7/8" OAK/MAHOG.
20—OARLOCK PADS—10" × 1¾" × 7/8" OAK/MAHOG.
21—OARLOCK SOCKETS—#1 TOP SOCKET
22—OARLOCKS—#1
23—OARLOCK LANYARD—TO SUIT
24—SEAT RISER—5/8" × 1¼" OAK/MAHOG.
25—THWARTS—7/8" × 10" CEDAR/WH. PINE
26—CENTER SEAT—¾" × 10" CEDAR/WH. PINE
27—FISHWELL BULKHEADS—¾" CEDAR/WH. PINE
28—FISHWELL PARTITIONS—¾" CEDAR/WH. PINE
29—SEAT HINGES—¾" BRASS PIANO HINGE
30—PAINTER—½" NYLON
31—BAILER—TO SUIT
32—OARS—7'-0" OR 7'-6"

+ — SEE ALTERNATE DETAIL FOR GUNNEL GUARD

FASTENINGS

PLANKING—AT LAPS—¾" COPR. CLOUT NAILS
TO STEM—1" #10 F.H. BZE. SCR.
TO CHINES—1" #10 " " "
TO TRANS. CL.—1¼" #10 " " "
FRAMES—TO CHINE—1" #8 " " "
TO PLANK—1" #8 " " "*
CHINES—TO STEM—1¼" #10 " " "
TO TRANS. CL.—1¼" #10 " " "
INNER BOTTOM TO CHINES, ETC.—1" ANCHORFAST NAILS
OUTER BOTTOM—TO INNER BOTT. ¾" CPR. CLOUT NAILS
TO CHINES—1¼" #10 F.H. BZE. SCR.
TO STEM—1½" #10 " " "
TO TRANSOM—1½" #10 " " "
OUTER STEM TO INNER STEM—2½" #14 " " "
STEM BAND TO STEM—¾" #6 " " "

TRANSOM CLEAT TO TRANSOM—1¼" #10 F.H. BZE. SCR.
KEEL—TO BOTTOM—1¼" #10 " " "*
TO SKEG—1" #10 " " "
SKEG—TO BOTTOM—1½" #12 " " "
STERN POST—TO TRANSOM—1½" #12 " " "*
TO SKEG—3½" #14 " " "
SKEG BAND TO KEEL—¾" #8 " " "
INWALE TO GUARDRAIL (THRU FR.)—#10 COPPER RIVET
GUARD RAIL—TO PLANK—¾" #8 F.H. BZE. SCR.*
TO STEM & TR.—1¼" #10 " " "
BREASTHOOK—TO INWALE—#10 COPPER RIVET
TO PLANK—1½" #10 F.H. BZE. SCR.*
JOIN 2 PIECES—¼" THREADED BOLT
QUARTER KNEE—TO INWALE—#10 COPPER RIVET
TO PLANK & TR.—1½" #10 F.H. BZE. SCR.*
TO TRANSOM—#10 COPPER RIVET

OARLOCK PAD—TO INWALE—#10 COPPER RIVET
TO PLANK—1½" #10 F.H. BZE. SCR.
OARLOCK SOCKET TO PAD—#12 MACH. SCREW
SEAT RISER—TO FRAMES—1¼" #10 F.H. BZE. SCR.
TO TRANSOM CL.—1¼" #10 F.H. BZE. SCR.
THWARTS TO SEAT RISERS—NONE
FISHWELL—TO FRAMES—1¼" #10 F.H. BZE. SCR.
TO SEAT—1½" #10 " " "*
TO BOTTOM—1½" #10 " " "*
TO PARTITIONS—1½" #10 " " "
SEAT HINGES TO SEATS—¾" #6 " " "
PAINTER TO STEM—SPLICE

* — SEE ORIENTATION OF FASTENINGS ON SHEET #3

DIMENSIONED PARTS

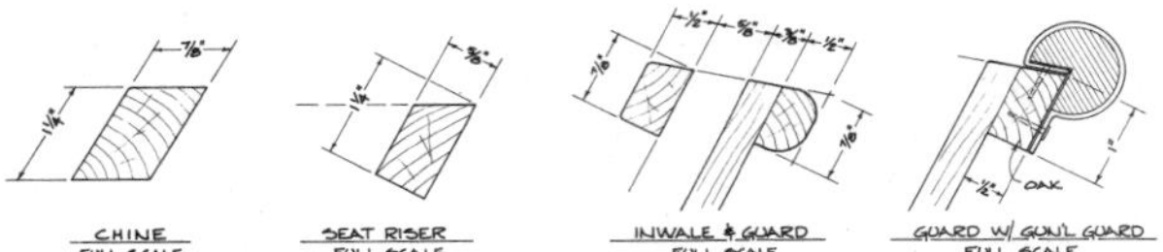

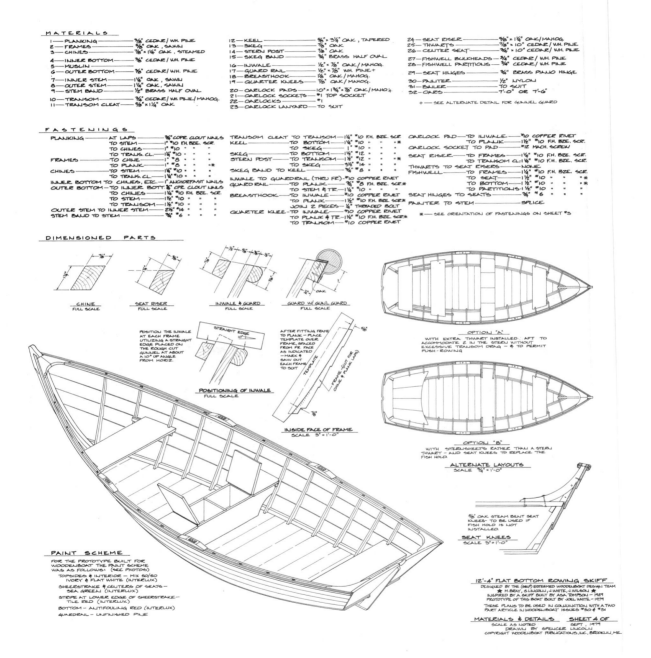

CHINE — FULL SCALE
SEAT RISER — FULL SCALE
INWALE & GUARD — FULL SCALE
GUARD W/ GUN'L GUARD — FULL SCALE

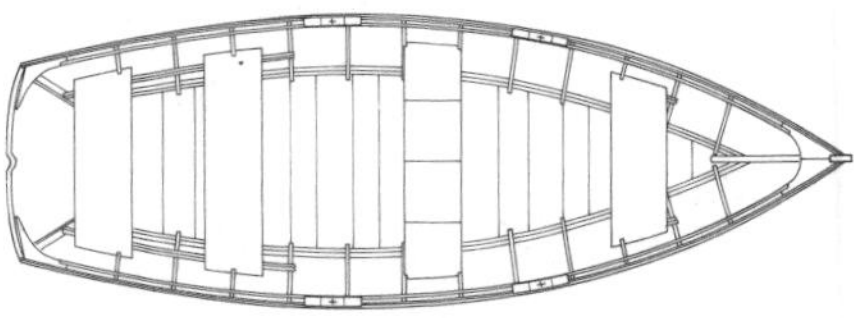

OPTION "A"
WITH EXTRA THWART INSTALLED AFT TO ACCOMMODATE 2 IN THE STERN WITHOUT EXCESSIVE TRANSOM DRAG — & TO PERMIT PUSH-ROWING

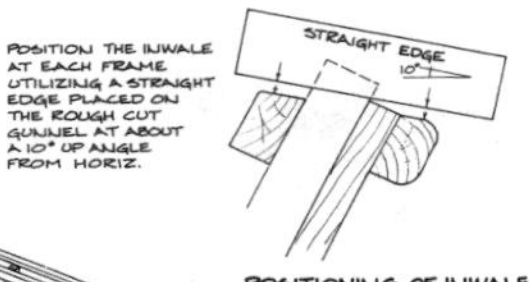
POSITION THE INWALE AT EACH FRAME UTILIZING A STRAIGHT EDGE PLACED ON THE ROUGH CUT GUNNEL AT ABOUT A 10° UP ANGLE FROM HORIZ.
STRAIGHT EDGE
10°

POSITIONING OF INWALE
FULL SCALE

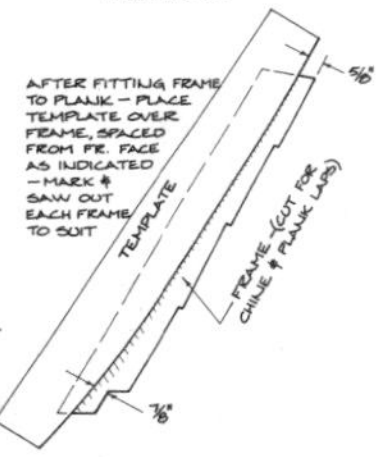
AFTER FITTING FRAME TO PLANK — PLACE TEMPLATE OVER FRAME, SPACED FROM FR. FACE AS INDICATED — MARK & SAW OUT EACH FRAME TO SUIT
TEMPLATE
FRAME (CUT FOR CHINE & PLANK LAPS)

INSIDE FACE OF FRAME
SCALE 3" = 1'-0"

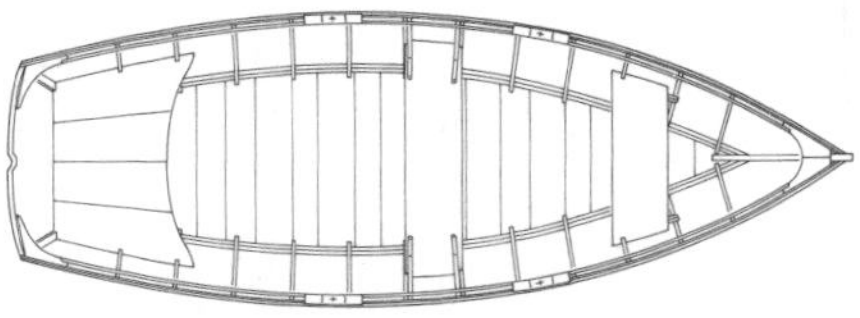

OPTION "B"
WITH STERNSHEETS RATHER THAN A STERN THWART — AND SEAT KNEES TO REPLACE THE FISH HOLD

ALTERNATE LAYOUTS
SCALE ¾" = 1'-0"

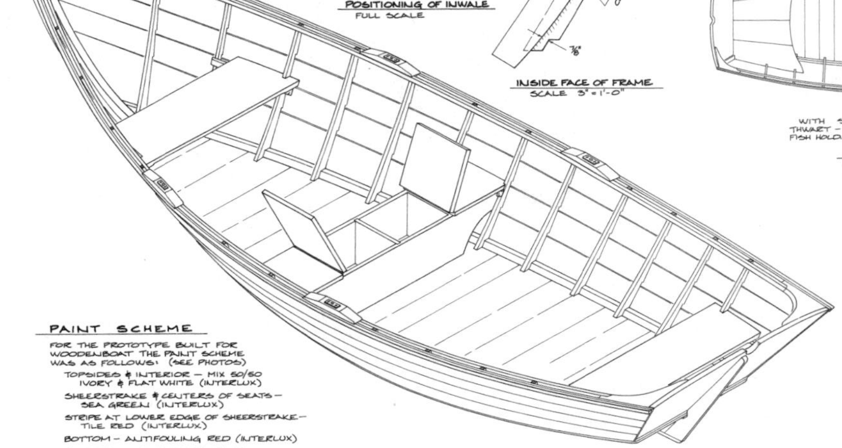

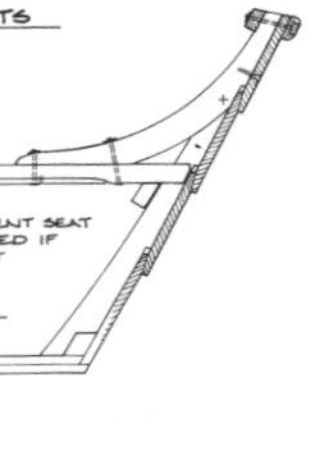
5/8" OAK STEAM BENT SEAT KNEES— TO BE USED IF FISH HOLD IS NOT INSTALLED.

SEAT KNEES
SCALE 3" = 1'-0"

PAINT SCHEME

FOR THE PROTOTYPE BUILT FOR WOODENBOAT THE PAINT SCHEME WAS AS FOLLOWS: (SEE PHOTOS)

- TOPSIDES & INTERIOR — MIX 50/50 IVORY & FLAT WHITE (INTERLUX)
- SHEERSTRAKE & CENTERS OF SEATS — SEA GREEN (INTERLUX)
- STRIPE AT LOWER EDGE OF SHEERSTRAKE — TILE RED (INTERLUX)
- BOTTOM — ANTIFOULING RED (INTERLUX)
- GUARDRAIL — UNFINISHED PINE

12'-4" FLAT BOTTOM ROWING SKIFF

DESIGNED BY THE (SELF) ESTEEMED WOODENBOAT DESIGN TEAM
★ M. BRAY, S. LINCOLN, J. WHITE, J. WILSON ★
INSPIRED BY A SKIFF BUILT BY ASA THOMPSON — 1929
PROTOTYPE OF THIS BOAT BUILT BY JOEL WHITE — 1979

THESE PLANS TO BE USED IN CONJUNCTION WITH A TWO PART ARTICLE IN WOODENBOAT ISSUES #30 & #31

MATERIALS & DETAILS — SHEET 4 OF
SCALE AS NOTED — SEPT., 1979
DRAWN BY SPENCER LINCOLN
COPYRIGHT WOODENBOAT PUBLICATIONS, INC., BROOKLIN, ME.

The seat knees, which are thought necessary in most open boats to help the seats hold their shape and generally strengthen them, can be eliminated if the storage compartment (detailed on the drawings) is installed beneath the middle seat. Asa Thomson built some of his boats this way, and they proved to be long lasting. The compartment can be either for dry storage, like the one shown, or can be made (as Thomson did) floodable for use as a bait well. Joel used ⅞-inch cedar for the two bulkheads that form the storage compartment and for the bow and stern thwarts. Partitions within the compartment and the top of the middle seat can be of thinner stock as shown on the plans. The compartment shouldn't leak, no matter whether used for a wet well or for dry storage. To ensure that it will stay watertight the edges of the bulkheads and the partitions are smeared with sealant before their installation.

This photo shows how the middle seat assembly is put together and how limbers are cut outboard of the partitions, allowing bilge water to drain through. Unlike the permanently installed middle seat, the bow and stern seats — or thwarts, as they are more properly called — are made to be removable. They rest on short seat risers fastened to the inner faces of the frames.

Smoothing up the hull and painting it, and perhaps some further work here and there on such things as the oarlock pads, finish this fine rowing boat.

Building plans for the Yankee Tender (plan #400-011) are available from The WoodenBoat Store, P.O. Box 78, Brooklin, Maine 04616. Call 1–800–273–SHIP (7447). The price is $35.

The Bolger Cartopper

BUILD A CONSTRUCTION MODEL,
THEN BUILD THE BOAT

———— by H.H. "Dynamite" Payson ————

Even though I build full-sized boats for a living, for years I always wanted to build model boats — not full-rigged ships or anything like that, but down-to-earth models that matched my levels of skill and patience. I watched others try their hand at modelmaking and learned a lot from their successes and failures. I saw the remains of a good friend's botched kit model go up in flames, for example, and decided then and there that, for me, stamped-out kits and working with balsa were out.

The type of modelmaking that appealed to me the most was that described by the late Weston Farmer in an article in the *National Fisherman*. His commonsense approach was to work with the plans of a full-sized boat — either a design in progress, to test it out, or a finished design — and to use materials for the model that you could find around the boatshop. So I started making construction models of my full-scale boats, put together from scratch in exactly the same manner as shown on the plans. Some models were built entirely for pleasure and are now on display on a shelf in my living room. Others were built to see how the lines of the boat checked out in three dimensions; I wanted to be able to hold the hull in my hand and eyeball the exterior (I usually skipped the interior on these models). Still others were built to test a set of plans; I wanted to check out the building

The full-sized Cartopper on her way to the launching ramp. Once there, she can be rigged for oar, sail, or outboard power.

procedure and discover where the difficult areas might lie before I started on the real boat.

No matter how experienced you are as a boatbuilder, building a construction model before tackling the full-scale boat is one of the best learning techniques around. The cost of materials is next to nothing, and cutting and shaping those small, flat pieces and transforming them into a model is bound to add to your abilities. The techniques for this type of modelmaking are virtually the same as for full-sized boatbuilding, and the satisfactions are every bit as high. If you make a mistake...so what? Better to make your mistakes on the model while you improve your skills for the real thing.

So come along with me on a minimum-risk adventure in boatbuilding. We'll build a model as if we were building a boat; then when we're done, we'll set the model on the shop bench and use it as inspiration to build a full-sized boat.

The Boat

Looks, lightness, and performance are built into this boat, the 11-foot 6-inch by 4-foot Cartopper, designed by Phil Bolger. Her centerboard and kick-up rudder permit shallow-water sailing, and should the wind fail she will take you home under oar or power. This isn't the first boat Phil Bolger designed for me this way. The 15-foot Gypsy is another, and as her owner John Garber put it, "Her spare plywood frame has all the structural elegance of a bird bone, or the inside of a green pepper." But not their lightness. The Cartopper is a vast improvement in that regard.

Since the purpose of this chapter is to cover how to build a simple construction model, followed by advice on how to build the full-sized boat with the tack-and-tape method, I will confine the discussion to the rowing version of the Cartopper. For ambitious builders, the sail rig, including the daggerboard trunk, the rudder, and other accessories, are shown on the plans.

Tack-and-Tape Construction

The full-sized Cartopper uses the tack-and-tape building method. Basically, this involves cutting out plywood panels to a predetermined pattern shown on the plans and shaping them to fit together edge to edge. No lofting or complicated jigs are required. The panels are temporarily fastened together on the boat's own frames with tacks, light-gauge nails, mechanic's wire, or hot glue, and the outside seams are filled with fiberglass putty. The temporary fastenings are then removed and replaced by long strips of fiberglass tape. The inside of the seams is then filled with putty and covered with fiberglass tape. The result is a smoothly curved hull with a multi-chine form that requires a minimum of

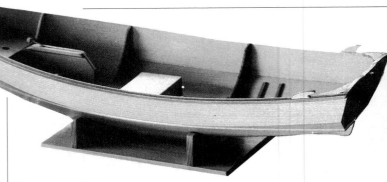

*The completed Cartopper
construction model, fitted for her sailing rig.
The instructions in this series are for the rowing version of this boat.*

framing and no chine logs for structural strength.

Your first question is probably the same as mine was when I first tried this out: How strong is such a puttied-and-taped joint? I gave one such joint — two pieces of plywood butt joined at an angle — the ultimate destruction test by driving my pickup truck over it. The 'glass joint came through intact; it was still clinging to a strip of plywood veneer that had ripped off neatly across the joint itself.

Your second question is: How accurately fitted do the joints have to be? My test proved that gaps up to ¼ inch are perfectly acceptable and even desirable. In fact, it's best to avoid wood-to-wood joints except at the inside edges. It's the 'glass putty filler that provides the strength and locks the joint together.

Of course, that's for the full-sized Cartopper. Tacking and taping the seams in the model is unnecessary. Glue will do for that.

The Plans

There are several ways to build a model of the Cartopper from plans. The easiest and most accurate way is to use a set of builder's plans at the scale drawn by the designer, 1½ inches equals 1 foot. You can cut up the plans and use them as patterns, which will produce a fine model that is one-eighth the size of the real boat, or 17¼ inches long. There is no transferring of measurements, no lofting, no bending of battens, virtually no way to mis-measure and ruin the project. Everything is done one to one.

If you want to keep your plans intact, you can measure all the parts of the plans and transfer their shapes to wood, but this means using rules, battens, pins, and a lot more time. But if you are looking at 10 feet of snow and a long winter out your shop window, you might want to consider this option.

The above two methods are viable if you have a set of builder's plans. The plans accompanying this chapter are exactly the same as the builder's plans, but they have been reduced to fit on the page and are therefore of no true scale. That's no problem if you don't mind

Cartopper Plans

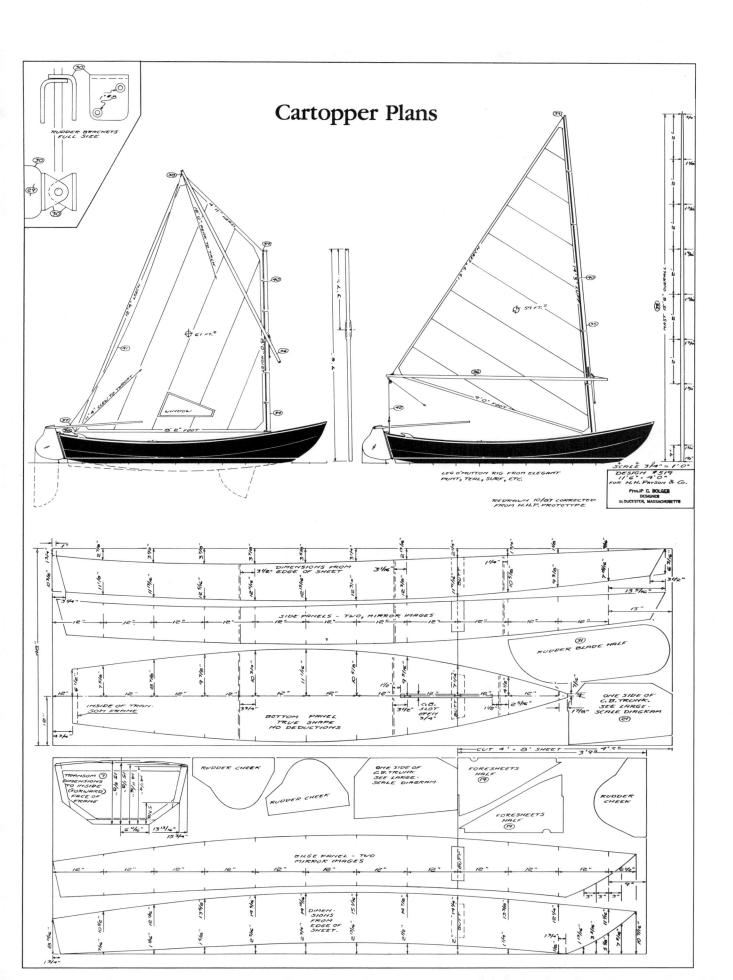

RUDDER BRACKETS FULL SIZE

WINDOW

8'2" FOOT

61 FT.²

LEG O'MUTTON RIG FROM ELEGANT PUNT, TEAL, SURF, ETC.

59 FT.²

9'0" FOOT

REDRAWN 10/87 CORRECTED FROM H.H.P. PROTOTYPE

MAST 15'6" OVERALL

SCALE 3/4" = 1'0"
DESIGN #519
11'6" × 4'0"
FOR H. H. PAYSON & Co.

PHILIP C. BOLGER
DESIGNER
GLOUCESTER, MASSACHUSETTS

DIMENSIONS FROM EDGE OF SHEET

SIDE PANELS - TWO, MIRROR IMAGES

INSIDE OF TRANSOM FRAME

BOTTOM PANEL TRUE SHAPE NO DEDUCTIONS

C.B. SLOT OPEN 3/4"

RUDDER BLADE HALF

ONE SIDE OF C.B. TRUNK. SEE LARGE SCALE DIAGRAM

CUT 4' × 8' SHEET

TRANSOM
DIMENSIONS TO INSIDE (FORWARD) FACE OF FRAME

RUDDER CHEEK

RUDDER CHEEK

ONE SIDE OF C.B. TRUNK. SEE LARGE SCALE DIAGRAM

FORESHEETS HALF

FORESHEETS HALF

RUDDER CHEEK

BILGE PANEL - TWO MIRROR IMAGES

DIMENSIONS FROM EDGE OF SHEET.

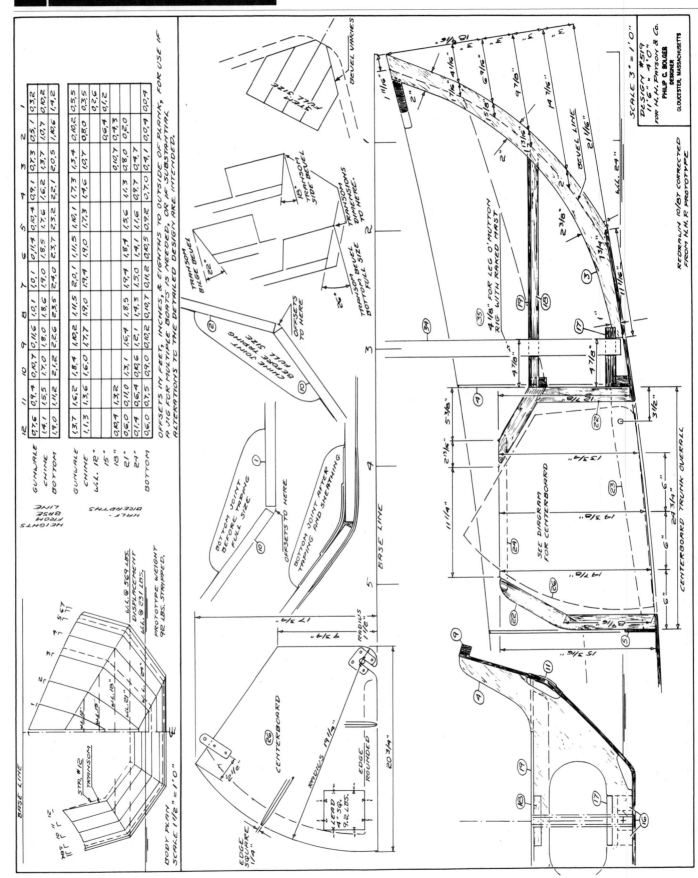

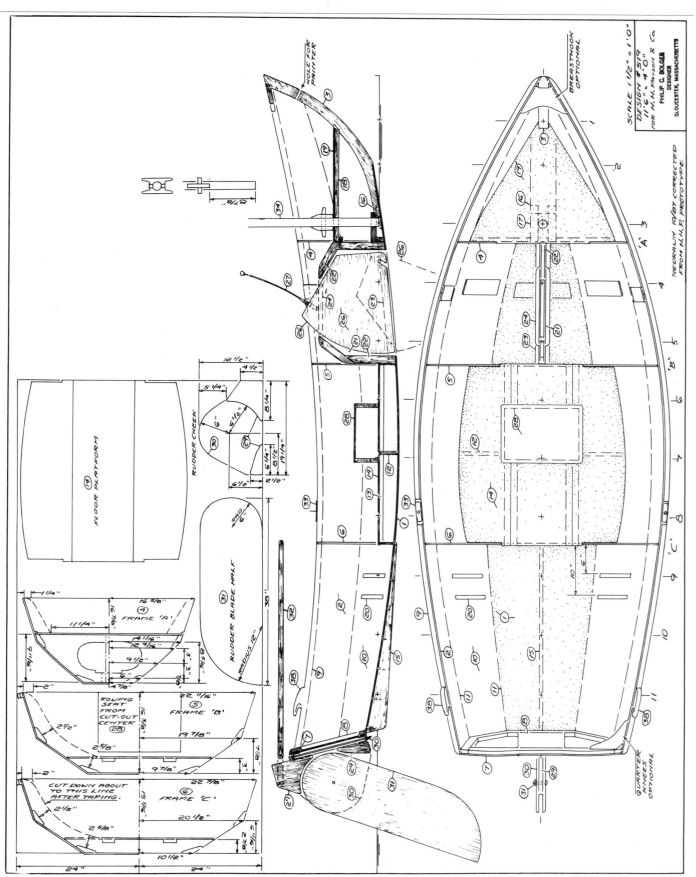

SCALE 1 1/2" = 1' 0"
DESIGN #519
11' 6" x 4' 0"
FOR H.H. PAYSON & Co.

PHILIP C. BOLGER
DESIGNER
GLOUCESTER, MASSACHUSETTS

REDRAWN 10/87 CORRECTED
FROM H.H.P. PROTOTYPE

BREASTHOOK
OPTIONAL

QUARTER
KNEES
OPTIONAL

HOLE FOR
PAINTER

FLOOR PLATFORM

RUDDER CHEEK

RUDDER BLADE HALF

ROWING
SEAT
FROM
CUT-OUT
CENTER

FRAME 'A'

FRAME 'B'

FRAME 'C'

CUT DOWN ABOUT
TO THIS LINE
AFTER TAPING.

— 43 —

redrawing them to the scale you want, especially if you are looking at 10 feet of snow out your window....

But at the risk of sounding like a promoter, I'd recommend ordering a set of 1½ inches equals 1 foot builder's plans and being done with it.

I might mention that building models this way — cutting up scale plans to produce patterns — will work for all of the boats in my Instant Boats series designed by Phil Bolger, and the instructions for the Cartopper apply to them as well. If you already have a set of plans for any other Instant Boat and you would like to make a model of it, then you have no need to buy more plans and therefore have a free run on me. Cut up the plans and have a go.

PLEASE NOTE: The dimensions I provide in this chapter are for the full-sized boat as shown on the plans. These must be translated into the proper scale for the model as you go along. As the scale of the model is 1 ½ inches equals 1 foot, the model will be one-eighth the size of the real boat. Where the sizes are stated on the plans or in the text, divide by 8 to get the size for the model. For example, I will recommend that you cut the framing for the transom from stock that is 1 ½ inches by ¾ inch. In scale model terms, that translates into ³⁄₁₆ inch by ³⁄₃₂ inch.

You can refer to the conversion table published here or use your architect's scale rule to get the proper dimensions straight from the plans.

Conversion Table

Boat	Model
⅛″	¹⁄₆₄″
¼″	¹⁄₃₂″
½″	¹⁄₁₆″
¾″	³⁄₃₂″
⅞″	⁷⁄₆₄″
1″	⅛″
1 ¼″	⁵⁄₃₂″
1 ½″	³⁄₁₆″
1 ¾″	⁷⁄₃₂″
1 ⅞″	¹⁵⁄₆₄″
2″	¼″

• The model is at a scale of 1 ½″ = 1′0″.
• Since 1 ½″ divides into 12″ eight times, the model is one-eighth the size of the boat.
• Where a full-size boat dimension is given, divide by 8 to get the dimension for the model.
• Where a full-size boat dimension is not given, use your architect's scale rule to determine the full dimension, then divide by 8 to get the dimension for the model.

[Courtesy of Dave Dillion]

Hand Tools for Modelmaking

The hand tools required for making the full-sized Cartopper are the usual ones for typical plywood boat-building projects. Most of these are useful for modelmaking, too, but should be supplemented with a few specialized tools. Here's a list of the modeler's hand tools I have been using:

• **Architect's scale rule**
  I consider this indispensable for modelmaking. Like a good compass you can trust, it lets you know where you are all of the time. Get one. Learn how to use it.
• **Steel rule**
• **2-ounce jeweler's ball-peen hammer**
  This is great for heading over brass wire or driving small pins.
• **Machinist's miniature vise**
• **Miniature hand drill**
• **Set of micro drill bits from Nos. 54 to 80**
• **Set of tool- and die-maker's files**
  Swiss pattern in the 12 standard needle shapes.
• **Jeweler's saw**
  For fine cuts in any material.
• **Razor saw with replaceable blades**
• **Micro plane**
  Indispensable for delicate planing jobs.
• **Extra-fine needle-nosed pliers**
• **Diagonal-cutter pliers**
• **Assorted sandpaper**
  220- to 320-grit production paper.
• **Emery boards**
• **Sticky-back tape**
• **½-inch and ¾-inch brass dressmaker's pins**
  Common pins can be used, but they tend to be too large for delicate work.
• **½-inch or ⅝-inch paintbrush**
• **Micro screw clamps**
• **Bellows-type glue applicator**
  Many of the above modeling tools can be found at a well-stocked hobby shop. Just about all, and more, are available from Micro-Mark, 340 Snyder Ave., Berkeley Heights, NJ 07922.

Power Tools for Modelmaking

The more power tools you have, the easier the job and the less dependent you will be on the hobby shops for materials of the proper size and thickness. For instance, I saw out all my model planking on an 8-inch table saw fitted with a hollow-ground planer blade, which is a cross/rip combination with no set to the teeth. There's nothing to resawing wood ¹⁄₁₆-inch thick with this blade; you can go down as far as ¹⁄₃₂ inch, too, but you have to be extremely careful.

A bandsaw is a great help, as is a scroll saw, which can be used for cutting small wood and metal parts where the fineness of the cut is of importance.

Glues for Modelmaking

For most modelmaking projects, I get by nicely with Franklin's Titebond, which is a quick-grabbing glue that will bond a joint in only a few minutes. (It is fast enough to allow "clamping" the joints with your fingers.) Titebond is not a waterproof glue, but it is fine for a mantelpiece model like this one.

Elmer's white glue, also not waterproof, is acceptable for modelmaking, but it is slower to grab than Titebond. But for a long seam that you have to fiddle with, the slow grab of Elmer's is a good feature.

Wood for Modelmaking

Most hobby shops sell modelmaker's plywood — so-called aircraft plywood — in both 12-inch by 2-foot and 12-inch by 4-foot sheets. This is nicely made out of basswood or birch veneers; it comes in various thicknesses starting as thin as $\frac{1}{64}$ inch. In addition, many modeler's catalog supply operations, such as Micro-Mark mentioned above, carry a very impressive inventory of solid wood veneers in varying thicknesses. You can purchase basswood, walnut, mahogany, cherry, and other species, usually in 2-foot lengths from $\frac{1}{32}$ inch to 2-inches thick. In terms of saving time building a model, buying a few sheets of this plywood or veneer can put you way ahead, especially since it is usually milled to within a cat's whisker and can be depended on to produce accurate results.

But if you are like me, you might find the usually flat grain — peeled from logs — of plywood and veneers boring to look at. For that reason, and also for economy's sake, I mostly mill my own modelmaking wood on my table saw. I use white cedar, because it is native to my area of the country and therefore easy to find, and because it is so flexible that I could tie thin strips of it in knots without steaming if I so desired. If you, too, decide to mill your own, use whatever wood that is native to your area — pine, spruce, cypress, whatever. The qualities you are looking for are no knots, straight grain, easy workability, no brittleness, and easy bending. Pick what you like to work with and go for it. What about balsa? Bahh! It's about as interesting as oatmeal.

How thick should your stock be? According to the full-sized plans drawn at 1 ½ inches equals 1 foot, the thickness of the planking panels (side, bilge, and bottom) is ¼ inch, which translates to $\frac{1}{32}$ inch for our scale model (see conversion table). I wouldn't go that thin, because $\frac{1}{32}$-inch stock is tricky to mill on a table saw and a bit too fragile for my liking. I use $\frac{1}{16}$-inch stock, which is safe to mill out and about right for bending, even though it is twice the scale thickness.

How much stock? Look at the plans, estimate the amount required, and then mill out more than that to account for wastage and the inevitable ruined pieces. The important thing to remember is this: Once you have your saw operation set up, run a test strip through to get the exact thickness you want, and then mill enough wood to do the job at this one setting. Nothing is more frustrating than to have to saw out another piece or two later and find you can't match the exact thickness you had before.

Of course, the width of your milled-out stock will depend on the maximum height you can raise the blade of your table saw. The maximum cut of my 8-inch table saw, for example, is only 1 ¾ inches. A piece of stock 1 ¾ inches wide isn't wide enough for some of my modelmaking, but that is no problem. I edge-glue pieces together to add on more width, and you can, too. Lay waxed paper down on a flat surface: your saw table, a Formica table top, whatever. Spread glue on the edges of the wood to be joined, lay the pieces on the waxed paper, make the joint, and wipe off as much excess glue as you can. If the pieces won't lie flat, cover them with another sheet of waxed paper and add weights. When the joint is dry, which is only about 10 or 15 minutes for Titebond used in a warm shop, sand the surfaces with 220-grit sandpaper to get rid of any excess glue.

Side Panels

We will start building the Cartopper construction model by making the side, bottom, and bilge panel templates and laying them out on the planking wood. The exact shapes for all these pieces are positioned together on two of the four sheets of plans. Note that in the full-sized boat, each of these pieces is made of two parts joined by a butt strap, but there is no need to build the model that way. We'll make each of the panels in one piece.

Start with the sides first. There are two identical side panels shown on the plans, but we only need to make one template, so we'll work with the panel at the top of the sheet. Cut along the lines representing the ends and the bottom of the panel, but for the time being do not cut along the line representing the sheer; rather, cut along the straight line above the sheer. This is done to avoid edge-set, or distortion, in the template while laying it on the wood.

Lay the side-panel template on the wood and trace around the bottom and the ends. Remove the template. Cut along the line representing the sheer on the template and lay it back down on the wood, aligning the bottom and the ends with the lines you have already traced onto the wood. Now trace along the sheerline.

Mark the locations of the three frames, A, B, and C, and label them. (Frame A is the one closest to the bow, C is closest to the stern, and B is between the two.) These are represented by dashed lines on the plans.

Cut out the side panel with a bandsaw or a scroll saw, being sure to leave the lines. Finish shaping the piece with a small plane and sandpaper.

You can use the template to draw out the second side panel, or use the finished first side as a template for the second. If the latter, remember that you will have made

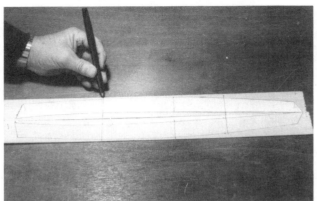

The side panels laid out on the planking wood. The vertical lines represent the locations of the frames.

Drawing the centerline on the face of the roughed-out stem. Note the notch that will take the forward end of the bottom panel.

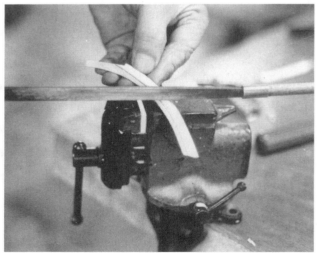

Using a file to cut a rough bevel on the stem. The bevel will be fine-tuned while planking the model.

the second side the width of a pencil point wider than the first, so after the second side has been cut out, put it next to the first and trim it to match exactly. Be especially sure that the angles of the ends are exact. Accuracy in later stages of the model depends on attention to accuracy here.

This brings up an important point: At a scale of 1 ½ inches equals 1 foot, the width of a dull pencil point equals about ⅛ inch. Unless you work with a sharp pencil at all times, you can add more than you might think to your model after you have traced around all sides of a template.

Bilge Panels, Bottom, and Transom

Follow the same procedures for the bottom and two bilge panels. Mark the locations of the frame and the longitudinal centerline on what will be the inside face of the bottom panel; the bilge panels needn't be so marked.

Make a template for the transom, trace it onto your wood, and cut it out. Then make the framing for the transom from stock that is 1 ½ inches by ¾ inch. Each piece of transom framing must be double-beveled (the same bevel on both the inner and outer edges), with the exception of the top transverse frame, the under edge of which should be left square. The bevel for the side frames is 18 degrees; the bilge panel frames, 22 degrees; and the bottom panel, 26 degrees. Don't forget the motorboard, which should be ¾ inch by 9 inches.

Stem

Make a template for the stem, using the same procedure as used for the side panel template. In other words, cut along the outside face of the stem and along the bottom edge, but for the time being do not cut along the inside of the stem. Rather, rough-cut up the line of the mast and along the sheer back to the stemhead. Don't forget the notch in the stem at the forefoot to catch the forward end of the bottom panel.

The stem should be made from a piece of wood that will produce a molded (profile) shape of 2 ½ inches and a sided (plan) shape of 2 inches. Try to find wood with sweeping grain that approximates the curve of the stem. If you can't find any and must work with straight grain, position the template so cross grain will be shared at both ends rather than be concentrated in the middle. Alternatively, use aircraft plywood.

Lay down the stem template on the wood and trace along the forward and bottom edges. Remove the template, finish cutting along the inside face of the stem, reposition the template, and trace along the inside face.

Sand the curved faces of the stem with an emery board, mark a centerline down the outside face, then mark two lines parallel to it, ⅛ inch from the centerline. Rough-cut the ever-changing bevels on each side of the stem right to these lines. It is better to under-bevel at first than to over-bevel. Later, when the frames are set up, a thin batten can be bent from the transom around the frames to the stem, and the bevel can be cut to its final, exact shape.

Frames

Make the templates for the three frames by cutting along the outside and straight across the tops. Do not cut along the inside edges yet. Following the same principles as for the stem, lay out the frame templates on your wood to best utilize the pattern of the grain.

Trace around the frame templates onto the wood. Remove them, and cut the outside shapes of the frames. Lay the template back on the wood and trace the inside shapes onto the wood. Mark the centerline of the frames.

Note that the bottom edge of Frame A, nearest the bow, is slightly curved to accept the curve of the bilge panel. Do not make it straight. This frame is in two halves, which are butted and strapped together at the bottom; and at the top — above the cutout — there's a cleat.

I made Frames B and C in halves for better grain layout and tied them together with butt straps that face each other under the floorboard in the boat. The plans show these frames notched to support the end of the floorboard, but such notches are hardly needed in a model, so I left them out.

Frame A has a notch to take the after end of the maststep. Since we are making the rowing model of the Cartopper, this notch need not be cut.

The plans also show limber holes in the bottom corners of the frames for the full-sized boat. I don't bother with these holes in the model. If you wish to put them in, make a tiny pattern for one hole and use it to mark all twelve. Don't completely cut out these holes at first. Leave tiny tabs (1/16 inch is fine) to hold the waste in place, since you need the corners for reference when assembling the hull. You can cut the tabs later.

Assembling the Hull

Begin assembling the hull by gluing the after end of one of the side panels to the transom. Franklin Titebond glue grabs quickly, so if you use it, you can hold the parts together with your fingers until the glue sets up. You could also use tiny clamps for this operation, hooking them on the transom frame. Then glue the other side panel to the opposite side of the transom.

Drop in Frame C, the one closest to the transom, aligning it with the frame position marks on the side panels. Do not glue it yet; use pins to hold it in place.

Pull in the bow ends of the side panels so they are touching, and hold them together temporarily with masking tape. Try Frames B and A in the positions marked on the side panels, beveling the edges of the frames so the side panels bear evenly on them. The frames are positioned properly when their lower corners are aligned with the lower edges of the side panels. Don't worry about any discrepancy in the alignment of the top of the frames with the top of the

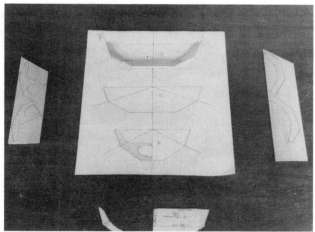

Frame pattern, laid-out frame parts, and the complete Frame B.

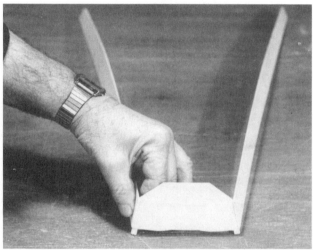

Gluing the after ends of the side panels to the transom.

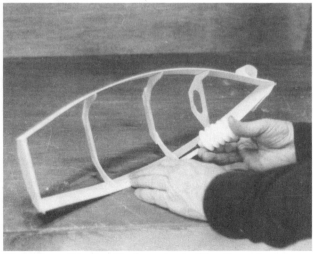

Gluing Frame B in place. The forward ends of the side panels are temporarily held together with masking tape.

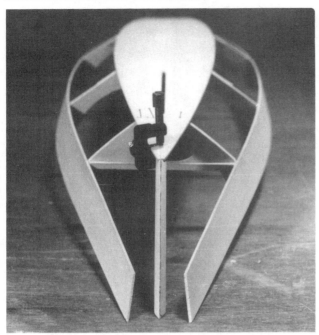

Gluing the stem to the bottom panel. Note the pins holding the bottom panel to Frame A.

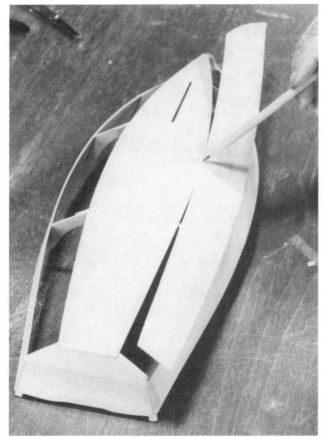

Fitting a bilge panel. Masking tape holds it in position, and a tick mark across the joint will ensure proper repositioning when the trimming and sanding are complete.

side panels; this can be taken out later at the same time you fair the top of the transom into the sides.

Fitting the Bottom Panel and the Stem

Release the masking tape at the bow, and temporarily fasten the after end of the bottom panel to the bottom of the transom and to Frame A, skipping Frames B and C. Check both positions for centerline alignment. Do not glue down the bottom yet; use pins.

Clamp the stem to the forward end of the bottom, making sure the bottom fits into the notch in the stem.

Pull the sides in to the stem and check the bevels on each side of the stem. Trim as necessary so the sides bear properly.

Take your time here. Adjust the assembly so the stem, the bottom, and the side panels fair into each other properly. When you are satisfied that all is okay, first glue one side panel to the stem and then the other. Hold the pieces together with your fingers until the glue sets, or pin them.

Remove the bottom and apply glue to the bottom of all the frames, the transom, and the stem. Lay the bottom back on and align the centerline of the frames with the centerline of the bottom. Hold or pin the bottom in place until the glue grabs.

Fitting the Bilge Panels

With the side panels and bottom in place, the model is really shaping up. Now it's time to close her in with the bilge panels.

Trial fit the bilge panels, using pieces of masking tape to hold them in position as you work. As you fit them between the sides and the bottom panel, think of them as the skins of orange sections and try to achieve a fit that is as close as that. If the panels seem too stiff at their forward ends to bend into place properly, sand them down a little thinner.

When you have each panel located properly in a fore-and-aft position, make a tick mark across the joint. This will allow you to reposition the panel exactly after you have taken it off for trimming.

To achieve a good fit, take a little off the inside edge of the bottom panel, the side panels, and the bilge panels together. Fit the middle of the panels first, then work toward the ends.

If you are in doubt about your skill here, the easy and safe way of doing this job is to cut the bilge panels wide enough to more than span the space they are to fill. Tape them in place on the outside of the hull, and from the inside mark off their shapes using the edges of the sides and bottom as guides. Do not assume that because you have made one that fits you can use it as a pattern for the other. It's highly unlikely. Fit each one individually.

Sand and fit, sand and fit, until the panels slip into place like a glove. From experience I can tell you that it pays to wait until both bilge panels are fitted before spreading glue on the frames.

Just as you must fit each bilge panel separately, glue them separately, too, but be certain that you are gluing the right panel to the right side of the boat. Apply glue to all the surfaces the panel will bear against. Rather than using Titebond, which grabs quickly, I suggest using regular Elmer's white glue for the panel's edges at the frames. Elmer's will give you time to adjust the panel before the glue sets. Save the Titebond for the ends of the panel, since they are the last points to be glued down and quick-grabbing will be an asset.

After the glue has been applied, lay the panel in place with your locating marks precisely aligned, and use a couple of pins to toenail the top edge of the bilge panel to the side panel. Then work from the middle toward the ends, checking for alignment as you go.

Follow the same procedure for the other bilge panel.

At this stage, your model looks like a real boat, and everything added to it will bring it closer to mantelpiece status.

Floor Platform and Seats

Cut the floor platform pattern from the plans and use it to make the floor platform from three pieces of 1¾-inch-wide strips of wood, ¾-inch thick, and fit it in. Don't glue it down in the boat, because it is supposed to be removable. Even though the plans show reinforcement under the floor platform, there's no need for it in the model.

Cut the bow seat pattern from the plans. Make the seat from two pieces of edge-glued wood. The projection of the after end of the seat misses its fit to the inboard edges of Frame A by quite a bit on each side, so make the template wider there to compensate. Note also that the sides of the seat to the stem are not a straight line as drawn in the plans, but are curved. Allow extra wood to fit and trim for this curve.

Fitting the bow seat is one of the trickiest operations in this model, much like fitting a breasthook in a full-sized boat. Work carefully. If you can make this seat fit in place all at one crack, without making any mistakes, chalk one up for yourself. If you bungle the job, don't worry. Throw the piece away, and try again. The great thing about modelmaking is that the wood is small and expendable.

The movable midship seat is an easily built box measuring 5 inches in depth by 1 foot by 1 foot 4 inches. The parts for it can be cut with your table saw fitted with a planer blade and an accurate miter gauge for making square cuts. If you don't have a table saw, use a miniature miter box and a modeler's razor saw.

False Stem

Using a sanding block, sand the forward ends of

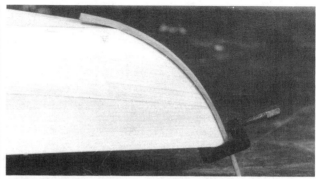

Gluing the false stem. Once the glue has set up, the top and bottom will be trimmed and the false stem will be faired into the planking.

the planking straight across, flush with the outside of the stem. Avoid rocking the sanding block as you go, or you won't get a good joint for the false stem.

For the false stem, cut a strip of wood about ½ inch by 2 inches. It should be wide enough to go across the stem and beyond the outside edges of the planking, and long enough to extend from the stemhead to the bottom panel with a little more to spare. Saw out this strip square edged, making no attempt to taper it or shape it to the sides.

The false stem is bent over the stem itself. To do this, wet the outside of the false stem with your tongue and prebend it with your fingers to the approximate curve of the stem. Then apply glue and hold the false stem in place with pins.

After the glue has set up, use your sanding block to fair the false stem into the side and bilge panels, and the bottom.

Gunwales

Rip out the gunwales. These can be 1 inch by ¾ inch rather than the two ½-inch layers laminated together called for in the plans. Make them a little longer than the length from the outside of the stem to the outside of the transom, taking into account the curve of the sides. For contrast, use fine-grained wood that is darker than the planking.

Actually, I made the gunwales from birch and soaked them in household ammonia to soften them up for bending. Ammonia stains light-colored wood a coffee color. You don't need a tank for soaking the gunwales. Simply wrap them in a paper towel, pour ammonia over them, then wrap the whole works in waxed paper and let it soak for a few hours or overnight. Maple also makes great gunwales. Save that old bureau or table that's headed for the dump and turn it into a model.

Cut and sand the planking so it is flush with the outside face of the transom. Be sure to leave the corners sharp.

Fasten the gunwales in place one at a time. Spread glue as evenly as you can on the back of the gunwale, clamp it at the bow, and feed it along the side, pressing it against the planking with your fingers as you

Trimming the gunwales. The next step is to mark the top of the transom and fair it into the gunwales.

Using sandpaper to fit the skeg to the curve of the bottom.

Scribing the waterline. The height of the block represents the distance from the baseline to the line.

go. Use a couple of clamps near the transom to hold the quick hook in the sheer back aft.

Trim the ends of the gunwales, then lay the transom template on the inside of the transom. Align the top corners of the template with the corners of the model's transom, then mark the shape of the top of the transom. Fair the ends of the transom framing down to the gunwales.

Skeg

Cut the skeg template from the plans along the edge next to the hull; leave extra paper underneath the skeg so the template won't edge set. Lay the template on the wood and mark the edge of the skeg that is going to fit next to the hull on your wood. Finish cutting out the template, and mark the rest of the skeg.

Cut out the skeg; then lay a piece of sandpaper, rough surface up, on the bottom of the boat where the skeg is to fit. Rub the bottom of the skeg fore-and-aft until it hunkers down for a tight fit. Glue the skeg in place.

Foot Stretchers

Make four foot stretchers from wood that is 7 inches by ¾-inch square. Determine their proper location in the boat from the plans, and put them in using temporary spacers to regulate their position. You could measure their position, but by being off by a mere fraction

you can ruin the looks of the final result. Spacers regulate the position of the stretchers quickly and easily.

Breasthook and Quarter Knees

According to the plans, the breasthook and quarter knees are optional. If you decide to fit them, follow the same procedures as for the bow seat, above. Make your templates from the plans, cut out your pieces, and trim with sandpaper until they fit like a glove.

Finishing the Hull

It's best to seal the hull before scribing the waterline. Will you use paint or varnish? It's your choice, of course, but I went with varnish for two reasons: it's easier to apply, and I feel the wood grain of this model is worth looking at.

At this stage, avoid handling the model more than necessary to avoid staining it. Check the surface over carefully; any sanding done from now on should be 320-grit or finer paper.

Use a good-quality brush. One that is about ¾ inch at the ferrule and about 1 inch at the business end is okay for a model this size.

I thin my varnish almost in half with turpentine and add a dash of japan drier to hasten the cure. This allows me to apply smooth, even coats, and the thinning cuts down on the gloss. I don't like high gloss on a model.

Don't forget to sand between coats, and clean up the surface with a tack rag.

Scribing the Waterline

The waterline is scribed by setting the model on a flat surface and using as a guide the top of a piece of wood that is as thick as the waterline height. The plans show both a boottop and a load waterline (LWL). We will mark the boottop first.

On the body plan, amidships, the top of the boot to the bottom of the boat measures 7 inches, so cut a block of wood that is 7 inches thick by 1 ½ inches by 3 to 4 feet in length.

Set the model on a flat surface, and raise the stern up or down until the top of the block of wood matches the extreme aft-end height of the boottop. Weight the model down so it won't skitter around while you work. With the sharp point of an awl or a pencil, scribe the boottop all the way around the hull. Use a light touch.

The thickness of the boottop is ½ inch, so take ½ inch off your guide block and go around again. You now have defined the top and bottom of the boottop.

The distance from the underside of the boottop to the LWL is 2 ½ inches, so take that much off the guide block and go around the hull one more time. That does it.

Mask off the boottop and the waterline with masking tape to keep their edges sharp for painting.

So that's it — a construction model built to the plans of a full-sized boat.

The Full-Sized Cartopper

There isn't much difference between building the construction model and the full-sized boat, except that in the full-sized boat we will be working with larger pieces of wood. The building method for the full-sized boat is what is known as "tack-and-tape" or "stitch-and-glue," in which the edges of the plywood panels are temporarily held together with small nails or wire and permanently joined with fiberglass tape over a putty of epoxy or polyester resin (your choice) mixed with a microballoon filler.

If you are a "gunk and goo" person and poor-fitting joints are your specialty, then this tack-and-tape method is the way to go. In fact, the hull gains strength from the builder's lack of skill, because the resin, putty, and tape used in holding the Cartopper together are much stronger than the wood itself. The basic parts of the boat — the sides, the bilge panels, and the bottom panel — are cut square edged and assembled that way. Beveling is required only for the stem and transom.

I'm excited about this method, because the rankest "all-thumbs" novice stands an excellent chance of putting together a shapely boat if he or she has an ounce of common sense, some basic skills, and the determination to get the job done. Even if you are dumber than a fence post, the Cartopper's pre-diagrammed parts guarantee that she will come out looking the way she was designed.

Materials and Tools

The basic materials for building the Cartopper are four sheets of ¼-inch by 4-foot by 8-foot plywood; waterproof glue, two gallons of resin (one with wax, one without); one roll of 3-inch fiberglass tape; and one gallon of Fillite powder. (I expect you to use common sense and protective gear when working with resins or solvents.)

Marine plywood, which has two good sides, is best if you are willing to pay the price. On the other hand, I have used AC exterior plywood — good on one side, not so good on the other — and have never lost a boat. At a price approximately half or more of marine grade, AC might be the way to go, especially if you live out in the middle of Kansas, where marine plywood might be difficult to find. After all, with AC, if you blow the whole project you won't be out a lot of money.

AC exterior plywood is more difficult to work with than marine grade, because you must be sure to lay out your parts carefully to avoid having the good side facing out on one side panel, for example, and the good side facing in on its mate. Lately, I've noticed that some AC exterior plywood has a tendency to curl. If you run across curled plywood and decide to use it anyway, make sure that the basic parts of the boat — the sides, the bilge panels, and the bottom — are laid out to curl in on the hull, not out.

For tools, it would be nice to have a small table saw, a portable circular saw, a sabersaw, and a bandsaw, but this doesn't mean you can't build the boat without them. If you don't have a bandsaw, for example, a sabersaw can do a lot that a bandsaw can do; it's slower, that's all. A friend with a table saw can rip out the gunwales from a clear 2 by 4 for you, and so on. The point is that you needn't be put off from building a boat just because you don't have a shop full of expensive tools.

In addition to the above, you will need a putty knife, a small ¼-inch electric drill with a ⁵⁄₆₄-inch bit, a block plane, a handsaw — the usual tools found in a small shop. You don't need heavy equipment at all.

As we go along in this building project, I'll be mentioning other tools; if you don't have them, substitute for them, or buy or rent them to get the job done.

Laying Out the Parts

Accuracy is important when laying out the parts of the boat on your plywood. Pay attention to your rule and straightedge, and by all means keep your architect's scale rule at hand for measuring dimensions on the plans where they haven't been given. Phil Bolger, the designer of the boat, shows just about all you need to see in the three different views — plan, profile, and body — so what you might not see in one view usually will be apparent in the next.

Let's begin with the first sheet of plans, showing the sides, bottom, rudder blade half, and centerboard trunk. These parts will be laid out on two sheets of ¼-inch plywood butted end to end. To make the job of sawing easy, and to protect your shop floor, lay 4-foot sticks under the plywood. Use a wider stick at the butt joint, and cover this wide stick with waxed paper. Now lay down the plywood, and fasten the butted ends to the wide stick with 1-inch No. 18 wire brads so the plywood can't move.

The major parts of the full-size Cartopper, cut out and ready to assemble. Note that the insides of the two middle frames in the photo, Frames B and C, have not been cut out yet.

Mark off 1-foot intervals from one end of the butted sheets to the other on both of the long edges, then connect your marks with a straightedge and draw each line right across the sheets. Plywood sheets are manufactured to be square, so it is best to mark off your lines by measurement rather than using a framing square. Just a speck of glue or a small imperfection of any kind can throw a framing square way out of whack without your being aware of it.

Now lay off the measurements defining the sheer and the bottom edges of the first side panel. (The principles for transferring the shape of this side panel from the plans to the plywood are the same as those for the rest of the parts; these instructions, therefore, apply to all parts.) At each of your 1-foot intervals, measure in from the edge of the sheet to the sheer and to the bottom the amounts indicated on the plans. For example, at the first interval the dimension is 2 ⅞ inches to the sheer and 11 ⅛ inches to the bottom of the side panel. Note that the same method is used to define the ends of the panel.

Drive small nails or brads (1-inch No. 18 will do fine) at each of the points you have defined. Now lay a ⅜-inch by 1-inch pine batten along the line formed by the nails, and mark along its length. Don't panic if the batten doesn't hit every dimension right on the mark; the idea is to fair a line through the majority of these marks. Don't hesitate to pull a nail to fair the curve and avoid a quick place, but remember the goal: to pull as few nails as possible to achieve a fair curve that represents as closely as possible the designer's measurements. When you are satisfied that the curve is fair, mark along the length of the batten with your pencil.

Follow the same procedure in laying out the other panels — the bilge panels, and the bottom panel. On each of these, mark the locations of the three frames — A, B, and C — for future reference. Frame A is the one nearest to the bow, Frame C is nearest to the stern, and Frame B lies between the two.

Keep in mind that when laying out and making such parts as the bottom, the transom, and the frames, you should carefully mark the centerlines. Centerlines are indispensable when you are assembling the hull to make sure it is in proper alignment.

The Fiberglass Butts

Before cutting out the side, bilge, and bottom panels, the butts must be joined. The plans call for plywood buttstraps, but I much prefer making a fiberglass joint, since I believe it to be simpler, stronger, and neater. I have found that just one layer of tape on each side of the joint is ample for ¼-inch plywood, but you can make the butt stronger if you want by hollowing out the joint and using a layer of fiberglass mat followed by a layer of fiberglass tape. If you have no

tape, make it from cloth cut on a bias. I use polyester resin and have had great success with it, but if you want to be extra sure about the strength of the joint, use epoxy.

Tape the joints with 3-inch fiberglass tape. Run it right out to the edges of the panel instead of holding it back 1 ½ inches as the plans show for the plywood butt. You will be taping both sides of the panels, but do only one side now. Use plenty of resin; apply it out from the joint about 2 ½ inches on each side. Place the tape in the fresh resin, spread more resin over the tape, and cover it with a strip of waxed paper wide enough to cover the entire area. Draw a wide putty knife over the waxed paper to smooth out the joint. Leave the paper in place until the resin cures. Then sand the joint carefully to remove all traces of wax residue from the paper.

With one side joined with fiberglass, now is the time to cut out the panels. A small portable circular saw does a great job. Even better is a special saw made by Makita for cutting plywood. But lacking these, you can also use a sabersaw and even a handsaw, though I consider the last to be the rock-bottom choice.

To save your circular saw blade, do not cut across the fiberglass butt. Rather, stop at this point, and use a sabersaw with either a conventional or diamond-toothed blade.

Once the panels have been cut out, turn them over, being very careful not to bend or break the joints, and tape the other side of the butts. Again, once the resin has cured, sand the joint carefully to remove all traces of wax residue.

The Transom

The transom is made from a piece of ¼-inch plywood and framed with ¾-inch by 1 ½-inch spruce, pine, fir, or mahogany — almost anything, as long as it isn't oak, which doesn't glue well. The top of the transom frame uses wider stock; I suggest 3 inches wide or something similar. Just keep in mind that it must be wide enough to accommodate the crown of the transom, with wood left over so the ends of the top of the frame can bear against the side framing of the transom.

The procedure for making the transom and its frame is to cut out the transom first according to the dimensions shown on the plans and bevel its edges to the amount shown on Sheet No. 3 (the bevel for the transom top is 21 degrees). Cut the framing and bevel it to match, and then glue and nail everything together. Clean up the excess glue right on the spot rather than having to face hardened lumps later. Note that the bevel of the transom top goes in the reverse direction from all the other bevels.

If you want a better-looking transom frame, instead of cutting the inside of the framing square-edged, bevel it to match the outside of the framing. In other words, make the inside and outside bevels alike. This not only improves the looks of the transom but also avoids a water pocket on the bottom piece of the framing, if it were cut square edged. All this is trickier to fit but is worth the effort.

The transom motorboard, No. 8 on the sheet showing the interior arrangement, should be made of two or more ¾-inch by 9-inch vertical planks.

By the way, I made the transom from a piece of plywood that curled out of shape after I cut it. If this happens to you, let nature straighten it out. On a hot, sunny day just throw the warped piece of plywood outdoors on your lawn, concave side down on the grass. Go back in your shop and drink a cool one while the plywood flattens. Dampness will swell the side of the plywood facing the ground, and the heat of the sun will shrink the other side. Check it in about 10 to 15 minutes. If it has flattened, grab it and frame it quickly, and the chances are good it will stay flat. You have to frame it right at the moment it's flat; otherwise, the plywood will revert to its original warped state.

The Stem

You can laminate the 2-inch stem from eight pieces of ¼-inch plywood if you want to take the trouble; I didn't and opted for four pieces of ½-inch plywood instead. Each piece is cut out separately with a bandsaw or a sabersaw to the shape of the stem's profile, and then all of them are glued with waterproof glue and clamped. No nails.

Sheet No. 3 shows the layout of the stem in profile and also shows the stemhead full size with the designer's notation: "Bevel varies." Well, it does, but not enough to worry about. The bevel shown at the stemhead is close enough to work with; it can be doctored if need be after the stem is set up on the hull, by running a batten around the molds onto the stem. Do this before the sides and bilge panels are sprung in place.

Lay out the stem according to the profile dimensions shown on Sheet No. 3, using a light batten to fair the line of the forward face of the stem, the bevel line ("bearding line" in boatbuilder's parlance), and the after face of the stem. Spring the batten around brads driven into the plywood at your reference marks. Note that the bottom of the stem is notched to accept the forward end of the bottom panel.

After the stem has been laminated, draw a centerline down the outside face, then mark off the actual ⁵⁄₁₆-inch width of the finished outside stem face. You can saw out the stem bevel with either a bandsaw or a sabersaw set at an angle of 21 degrees, which will make a cut well clear of the final ⁵⁄₁₆-inch width of the outside stem face; the excess is then worked off to the ⁵⁄₁₆-inch width.

Clamping the motor board to the inside of the transom. The ends of the transom frame pieces will be cut all at once.

The stem is laminated from four pieces of 1/2-inch plywood. Alternatively, you can use eight pieces of 1/4-inch ply.

Cutting the stem bevel with a bandsaw.

The inside of the frames is partially cut before the hull is assembled.

Temporary legs for supporting the hull while you work on it.

Clamping the frames to the legs.

The Frames

The three frames are made from ¼-inch plywood to keep down the weight of the boat, but it is okay to make them heavier if you like. If you think ¼-inch frames don't seem like much in the strength department, you are right; but their lack of strength is offset when the boat has been assembled. With the hull seams taped with fiberglass and the outside of the hull sheathed with fiberglass cloth, you essentially have a tough, one-piece structure. But until the frames are fiberglassed into the hull, they are pretty flimsy, so for setting up the hull we will make the frames in one piece for the sake of rigidity.

On the plans, the height of each frame at the sheer is given at the centerline, so lay out each frame to all the outside dimensions first, then cut it out across the top, full height, in one piece, square edged. The frame's inner shape is shown by curved, dashed lines; this shape must be taken off with an architect's scale rule, plotted on the frame, and then drawn with a light batten or ship's curve. But don't cut out the inner shape yet. Rather, bore ½-inch holes 5 or 6 inches apart outside the line on the "waste" side, and with your sabersaw, saw along the line between the holes but not all the way, leaving just a tab between the holes. After the frames have been fiberglassed to the hull, you can finish cutting with a handsaw.

The same principle applies for the limber holes in the corners of the frames. Unlike the inside waste of the frames, which must be left in place for strength until the frames are fiberglassed to the hull, the corners of the frames must be left intact so you can use them to align the edges of the sides, the bilge panels, and the bottom when assembling the hull. So make a pattern of a limber hole and use it to mark off the others, and saw each limber almost out, leaving a tab to hold the waste in place until the hull has been assembled. Finish cutting the limber holes when you are ready to fiberglass-tape the inside seams.

Note that Frame A is curved in the area of the bilge panel. You can cut out the portion of Frame A that provides access to the under-the-seat compartment, but be sure to leave the top of the frame intact. Frames B and C are notched ¼ inch to accept the ends of the floor platform. The frames' ¼-inch thickness here doesn't seem to offer much support to the floor platform, so I added ¾-inch by 2-inch framing later after taping the frames to the hull. I let the ends of this extra material extend out almost to the bilge panels.

Assembling the Hull

While construction to this point has taken a day or two, the actual assembly of the hull will only take a couple of hours or less.

The hull is built upside down, just like the construction model, and is supported on four legs to provide a comfortable height for working; I made the legs from 2-foot 2 by 4s. To provide a lip or ledge to temporarily support upside-down Frames B and C, I nailed to each 2 by 4 a board measuring ¾ inch by 3 ½ inches by 18 inches, which automatically sets the tops of Frames B and C precisely 18 inches off the floor. I'm on the short side, and this height works perfectly for me. But if you are 6 feet or taller, you might want to make the legs 2 feet 6 inches long and fasten a 2-foot board to them. In either case, the lips support the tops of the frames, which are clamped to the 2 by 4 legs. Fasten feet to the bottom of the 2 by 4s to keep them from toppling over while you begin to assemble the hull.

Fasten temporary cleats made of scrap wood (¾ inch by 1 inch, of various lengths) along the outside edges of the frames where the side panels, the bilge panels, and the bottom meet them. These are used for temporarily holding the panels to the frames until the outside seams are ready to be fiberglassed. I use 1-inch No.18 wire nails for this, nailing through the frames into the cleats. These nails are adequate when plenty are used and they are driven in well, and they are easily pulled out without wrecking things when the cleats are removed for taping the interior seams.

But if you have your doubts about the temporary nature of this procedure, use sheetrock screws instead of small nails. I mention this because a friend of mine had a minor disaster when he built a boat similar to the Cartopper, using the same construction method. He spent hours carefully setting up the hull in his garage, took one more admiring look before quitting for the day, went out and slammed the garage door behind him, and the whole temporarily nailed assembly slithered to the floor like a deck of cards!

Fitting the Sides

The sides go on after Frames B and C are clamped to the supporting legs. Position them against the frames, aligned with the frame-positioning marks you put on the panels when you laid them out; align the bottom edges with the corners of the frames where the limber holes will be; and when you are satisfied all is right, tack them to the cleats (no glue yet).

Fitting the Transom and Bottom

Spread glue on one side of the transom framing, and nail the after end of the appropriate side panel to it with ⅞-inch or 1-inch bronze ring nails. Let the other side of the transom lie where it wants while you do this. Apply glue to the other side of the transom and pull the end of the other side into it by hand — no Spanish windlass is required, though you will need a couple of clamps to hold the side to the transom frame while you nail it.

Now for the bottom panel. Line up its centerline with the centerline of the transom, and tack it there. Then

Nailing the ends of the side panels to the transom framing.

Nailing the after end of the bottom to the transom framing.

do the same thing at Frames C and B. A helper here to spot the centerline to the frames from underneath, while you tack from the outside, will speed up the process.

Take care at this point to be sure everything is lined up correctly. Sight down the centerline of the bottom and across the tops of the frames; check to be sure the frames lie in the same plane. Though this type of construction is more or less self-aligning, it is still possible to put a slight twist in the hull if the floor you are working on is extremely crooked. A peek takes only a second but pays off in the long run.

Fitting Frame A and the Stem

Tack temporary cleats to the after face of Frame A so they will be out of the way of the bottom panel when it is bent into place. Tack a temporary cleat to

A Spanish windlass is used to bring the forward ends of the side panels together.

Fitting the side panels to the stem.

the forward end of each side panel to catch a Spanish windlass. (These cleats should be positioned far enough back so they don't interfere with nailing the sides to the stem.)

The Spanish windlass is nothing more than a length of line that is used to pull the sides in at the bow and hold them there while you align Frame A in its proper position on the side panels and tack it to the frame cleats. Not much pull is required on the line; in fact, you can pull the sides in by hand and hold them while you tie a knot in the line. It's that easy.

Now ease in Frame A; clamp it to the bottom panel. Carefully match the centerline of the frame with the centerline of the bottom; make sure it is positioned properly in relation to the side panels; and tack it in place.

Fitting the Stem

Put the stem in place on the bottom panel, align both centerlines, and clamp it in place — no glue and no fastenings yet.

Apply glue to both surfaces of the stem where the sides are to bear, and bring the sides in together to land on the stem; adjust them so they are positioned correctly. I emphasize that both sides must be brought in to the stem together — do not bring in one side and nail it, then bring in the other. Hold both sides against the stem, and tack a 1-inch No.18 nail at the top of each panel into the stem. Adjust the stem slightly, if needed, and tack the bottom edges. When you are satisfied that everything is lined up correctly, permanently fasten the sides to the stem with 1-inch or 1 ¼-inch bronze ring nails.

Unclamp the stem from the bottom panel, spread glue on the bottom of the stem, push the bottom panel down to the stem, and fasten it in place with bronze ring nails.

Pull the temporary nails from the bottom at the transom, letting the bottom spring up, spread glue along the bottom edge of the transom framing, push down the bottom, and fasten it with bronze ring nails.

Fitting the Bilge Panels

Fitting the bilge panels is the most difficult part of building the Cartopper, so take your time and work them in a little at a time. There is quite a bit of twist in these panels, and they don't mind giving you a hard time. Sooner or later as you go you're likely to swear they will never fit, but the nice part of this type of construction is that they don't have to fit edge-to-edge. If the edges of the bilge panels are within ¼-inch of their neighbors, you are still in good shape. Open seams can be dealt with by getting underneath the hull and running masking tape along the inside of the seams to keep fiberglass putty from oozing through.

There are only two things to watch for when fitting the bilge panels. One is to be sure the middle of the panels is down before gluing and nailing their ends. The other is to be sure that the edges of the bilge panels lie on the same plane as the edges of their neighbors. This is necessary so the panel edges meet and flow in a fair curve without quick places caused by one edge being higher or lower than its neighbor. This is more difficult to explain than it is to see as you fit the panels.

You will discover tight and loose places when you put the bilge panels on. The loose places are no trouble, but the tight places must be freed so the panel can be adjusted. Do this by running a handsaw or a sabersaw down the joint.

If a bilge panel won't lie down properly next to its neighbor, drill small holes in the edges of both panels, force the bilge panel in place, and temporarily wire it. Soft mechanic's wire, 18 gauge, works the best; you can get it at an automotive supply store. You can also use hot-melt glue, duct tape — anything that will do the job. After the seams are filled with fiberglass putty from the outside, the temporary fastenings can be pulled.

Clamping the first bilge panel to the stem is easy, because you can hook the clamp to the stem. Your luck runs out on the second panel, as the first panel will interfere with clamping. So for this one I nail a stick on the side panel and use it as a button to hold the top end of the bilge panel while I nail it.

As with the side and bottom panels, spread glue along the transom edge and framing, and on the stem, and then nail the bilge panels with bronze ring nails.

Puttying and Taping Resins

It's time to begin the "tape" part of this "tack-and-tape" construction method. The edges of Cartopper's plywood panels must be permanently joined with fiberglass tape over a putty of epoxy or polyester resin mixed with microballoon filler.

Let's talk about resin for a minute. I use polyester resin because I'm used to it, it's available just down the road at Spruce Head Marine (and at a far cheaper price than epoxy), it's more than adequate for the job, and I've learned how to doctor it to suit my needs. If you'd prefer to use epoxy resin on your boat, go to it, but be sure to follow the product instructions carefully; epoxy is a little more temperamental than polyester, but it will do a good job.

I like to use a thin "laminating" resin, the waxless polyester resin found in most boatyards, because the absence of wax in the resin keeps the surface ready for more bonding without further prep work. I can stop work and even go off sailing for the rest of the day, then get back to work on the boat the next morning without having to sand everything first.

With the thicker "finishing" resin containing wax, even a half-hour pause on a warm day will allow the wax to float to the surface as the resin cures, and your bonding surface is lost until the wax is removed by sanding. I use this waxed finishing resin for my final coats on the boat, so I can sand everything smooth for painting. Laminating resin doesn't sand as well. Although you can smooth bubbles on the edges of 'glass cloth with coarse 20-grit sandpaper in a slow-turning variable-speed drill after the resin has cured, I've never had any luck sanding large areas of laminating-resin-coated cloth with a high-speed vibrator or belt sander; the sandpaper loads up too quickly. If you need to smooth things up with some sanding, take the time to apply a coat of finishing resin first.

Puttying the Outside Seams and Stem

Begin by checking the hull seams over once more to be sure they all lie together in fair curves that are

Nailing the bilge panel to the stem.

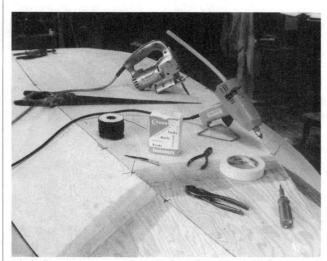

The hull is all closed in, with mechanic's wire used to hold the panel edges together.

pleasing to the eye. Then take a roll of 1-inch-wide masking tape and tape all the seams from underneath. The masking tape will keep the putty from falling through the wider seams, and it pulls off easily when the job is done (one of the few lucky breaks for boatbuilders that Murphy missed...).

With the masking tape in place, go back to the outside of the hull and mark each seam for the 3-inch-wide 'glass tape using a 1 ½-inch-wide block of wood as a guide to make a line parallel to each seam. You only need to mark one side of each seam. Brush the seams with polyester or epoxy resin, extending the resin out a couple of inches on each side of the seam. The edges of the plywood will soak up resin, so coat them liberally now so that they don't pull resin out of the 'glass putty that's going in next, weakening the bonding.

Use a block of wood as a marking gauge to help you run the tape straight along the seams.

Fill out the stem area with plenty of putty.

Use a rasp to round the puttied stem to shape.

When you're puttying or taping, you need to work with clean tools. The easiest way to keep them clean is to place them in a bath of acetone or lacquer thinner and clean them well between uses. If you get lumps of hardened resin on your smoothing tools, you have lost the whole show as far as neatness goes. The same goes for yourself; learn to work clean. Use gloves to protect your skin, be sure there's plenty of ventilation, take extra precautions when you handle solvents, and wear a face mask when you mix fillers or do any sanding. To give yourself more time, don't do fiberglass work in the sun; the resin sets up too quickly. If you are blessed with hot hands, remember to hold the containers at their edges, not in the palm of your hand.

With additives such as Cab-O-Sil, talcum powder, microballoons, or Fillite powder, I can doctor my resin into a tough 'glass putty of any consistency I want. Fillite is my favorite thickener; you can get it from Spruce Head Marine just like I do, along with the other 'glass supplies and hardware for Cartopper (Spruce Head Marine, Spruce Head, ME 04859; 207-594-7545). Fillite powder is easy to work with, strong, and cheap.

To begin filling Cartopper's outside seams, pour about ¼ inch of resin into a pint milk-carton container and mix in some hardener; a teaspoonful of hardener to a full pint of polyester resin is a good average. Use a little more in cold, damp weather, and a little less in warm weather. In all cases you'll need just a few drops for this small quantity of resin. Mix the resin and hardener well before you add the Fillite. Use just enough Fillite to make a good putty — not too drippy, not too stiff. Smooth the putty into the seam using a clean putty knife. We're trying to create a smooth, solid foundation for the tape that comes later, and after the putty dries, we'll sand the panel edges smooth, too.

Mix more putty as you need it, but if a batch starts to stiffen up a little, move to the stem and quickly apply the putty there. The stem is going to need a lot of putty, since it's easier to fill out the stem area with putty and then round it with a rasp, than it is to round the plywood edges. As soon as the stem filler putty hardens enough to shape, round it with a rasp. The rasp will quickly fill up with putty, but a wire brush will clean the rasp just as quickly.

Let the seams harden a few hours or so; overnight is better. Avoid bumping or disturbing the boat at this vulnerable stage, and don't remove any wire, tape, or glue or a bilge panel might part company from its neighbor. After the resin cures overnight, it's safe to take out the wires or "tacks," but don't move the hull around or turn it over until the outside seams are taped.

To prepare for the tape, sand all corners round with very coarse 20-grit sandpaper stapled to a stick hollowed on one side and made long enough to accept a sheet of paper. If you can't find 20-grit paper at your hardware store (and chances are you won't), go to a tool-rental store and buy sheets of coarse sandpaper made for floor sanders.

Taping the Outside Seams

A 2-pound roll of 3-inch-wide fiberglass tape is fine for the rest of the boat, but a strip of 4-inch-wide tape does a better job on the stem. If you don't have it, a scrap of your 10-ounce cloth will do.

We'll start at the stem, cover the entire transom next, and then run 3-inch tape along the outside seams in between. Doing the sheathing in pieces this way is a lot easier than trying to get one piece of cloth to cover the entire length of the hull as well as the transom and the stem. If you try to do it all with just one piece of cloth, you'll find yourself spending too much time trying to get sags and wrinkles out around the stem and transom, and you'll feel your composure slipping as time runs out. Don't tempt Murphy. Do the most difficult places first: the stem, the transom, and the seams. And then fill in between with the larger pieces. No sweat.

Do a little cleaning up before you begin. Sweep the hull off first, then the floor. I can guarantee that if you drop a piece of wet cloth on a dirty floor, it will pick up everything there. You might find yourself getting a little nervous as you pick out the bits of dirt while the catalyzed resin you so thoughtfully mixed up beforehand is hardening.

Dry-fit the length of 4-inch tape or cloth to the stem, then use a brush to liberally coat the stem area with laminating resin. Brush it out a little past where the tape will end. Lay the tape or cloth into the resin, and wet it out thoroughly with more resin, using a 3-inch roller and a brush. The tape should smooth right out and take the shape of the stem. The trick here is using enough resin to wet the tape out thoroughly and fill the weave of the cloth.

You're going to need about nine yards of 10-ounce, 38-inch 'glass cloth for Cartopper. Measure out two 12-foot lengths of cloth for the hull sides' sheathing and set them aside. Then drape a piece of cloth over the transom and let it flap over the transom corners onto the hull about 3 to 4 inches and hang down past the top of the transom about the same amount. Don't trim it any smaller yet. Mix up some resin and roll it on the transom and around onto the hull a few inches. Then put the cloth right in the fresh resin and, with either a paintbrush or a 3-inch roller, smooth and wet the cloth out. A roller does the best job of spreading resin evenly.

After the cloth is smoothed across the transom, concentrate on wetting out the corners and make the cloth lie around the corners smoothly. This is easier than it sounds, but the cloth must be well saturated with resin. After working the cloth around the corners, eyeball the length you want the cloth to run around onto

Lay the stem tape or cloth into wet resin and wet it out with more resin until it lies smoothly in all directions and the weave is filled.

Cut a piece of 10-ounce cloth for a generous fit over the transom.

Roll resin onto the transom, extending around the sides and bottom a few inches.

Position the cloth in wet resin; smooth and wet it out with more resin, working from the center out to the edges and around the corners.

Coat the puttied outside seams with resin, position the tape to the gauge marks, and wet out the tape with more resin.

With the top cleat removed, use putty to create a fillet between the frame and the side panel.

the hull sides, trim the cloth, and roll it down snug in place with more resin.

Make sure there are no white-looking places in the cloth; they indicate trapped air and not enough resin. When you're satisfied that the cloth is evenly saturated, wait a half hour to an hour until the resin kicks off (hardens), then give it another coat with either a brush or roller to fill the weave of the cloth. A brush gets on more resin, but the price you pay for using it on this nearly vertical surface is sagging of the resin, which can mean extra sanding before you paint. Three coats of laminating resin do the basic job; then, when the whole hull is covered, you can add a finish coat of resin with wax in it.

Now for the long, outside seams. As you did with the stem, dry-fit a length of tape (3 inches this time), liberally coat the seam area with laminating resin extending out beyond your gauge marks, then lay the tape in the resin and wet it out thoroughly with more resin. Use enough resin to fill the weave of the cloth.

Why not go ahead now and cover the rest of the hull with cloth? Because the nails driven through the hull from outside holding the frames to the cleats were left sticking out for easy removal; remember, these cleats were nailed two ways. If you were to drive these nails in from the outside so you could 'glass over them, you would be locking the cleats in and wouldn't be able to get them out when you got around to taping the frames to the hull. You can't pull them out now because the frames could shift, changing the boat's shape.

Puttying and Taping the Frames and the Inside Seams

The long fore-and-aft inside seams are going to take the longest time to tape and will be the trickiest to do because they take more putty than the outside seams. Here it pays to gain yourself some time by paying attention to temperature. I'd leave these seams until the coolest time of the day, or have a helper who knows what he or she is doing, so these seams can be done in one smooth motion.

The procedure for puttying and taping the long inside seams is about the same as for the outside seams: Mark your tape guideline with the 1 1/2-inch parallel guide block, apply resin to the seams, putty, and tape. We want to create a smooth fillet along these seams for the tape, and accommodating the ever-changing lay of the planks takes a little extra concentration. While you're thinking about this you can work on taping the frames, even in the middle of a hot day.

The frames get taped on both sides to the panels, using short lengths of tape between the limber holes, so you're not likely to get into trouble here. Figure on about four hours, total, for this operation.

Start out by carefully turning Cartopper over, and place her on sawhorses, right-side up. You can start taping the frames to the panels anywhere you want, but only remove cleats from the area where you're working; don't take all the cleats off any one frame all at once. Let's start by taking the cleats off the side panels; 'glass-tape both sides of the frame to them, then tape them to the bilge panels and the bottom panel.

Remove the masking tape from the seams, and take the top cleats off the frame. Measure the distance from the edge of the top limber hole to the sheer, and cut four pieces of 3-inch 'glass tape, enough for each side of the frame and for both sides of the boat. It makes sense to cut these pieces beforehand, instead of later while your resin is hardening up. Think ahead all you can.

Mark the tape line with the 1 ½-inch parallel guide, coat the seam with resin, then mix up a small amount of putty (about a quarter pint). Lay Cartopper over on her bilge to make spreading the fillet along the seam easier. Use a tongue depresser, available from a drugstore, to spread the putty; it makes a neat, coved application. If the putty is mixed a little on the stiff side, you can shape the fillet and it will stay put.

When each fillet is smoothed to your satisfaction, coat the area with resin, position the tape, and wet it out thoroughly with more resin. As each frame is taped to the side panel, the frame is locked in place enough so that the rest of the cleats can be taken out. One of the nice things about "tacking" with small No. 18 wire nails is that if your claw hammer won't pull them out, a pair of pliers will do the job without causing misalignment. Tape each frame and bilge panel with the boat heeled over, then heel her the other way to work on the other side.

The day after all my frames were taped, it was 65 degrees F in my shop at seven in the morning — exactly right for taping those long seams. You're going to need a 1 ½-inch putty knife to spread the putty on the seam, then a couple of shaped wooden blades that you make yourself to shape the fillet. One should be rounded more than the other for the sharper angles from amidships to the after end of the boat. Better yet, if you can get your hands on one, is an auto-body repairman's putty spreader made from flexible rubber; this easily accommodates its shape to any change of angle.

Begin by cutting out the limber holes; they're just hanging from their tabs and can be easily sawn out with a handsaw. Cut the 3-inch tape to length and use the 1 ½-inch parallel guide to mark the tape line on one side of the seam. Saturate the seam with resin, then mix up a batch of putty. You'll want to mix enough putty to do each seam with one batch, so mix a half pint or more per seam. You want to get the putty in the seam fast, smooth the fillet, lay the tape in the fresh putty, coat it with more resin, and wet it all out so that the whole job sets up together. Work quickly, but carefully. Working alone, it's going to take about four hours to do all four long inside seams.

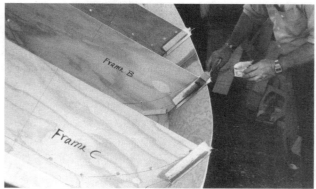

The frames are taped to the panels with short lengths of tape between the limber holes.

Try to make a smooth fillet along the long inside seams.

Coat the long seam fillets with resin, position the tape, and wet it out thoroughly with more resin.

With the inside taping done, you can finish cutting out the inside of the frame panels.

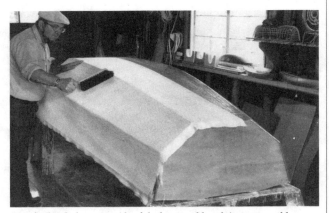

Dry-fit the cloth on one side of the boat, and brush it out smoothly.

Working with a roller, wet out the cloth with resin, starting in the middle so that any air is forced out to the edges.

With the inside seams and frames taped and cured, you can finish cutting out the inside of the frame panels. This is a good time to put the foot stretchers in, too. Those are the cleats that are fastened to the bilge panels. Be sure they're positioned to suit your height. Now turn Cartopper upside down to sheathe the hull.

If you think your outside taping is going to need some sanding before the hull sheathing goes on, give the areas a coat of finishing resin or resin that's been doctored with a "surfacing agent." I sometimes use a surfacing agent made by Advance Coatings Co. (Depot Rd., Westminster, MA 01473). I add a heaping tablespoon to a pint of resin. This makes sanding a lot easier.

Put a coarse 20-grit disc in your variable-speed electric drill and grind off any 'glass bubbles in the tape or hull in preparation for laying the cloth. When you've finished sanding, give the rest of the hull a coat of laminating resin and let it sink into the plywood and set up.

Sheathing the Hull

I picked a 60-degree-F morning for sheathing Cartopper, and it couldn't have been better for handling those larger pieces of cloth. Some manufacturers used to recommend laying cloth in fresh resin, then smoothing it out. But they never said how much cloth was easy to handle at one time or at what temperature. Sure, you can put a yard of cloth into fresh resin and get it laid down fast enough to stay out of trouble, even in warm weather. And that technique can be useful on a vertical surface. But there's no way I would try it on a hot day with a piece of cloth 38-inches wide and 12-feet long, such as the one we're going to use on Cartopper. Imagine getting a piece of cloth that size half stuck, full of wrinkles, and finding you're powerless to do anything more about it!

Take the two 12-foot lengths of your 38-inch, 10-ounce cloth, and lay one of the pieces on one side of your dry hull, with an overhang at the sheer. Trim the selvedge edge (the factory binding) at the sheer, leaving an overhang of an inch or so. Getting rid of the selvedge will allow the cloth's weave to move more freely in all directions. Smooth out the cloth with a dry brush, getting rid of wrinkles. Brush the cloth from amidships toward the bow, and then toward the stern, and the cloth will fit like a glove. Don't hesitate to give the cloth a tug with your hand if brushing alone won't do the job.

Mix a pint of laminating resin, pour some right in the middle of the cloth, and start to work with a roller. Work it in an ever-widening pattern, starting in the middle so that the air is forced out to the edges. Cloth stretches when it is saturated with resin, and you want to avoid creating bubbles. When everything's smooth, roll on a second coat of resin to fill the weave, and let it all set up before you start on the second piece of cloth. This is safer than trying to cram on the last piece of cloth and finding you can't brush it out because it's sticking to the first piece.

When you're ready to position the second piece of cloth, look for the selvedge edge showing through from the first piece. You can match the two edges with an overlap of a couple of inches, or simply butt them. Smooth out the cloth carefully, wet it out as you did with the first piece, then treat it to a second coat of resin.

Use resin with wax in it for the finishing coat, and put it on lavishly with a 4-inch brush. If the temperature is up around 70 or 80 degrees, you can start sanding within an hour if the resin looks dull and feels hard to your thumbnail. To hasten drying even more, take the boat out in the sun; you'll want to do your sanding outdoors, anyway, if you have a small shop like mine.

Get at this sanding as quickly as you can — when the resin is cured enough so that it doesn't clog your sandpaper, but before it sets up rock hard. This will save you a lot of time, and makes doing a good job much easier.

I trim any excess cloth away and then start sanding the bottom of the hull first, because it's always the first to set up. I put on a face mask and use a belt sander with a 50- or 60-grit belt for sanding the entire outside of the hull; then I switch to a Rockwell vibrator sander (which takes a half sheet of paper) and use 60-grit for final smoothing. I see no point in using a finer grit, because the coarser paper leaves some tooth for the paint to grab onto, and that's what I want!

You don't really have to sheathe the entire outside of Cartopper with cloth, but you should at least double up on the taped seams. I'd use 4-inch tape for the first layer and 3-inch for the second. You may save some weight or money doing this, but you'll be losing abrasion protection and a good base for paint (paint over fiberglass seems to last forever without cracking or peeling). For me, that alone is worth the trouble and expense.

The Skeg

Make the skeg from ¾-inch pine, spruce, fir, mahogany, or even oak, if you want. Scribe-fit it to the hull, bore through the hull from the outside along the centerline, bed the skeg in a marine bedding compound or in epoxy thickened with Cab-O-Sil or talcum, and fasten the skeg from inside using 2-inch No. 14 stainless steel pan-head screws with washers. Use shorter screws at the skeg's thinner end. Later, after painting, add a piece of ⅝-inch half-oval brass to the skeg for protection.

If you don't have a helper to hold the skeg in place while you fasten it, clamp a couple of 2 by 4s together side by side to the skeg and weigh them down to hold the skeg in place. I use a couple of pieces of railroad track for weights.

Gunwales

You need four gunwales, two to a side, made from ½-inch by 1-inch by 12-foot 6-inch stock. Mine were

Trim the cloth overhang before your final coats of resin.

Scribe-fit the skeg to the hull.

Bore from the outside for the skeg fastenings.

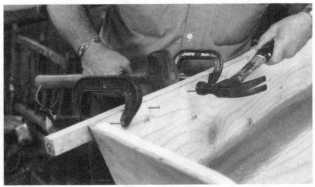

The gunwales, made of two pieces to take the bend more easily, are clamped and fastened along the sheer.

Use a homemade T-square to mark the waterline and the boottop.

The floor platform can be built in three pieces, as shown in the drawings, or in one piece, if you have a piece of plywood large enough.

ripped from slices off a clear (as clear as I could get) 14-foot 2 by 4. Fir or spruce, it doesn't matter.

Why are the gunwales cut 12 feet 6 inches when the boat's length is only 11 feet 6 inches? The latter length is down the centerline, but the length around the sheer is about 12 feet 1 inch. Add another 5 inches for trimming, and 12 feet 6 inches is the size to start with. Usually the outside edge of a 2 by 4 plank has the best grain and is freer of knots, so keep the best slices for the outside course.

Pick a pair of gunwales — outside and inside — and spread glue on their inside faces. Position them along the sheer, and start clamping them in place, working from the bow aft, or from amidships toward the ends. Fasten them from inside the hull with 1 ⅛-inch bronze ring nails, spaced about 6 to 7 inches apart. Wipe off any excess glue immediately, and trim the ends when the fastening is completed.

Corner knees and a breasthook are optional on Cartopper. They add something to her looks, and the breasthook is a handy place to grab onto when you want to haul Cartopper out, but they add little structural strength.

Finishing

Give Cartopper's interior a coat or two of sealer, and worry later about painting her. Since I'm already using polyester resin for the taping process, I generally thin some waxed resin about 30 percent with acetone and keep on going with it to seal the rest of the hull.

While you're waiting for the sealing coat of resin to set up, you can add a touch of class to Cartopper by striking her waterline and marking her boottop. If it weren't easy to do, I'd never bother to do it myself or mention it. Scribing the waterline on the full-sized boat is done the same way it was done on the construction model.

I put Cartopper on a sheet of 14-foot plywood resting on boards across sawhorses, but a garage floor, a paved driveway, or any good, flat surface will do as well. (On the hull I'm finishing in the accompanying photograph I'll try a rockered waterline, since the boards the plywood is resting on have sagged a bit. It should complement Cartopper's pretty sheer....)

After leveling the hull, I'll make a sort of T-square that's the height of the boottop, mark the boottop's height around the hull, cut the depth of the boottop off the T-square (the distance to the load waterline at 231 pounds), and then mark the waterline around the hull. I should be finished in about an hour; and I'll be sipping a cool one while anyone using the string-and-level method is still hard at work. You can skip the boottop and just put the waterline on using this method. It's so easy, it's fun.

To get the height to the 231-pound waterline, see

Cartopper's body plan on sheet No. 3. The measurement from the hull's bottom to the waterline is 4 inches; to the top of her boot (measured at a scale of 1 ½ inches equals 1 foot) is 7 inches. The depth of the boottop isn't shown there, but does show on the sail plan (sheet No. 4), drawn to a scale of ¾ inch equals 1 foot; it measures about ¾ inch in depth. That's a personal choice, however; you can make the boot deeper or shallower, as you wish.

Mark the waterlines on your T-square and level the boat fore-and-aft. Note that on sheet No. 2 the 231-pound waterline strikes the aft end of the skeg 2 inches below her planking. Using that height on your T-square, pull Cartopper's stern down to the plywood she rests on until both heights match — or maybe you'll need to shim her up a bit. Check both the bow and stern for proper height from the plywood, and when you're satisfied, go for it.

Tape the waterline and the boottop with masking tape, give her a coat of sanding primer, and then paint. I'm not going to go into any special finishing techniques, because that information is readily available elsewhere. My own experience tells me that the base that's under the paint makes the biggest difference in a paint job that lasts and lasts — more so than the paint itself. Sheathing Cartopper's outside, as I mentioned before, provides that good base.

The Seats and the Floor

While the sanding primer dries, you can finish building Cartopper's interior. We have a bow seat to install, and we should put the mast partner support under it in case we decide to convert her to sailing later. The mast partner support is made from pine or spruce, and is shown on Cartopper's profile plan, sheet No. 2.

The floor platform is shown as No. 14 and is built in three pieces; this seemed like more work to me, so I built it in one piece, since I had a piece of plywood large enough to do it. To fit it in one piece, measure its overall length (3 feet 1 inch) and its greatest width (2 feet 9 inches) with your scale rule, cut it a little larger, and scribe-fit it all around. Three pieces work pretty much the same way. Frame the platform as in the drawings, and give it a coat of sealer.

The movable box seat shown as No. 28 (sheet No. 2) is as easy as anything you will ever make that is part of a boat, so I'll spare you the how-to, other than to mention that instead of making its top flat, I curved it for a little more seating comfort.

A pair of Wilcox Crittenden sidemount oarlocks, placed about 3 inches farther aft than shown, suited me, along with a pair of 6 ½- to 7-foot Shaw & Tenney spruce oars and a Dacron painter.

Cartopper's complete, and I've enjoyed building her!

Install the bow seat, coating, puttying, and taping the seams.

The finished Cartopper has it all — looks, lightness, and performance.

Building plans for the Cartopper, which include assembly instructions, are available from Harold H. Payson & Co., Pleasant Beach Rd., South Thomaston, ME 04858. The price is $35.

The Cape Charles Sea Kayak

Text and photographs by Chris Kulczycki
Drawings by Carl Ulanowicz

I built the Cape Charles because I wanted a big, stable sea kayak for long trips, particularly for the trip to Newfoundland that I had been planning. Not satisfied with any of the plans or kits I'd seen, I made a list of design goals for my perfect kayak. These included light weight, high initial and secondary stability, a big payload, a roomy cockpit, good performance in a wide variety of sea conditions, and fast plywood construction. Aesthetics were also high on my list; it is too easy to draw a hard-chined boat that looks like a packing crate, and I was determined not to launch an eyesore. I drew and redrew my design, eventually settling on a kayak that was 18 feet long, 25½ inches wide, and 38 pounds.

The Cape Charles has a long waterline and therefore a high hull speed. Because of its greater waterline beam, larger wetted surface, and hard-chined construction, it is not as effortless to paddle as some of my compounded plywood designs; but it is roomy and comfortable. At 38 pounds it weighs about a third less than comparable fiberglass or plastic boats.

The author tests his newly built 18-foot stitch-and-tape kayak in the Chesapeake Bay.

The hull is built stitch-and-tape fashion from two sheets of 4-millimeter plywood and the deck from one sheet of 3-millimeter. It is built without any strongback or station molds. Building time is about 60 hours, not including finishing. While building the boat, I was surprised by how easily it went together. It is a little more labor-intensive to build than a compounded plywood boat, but certainly much less complicated than a skin-on-frame kayak or a plywood kayak built over a frame.

Here's how you can build your own Cape Charles.

Tools and Materials

You'll need relatively few tools to build the Cape Charles. A saber saw and a drill are the only power tools you must have. You'll also need a block plane, a staple gun, a handsaw, pliers, a screwdriver, a tape measure, and a carpenter's square. Clamps are mandatory for any boatbuilding project — buy or borrow as many as you can, at least 20. A table saw would be helpful for ripping long pieces, such as the ¾-inch-square sheer clamps, but if you don't have access to one you could pay a lumberyard a few dollars to do the millwork for you. An electric sander is useful when preparing the boat for painting or varnishing, and a portable circular saw is handy, though neither is essential.

The cost of the materials, listed in the accompanying table, should be around $400. The two 4-millimeter plywood sheets for the hull should be of marine grade; okoume, sapele, meranti, or lauan is fine. The deck should be 3-millimeter marine-grade okoume. Other species of marine-grade plywood, or even exterior-grade, could be used if they don't contain any voids and are of the proper thickness; but the extra time you'll spend to obtain a nice finish on cheap panels might be worth more than the few dollars you save.

You will use about three quarts of marine epoxy resin. Although there are many good brands of epoxy on the market today, I've had fine results with WEST System, System Three, and MAS brands. Whatever brand you buy, make sure that it is formulated for marine woodworking. Also, buy the small metering pumps that accurately measure the epoxy and hardener; they'll save you much time and irritation. Most epoxy manufacturers have short manuals explaining the use of their products and the precautions that need to be taken. Read them.

Because epoxy is readily absorbed by wood, it will affect the wood's bending properties. Wipe up any epoxy that oozes out of joints before it fully hardens. It is also important not to starve the joints — if you use too little epoxy, most of it will be absorbed by the wood, leaving a dry and weak joint. Let the epoxy sit on the joint for a few minutes to determine if more is needed before clamping or joining the parts permanently.

Materials

2 sheets of 4mm plywood (4 x 8')

1 sheet of 3mm plywood (4 x 8')

3 x 2' of ¼" plywood

3 x 2' of ⅜" plywood

40' of ¾"-square spruce or fir

17' of ¼ x 1 ¼" lattice

37' of ¼ x ¾" ash or other clear wood for rubrails

1 gallon of marine epoxy resin and thickening agents for epoxy

2 rolls of 3", 9-oz fiberglass tape

50' of copper wire (18 gauge is best)

8, #8, ¾" stainless-steel wood screws and finish washers

6 yds. 6 oz glass cloth

8, 1 ½" thin stainless-steel sheet-metal or wood screws

½ lb ¾", 14-gauge bronze ring nails

The following items are needed if you plan to install bulkheads and hatches:

8' of 1" foam weatherstripping

4, 1" plastic Fastex buckles

14' of 1" nylon webbing

8, #8, ¾" stainless-steel wood screws and finish washers

2 x 2' of 3" closed-cell foam or ¼" plywood for bulkheads

7' of ¼ x 1 ¼" lattice

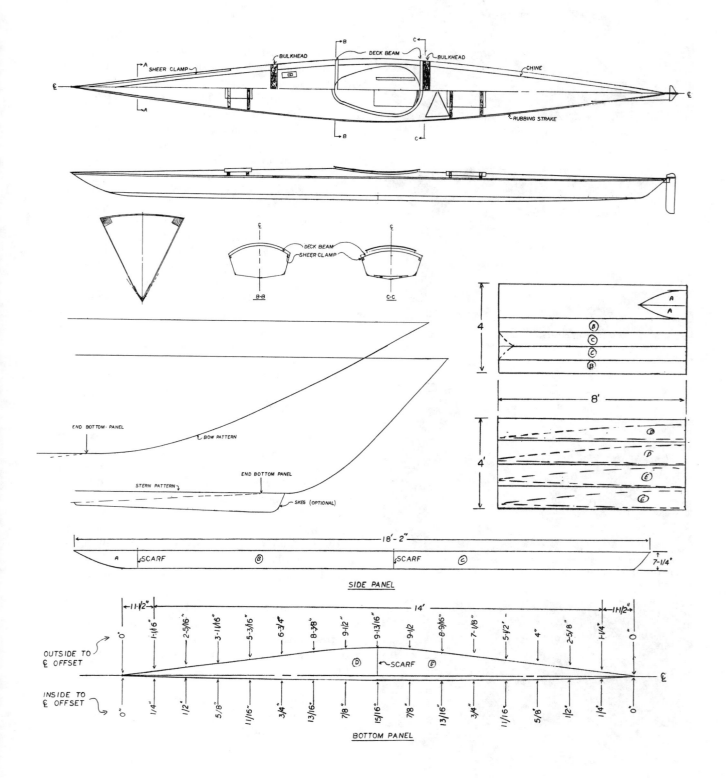

BULKHEAD   DECK BEAM   BULKHEAD

SHEER CLAMP

CHINE

RUBBING STRAKE

DECK BEAM
SHEER CLAMP

B-B   C-C

END BOTTOM PANEL

BOW PATTERN

STERN PATTERN

END BOTTOM PANEL

SKEG (OPTIONAL)

4'

A
A
B
C
C
B

8'

D
D
E
E

4'

18'-2"

A   SCARF   B   SCARF   C   7-1/4"

SIDE PANEL

11-1/2"   14'   11-1/2"

OUTSIDE TO
℄ OFFSET   0"   1-1/16"   2-5/16"   3-1/16"   5-3/16"   6-3/4"   8-3/8"   9-1/2"   9-13/16"   9-1/2"   8-9/16"   7-1/8"   5-1/2"   4"   2-5/8"   1-1/4"   0"

D   SCARF   E

INSIDE TO
℄ OFFSET   0"   1/4"   1/2"   5/8"   11/16"   3/4"   13/16"   7/8"   15/16"   7/8"   13/16"   3/4"   11/16"   5/8"   1/2"   1/4"   0"

BOTTOM PANEL

As you cut the scarfs, the plywood's veneers will appear as bands. Here, four panels are stacked with their edges staggered, and the scarfs are being cut all at once.

This scarf was cut with a belt sander; it needs to be touched up with a block plane.

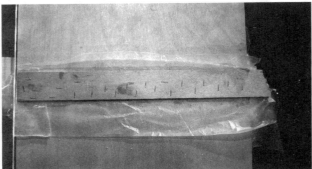

Clamping the scarf by stapling it to the work surface is quick and easy. The piece of scrap plywood will be pulled up with all the staples once the epoxy has cured. Notice the string line used to check alignment.

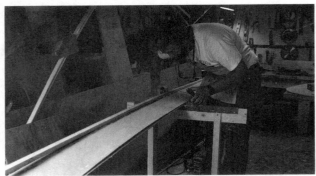

You can glue on both sheer clamps at once by laying the side planks back-to-back.

Scarfing the Hull Panels

Cut one of the 4-millimeter plywood sheets into four 11 ¾-inch by 8-foot strips for the bottom panels. Cut the other sheet into four 7 ¼-inch by 8-foot strips and two 7 ¼-inch by 28-inch strips. The 8-foot strips will be glued together, using an 8:1 scarf joint, forming four long planks from which the two side panels and the bottom panels of the kayak will be cut.

Start by making a pencil line 1 ¼ inches in from one end of the panel to be scarfed (4 millimeters multiplied by 8 is 32 millimeters, or about 1 ¾ inches). Lay the panel on your workbench with this end flush with the end of the bench. Plane away the wood between the penciled line and the bottom face of the sheet where it meets the workbench. Soon the layers of the plywood will appear as bands; try to keep these parallel as you plane. When you have a smooth surface between the line and a feather-like edge at the bottom of the plywood, you're done. This isn't as difficult as it sounds, but practice on a piece of scrap first. Several panels can be lined up in staggered fashion and their scarfs cut at once; the end of each sheet rests on the pencil line of the sheet below it. You can also cut the scarfs with a belt sander to save time.

Mix up a couple of ounces of epoxy and thicken it to the consistency of jam. Lay the first panel down, taper facing up, with the scarf resting on a sheet of plastic film. Spread half the epoxy on the joint, then place the second panel in position. Cover the joint with another sheet of plastic. Now, lay the next two similar panels over the first ones, taking care that they are all precisely aligned. Stretch a piece of string along the long edge of each plank to check the alignment of the joint.

Cover this second joint with another sheet of plastic and then lay a strip of scrap plywood over the scarf; drive a staple every inch along the joint. Tap each staple with a hammer to ensure that it is fully driven. Repeat these steps with the other planks.

When the epoxy in the scarf joints has fully cured (overnight), pull up the sheet of scrap plywood, and the staples should pull out with it. Sand or plane off any epoxy that has squeezed out of the joint.

Laying Out and Cutting the Hull Panels

You should now have two 15-foot 11-inch by 11 ¾-inch planks and two 18-foot 1-inch by 7 ¼-inch planks. Carefully mark a centerline 1 inch from the edge of one of the short planks. Mark the offset points to the left and right of that line, as shown on the layout diagram on the plans. Use a batten to draw a fair curve connecting these points. Drive small brads at the measurement points, and hold the batten against them.

Use the patterns on the plans to draw the curves of the bow and the stern on the longer planks from which the side panels will be cut.

With a jigsaw, cut out the panels just outside your pencil line, and then carefully trim them to the line with a block plane. Clamp or temporarily nail the similar panels together, and cut and trim them as pairs at the same time to ensure they are identical.

Installing the Sheer Clamps

The sheer clamps provide a gluing surface for joining the deck to the hull. Make or buy two spruce or fir strips 18 feet 2 inches long by ¾ inch square. It may be more economical to join shorter sections with an 8:1 scarf to form the full-length sheer clamp.

When the epoxy in the hull joint and sheer clamps has fully cured (overnight), glue the sheer clamps onto the inside top edge of the side panels. Both sheer clamps can be installed at once by laying the panels back-to-back and clamping the sheer clamps to them. If you don't have enough woodworking clamps to hold the sheer clamps in place, you can staple them individually while the epoxy sets.

Assembling the Hull

Lay the side panels sheer clamp to sheer clamp, and drill several ¹⁄₁₆-inch holes 4 inches apart and about ⅜ inch from the edge at both ends of the panels. Wire the bow and stern loosely together with short pieces of copper wire (keeping all the twists on the outside). Use a piece of scrap wood to spread the sheer clamps apart near the center of the panels. They should be 25 inches apart at the center. Now, you'll have to cut a bevel at the inside edge of the ends of each sheer clamp so the panels can be neatly brought together. Cut these bevels carefully with your handsaw.

Drill ¹⁄₁₆-inch holes ⅜ inch from the edges at 4-inch intervals along the inner and outside edges of the two bottom panels. Drill these holes with both panels stacked so they are in identical positions. Wire the panels together loosely along the inner edge (keel line). Cut pieces of wire about 3 inches long and thread them through the tie holes. Twist the wire under the hull so the panels just touch.

Lay the side panel unit upside down and place the wired-together bottom panels on top of it. Drill a corresponding ¹⁄₁₆-inch hole in the side plank for each hole you've drilled on the outer edge of the bottom plank. Wire the bottom panels loosely to the

You'll need lots of C-clamps to glue the sheer clamps.

First, wire together the ends of the side panels and the keel line of the bottom panels. A spacer of scrap wood spreads the sides to the proper beam width.

Wire the bottom panels to the sides.

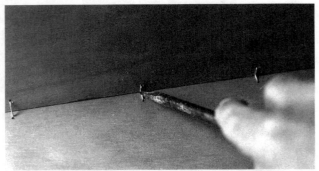

Press the wires against the wood on the inside seams. This tightens the wires and prevents little bumps under the tape.

Tape the inside seams with two layers of 3-inch, 9-ounce fiberglass tape.

Fully saturate the tape with unthickened epoxy. Work it into the tape with a disposable brush to eliminate dry spots and air pockets.

After turning the hull over, cut off the tie-wires, sand off any epoxy that's dripped through the edges, and clean up the outside seams with a plane.

side panels. Gradually tighten all the wires until the panel edges come together. Carefully turn the hull over and push each tie-wire down against the hull with a screwdriver point so the wires lie flat against the wood. Tighten or loosen the wires until the wood-to-wood joints are smooth and even, and without lumps or hollows.

Taping the Hull Seams

Set the hull right-side up and see that it is carefully supported so there is no distortion where it touches the sawhorses or the workbench. At its widest point, which is 9 feet 6 inches from the tip of the bow, the hull should measure 25 inches at the top of the side panels and 21 inches at the chine. If these measurements are true, the hull will assume its proper shape, except at the ends. Near where the four panels join at the bow and the stern, the bottom panels will tend to "flatten out." Use a spring-clamp to squeeze them into a sharp vee; the angle should be about as shown on the plans. You're now ready to tape the inside hull joints.

Mix about 8 ounces of thickened epoxy and spread a bead along the joints so it just covers the wires. Cut a piece of fiberglass tape, and lay it over each joint. Mix about 16 ounces of unthickened epoxy and brush some of it over the tape until it is saturated; use a disposable brush to work the resin into the tape. Lay a second piece of tape over the first one. Work more unthickened epoxy into both layers of tape, being careful to eliminate any air bubbles and dry spots.

When the epoxy has hardened, gently turn the hull over and cut the tie-wires off flush with the plywood. Scrape or sand any epoxy that has squeezed through the joint. Sand or file down any projecting ends of the copper wire. Cover the outside joints with fiberglass tape and saturate it with unthickened epoxy applied with a foam roller.

Tape the outside seams, and saturate the tape and wood with unthickened epoxy applied with a foam roller.

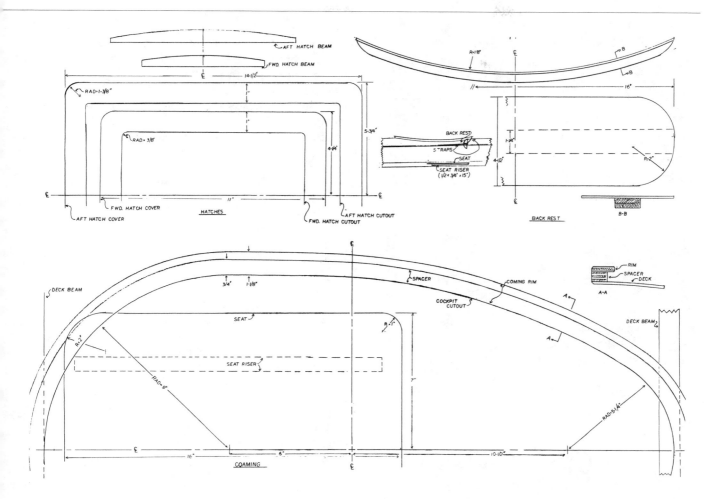

When the first coat of epoxy has cured, brush on a second coat to fill the weave of the tape. If paddling in rocky areas add a layer of glass cloth on the bottom panels.

Making and Installing the Deck Beams

Each deckbeam is laminated from three 26-inch strips of ¼-inch by 1 ½-inch lattice or furring. Make two simple bending jigs by drawing the 24-inch and 18-inch radii on pieces of scrap board, cutting them

Simple jigs are used to laminate the deckbeams.

out, and drilling holes for the C-clamps as shown in the photo.

Spread some thickened epoxy between the furring strips and wrap them in plastic so they won't stick to the jig. Clamp the furring strips into place and allow the epoxy to cure overnight.

When the epoxy in the hull joints has cured, hold the hull at the maximum beam of 25 inches at a point 9 feet 6 inches from the bow as you did earlier, and trim the deckbeams so they fit 15 ½ inches forward and aft of this point. Glue the deckbeams to the sheer clamps, and hold them in place with two 1 ½-inch screws driven into the sheer clamp. Be sure to pre-drill the holes for the screws.

Installing the Bulkheads

Recently I've started using 3-inch flexible, high-density, closed-cell foam, such as Minicell, for bulkheads. It is easier to install than plywood and provides additional flotation. Closed-cell foam can be cut with a large, serrated knife or a long blade fitted in your saber saw. You could also make bulkheads from ¼-inch plywood.

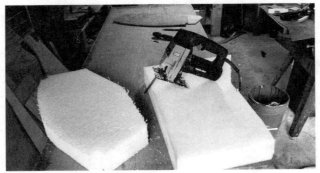

Bulkheads made from 3-inch closed-cell foam are easily installed.

Coat both the inside of the hull and the underside of the deck with epoxy just prior to installing the deck.

Bronze ring nails hold the deck down until the epoxy cures.

With the deck just installed, my Cape Charles looks like a strange submarine.

Using a piece of cardboard, make a mockup of the bulkhead and check its fit. Fold the cardboard along the centerline to ensure that it is symmetrical. Trace the shape onto a piece of 3-inch closed-cell foam or plywood and cut out the bulkhead. The top edges of the bulkheads should be the same radius as the closest deckbeams. The after bulkhead should fit just behind the deckbeam. The position of the forward bulkhead can vary depending on the length of your legs.

Glue closed-cell foam bulkheads into place with a generous bead of 3M 5200 sealant on each side of the bulkhead. If you use plywood bulkheads, install them with short lengths of fiberglass tape folded at the joint and epoxied into place. Add a fillet of epoxy at the hull-to-plywood bulkhead joint, as you did when taping the hull joints.

Installing the Deck

The deck is cut in three sections from a sheet of 3 millimeter plywood. The after section extends 8 feet from the tip of the stern to the cockpit. The middle deck section extends almost to the bow; it will be attached to the after section with a butt joint. A short piece covers the bow, and it is scarfed to the middle section.

Mark the deck panels by holding or stapling the 3-millimeter plywood sheet on the hull and tracing the hull's shape onto it. All three pieces will fit on one 4 by 8-foot sheet if they are laid out end-for-end. Cut out the deck sections about ½ inch proud. You can cut the cockpit and hatch openings now, or you can wait until the deck is glued into place. Scarf the short bow section onto the middle deck panel so they can be installed as a single panel.

Lay the deck sections on the hull for a trial fit. You will notice that they don't lie squarely on the sheer clamps. Plane the top of the sheer clamps so they match the radius of the deck. Take your time planing, and you'll be rewarded with a fair deck line.

Saturate the inside of the hull and the underside of the deck with epoxy just prior to installing the deck. Apply two coats of unthickened epoxy resin with a foam roller. Finally, glue the two deck sections to the sheer clamps, deck beams, and bulkheads. Hold the deck down with ¾-inch bronze ring nails every 4 inches. Be sure to nail on alternate sides as you go, port and then starboard, or the deck will creep off to one side.

After the epoxy in the hull-to-deck joint has hardened, cut off the excess deck with your saber saw. Finish up by trimming it flush to the hull with a block plane. Because a kayak's hull-to-deck joint can take quite a beating, I suggest that you add rubrails. Ash, teak, or white oak will work well. Select a piece with straight grain, and rip it into ¼-inch by ¾-inch strips. Spread thickened epoxy on the strips, and tack them into place with ¾-inch brass brads spaced 4 inches apart. Cut and finish the rails just short of the boat's ends.

Installing the Coaming, Seat, Backrest, and Footbraces

Make the Cape Charles's coaming by laminating a ring of ¼-inch plywood onto a spacer that is glued to the kayak's deck. The coaming shown on the plans will accommodate many popular brands of sprayskirts, but you could easily change the dimensions to accommodate odd-sized sprayskirts or odd-sized paddlers.

First, cut the spacer to which the rim will be glued. Make the spacer from ⅜-inch plywood; this can be exterior grade since it will be barely visible and will be sealed with epoxy. You could also make the spacer from two layers of the ¼-inch plywood used for the rim, or from four layers of leftover 3-millimeter plywood. It is more economical to cut the spacer in two pieces. If you lay out the two pieces so they nest, you'll avoid ending up with a large, useless piece of wood cut out of the center of a one-piece spacer.

The top ring or rim should be made from ¼-inch plywood. I usually use ¼-inch lauan. Marine-grade lauan looks a bit better than the exterior grade, but both seem to hold up well. Of course, you could use any waterproof ¼-inch plywood, or even solid wood. If you tend to abuse your kayak, laminate a second ring or sheathe the rim with fiberglass cloth to increase its strength.

After you've cut out the spacer and rim, spread thickened epoxy on both sides of the spacer and position it on the deck, then position the rim on top of the spacer. Clamp the pieces into place, placing pads of scrap plywood between the clamps and the rim to avoid denting the rim. Wipe up any epoxy that squeezes out from under the rim so your sprayskirt won't catch on gobs of hard epoxy later.

When the epoxy has cured, sand the inside of the cockpit opening. If you weren't precise when you cut the pieces, there will be lots of sanding to do before the inside is smooth and even. When you're finished, the inside of the opening should show a handsome pattern of plywood layers. Brush a coat of unthickened epoxy onto all the exposed plywood edges around the coaming. When it has soaked in, brush on a second coat.

Glue the two small seat risers into the hull, then

Use a paper template to mark the cockpit opening.

Protect the deck with masking tape when you glue on the cockpit spacer and rim.

The seat is a simple plywood rectangle glued to two risers. This arrangement of scrap wood keeps the seat curved until the epoxy cures. A pad of closed-cell foam will make the seat quite comfortable.

Laminate the backrest on the same jig as the forward deck beam.

This arrangement of nylon straps adjusts the position of the backrest.

Form the hatch covers to the correct camber with small beams running athwartships. The frame adds stiffness. Weatherstripping glued around the perimeter forms a watertight seal.

After varnishing the deck, attach the hatch hold-down straps, grab handles, compass, and other deck gear.

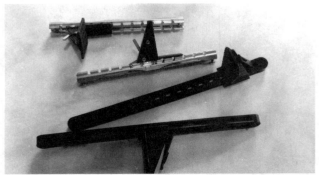

Although wooden blocks can be used as footbraces, adjustable footbraces such as these are better.

glue the plywood seat on top of them as shown on the plan. Don't forget to seal the underside of the seat before gluing it into place.

The curved backrest is laminated on the same jig as the forward deck beam. Two pieces of ¼-inch by 1 ¼-inch lattice are laminated onto the back of the plywood piece to give it its shape. It is attached to the boat with a 1-inch nylon strap screwed to the back of the lattice strips and to the sheer clamps (just forward of the seat). Adjustable buckles can be added to these straps so you can vary the angle of the backrest. A small loop of shock cord or strap connects the backrest to the coaming to keep it from sliding down when the paddler leans forward.

Strong and properly positioned footbraces are essential to efficient paddling. Kayaks with rudders must have footbraces that slide or pivot to control the rudder. If more than one person will be paddling your kayak, it should be fitted with adjustable footbraces.

Simple, nonadjustable footbraces can be made from scrap ¾-inch board. However, I install commercially made adjustable footbraces in most of the kayaks I build, because they work better than any that I can easily make. Footbraces are subject to considerable loads, and these loads must be distributed by backing plates glued under the footbraces. The backing plates are simply rectangles of 3-millimeter or 4-millimeter plywood that are a couple of inches wider and longer than the footbrace. The footbraces, whether homemade or store-bought, should be both glued to the backing plate and secured by two screws passing through the hull.

Making the Hatch Covers

The hatch covers are simply rectangles of plywood to which two small frames are glued to give them the same camber as the deck. Wide weatherstripping is glued to the hatch cover's perimeter as a seal. Nylon straps with Fastex buckles screwed to the deck and sheer clamps hold the hatch covers in place.

Cut the hatch openings and the hatch covers, using the full-sized patterns in the plans. Make two stiffeners for each hatch cover from short pieces of lattice, cutting them to shape with a saber saw; trace their curve from the pattern on the plans. The stiffeners should just fit into the deck opening when glued to the underside of the hatch covers. Two more stiffeners glued forward and aft as in the photo will add rigidity. Don't install the hold-down straps until you've varnished the deck.

Installing a Rudder or Skeg

I recommend fitting a rudder on any kayak intended for long-distance touring. Chesapeake Light Craft (address below) sells a rudder kit for the Cape Charles, and some other kayak rudder systems could probably be adapted as well. Installation details will, of course, vary depending on the brand of rudder you select.

Since the Cape Charles is designed for loads of over 200 pounds, it may not track well if paddled unloaded by a light paddler. This problem is normally solved by using a rudder. However, if you prefer not to fit a rudder and often paddle with a light load, fit a small skeg instead. It should be made of ½-inch plywood and fiberglassed to the hull as shown on the stern layout pattern on Sheet 2 of the plans.

Finishing

Prior to painting or varnishing your boat, apply a coat of unthickened epoxy to the outside of the hull and deck. This will substantially improve the stiffness, abrasion resistance, and strength of the wood. Again, the best tool to use is a disposable foam roller. Unfortunately, cured epoxy has an amine-blush surface film that prevents varnish and some paints from drying. Allow the epoxy to fully cure, then wash the boat with soap and water to remove this film. Some brands of epoxy will continue to produce this effect for up to two weeks after they are applied, so it is a good idea to test the varnish or paint you plan to use on a small section before covering the entire boat. Don't leave your kayak in the sun for long periods before you varnish or paint it, because the sunlight will cause the epoxy to turn milky.

My favorite finish is six coats of good-quality marine varnish on the deck, and a painted hull. If you choose to paint your hull, I recommend using two-part polyurethane paint. It is expensive and a bit tricky to apply, so follow the manufacturer's instructions precisely. I've had good luck with Interlux's Interthane Plus; the gloss is remarkable and the finish very hard. Of course, you could also paint your kayak with marine enamel or regular polyurethane, but they don't hold up nearly as well as two-part polyurethane.

After the last coat of paint and varnish has dried, attach the nylon webbing grab handles with ¾-inch screws and finish washers. Cut the webbing into two 8-inch lengths and melt the holes for the screws in the webbing with a nail heated over a flame. Screw the webbing to the sheer clamps in the position shown in the photos. Also attach the elastic cord hold-down straps.

Some paddlers will find a rudder helpful.

This simple arrangement is used to lift and drop the rudder. Notice also the fold of nylon webbing used to hold the deck tie-downs.

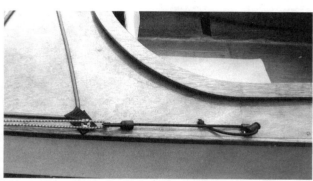

Saturate the hull with epoxy resin, using a foam roller, then tip out any runs and bubbles with a disposable bristle brush.

A couple of hours of sanding and fairing will produce a smooth hull.

Pad the seat and backrest with closed-cell foam, which is available at camping stores. Glue this in place with contact cement. Do not be tempted to use overly thick foam padding; it will raise the seat height too much and have an adverse effect on the center of gravity of the boat.

Remember, the Cape Charles 18 is designed for large paddlers (over 200 pounds). If you are lighter, consider building a Cape Charles 17, 15.5, or 13.5 version.

This chapter was adapted from the author's book, *The Kayak Shop* (Ragged Mountain Press, Camden, Maine), a thorough treatise on the author's building method. The book contains plans for three kayaks.

Large-scale plans ($45) for the Cape Charles, and the book The Kayak Shop *are available from the WoodenBoat Store, P.O. Box 78, Brooklin, Maine 04616. Call 1–800–273–SHIP (7447).*

Two-part polyurethane paint leaves a hard, shiny surface. Wet-sand between coats.

A Double-Paddle Canoe

—— by Henry "Mac" McCarthy   Construction photos by Gary Crowell ——

My first experience with canoeing was on Tupper Lake in the Adirondacks. My father used to take me out on the lake early in the morning. We would look for deer, then watch the flag being raised at the camp where we vacationed. As this is one of my earliest memories, I guess you could say I have always loved canoes.

Many years ago, when I started building canoes, I made several cedar strippers 16 to 18 feet long. They were all right, but not really what I wanted. What I did want was a light-weight, good-looking canoe just big enough to carry one person anyplace there was enough water to float it. My search led from John Gardner's articles in the *National Fisherman*, to Atwood Manley's book, *Rushton and His Times in American Canoeing* (Syracuse University Press, 1977). It was in Manley's book that I first found the Wee Lassie canoe. I knew I had to have one, so I built the little canoe. I enjoyed paddling it. So did two of my sons, and so did a little 78-year-old lady, who bought it on the spot because she could pick it up by herself. In a very short time, I had built four Wee Lassies, each a little different. I was thoroughly hooked.

Since then I have built many more Wee Lassie-type canoes. Most of them were 10 feet 6 inches in length, but some were a foot longer (no wider) for the person who weighs more than 175 pounds or

The author in one of his elegant Wee Lassie double-paddle canoes.

wants to carry more than 40 pounds of gear or just plain has longer legs. I have modified the original design; the boat I build now is asymmetrical, with the stern sections fuller than the bow. I did this in an effort to increase ease of paddling in shallow water.

With a double-bladed paddle you can go upstream in shallow creeks. A regular canoe paddle becomes almost useless in these conditions, unless you use it as a pole, which will destroy a good paddle in nothing flat. A double paddle requires only as much water as the canoe needs. You don't have to worry about pickup times, or ferrying cars back and forth. Just paddle against the current for as long as you want, then drift back downstream.

You sit down low in the Wee Lassie, but it is easier to get in and out of than a sea kayak because it is undecked, which also helps to keep the weight of the finished boat down. Because your center of gravity is low, the little craft is surprisingly stable. I have paddled hundreds of miles in a Wee Lassie and have never been dumped, except when playing in the surf at Lido Key, here in Sarasota, Florida. The Wee Lassie handles rough water well, but, as with any small boat, reasonable care should be taken.

If there is anything better than one Wee Lassie, it has to be a pair of Wee Lassies, cruising along in company with each other. I have often felt that there would be less husband-and-wife bickering on "canoe-athons'" if each person had his or her own canoe. It is nice to look over and see how pretty the other Wee Lassie is, and know that your boat looks just as neat.

From the pine barrens of New Jersey, to the mangrove tunnels on the west coast of Florida, I have found many fantastic places to slide a Wee Lassie into the water for small explorations. When you can glide up close enough to an otter to hear the crunch of his jaws as he eats a crawfish, you know you have the right boat.

A light double-paddle canoe is not expensive, doesn't require a lot of room for building or storage, and is not too difficult to put together. Working from a set of my patterns, an eighth-grade class turned out a presentable little canoe. You don't need to be an expert woodworker to do the job.

You do need a small, well-ventilated area to work in, or the ability to slide the boat outdoors for some of the sanding operations. To rip your strips, you'll need the use of a table saw. The only other expensive tools required are sanders (a dual-action sander would be the most helpful) and as many small clamps as you can find for clamping the rails. With a small assortment of hand tools — a hammer, a small handsaw, a sharp block plane, and a staple gun — you are on your way to a very enjoyable experience. There is no heavy lifting, no steam bending, no complicated lofting — none of the things that can bog down the amateur or one-time builder. Because of the canoe's small size, you finish each operation before it gets tedious or boring.

In this chapter I will show you how to build one of these little craft. For less than $300 for materials (1991 prices), and 60 to 80 hours of your time, you can create a boat you will be proud to be seen using for years to come.

The man who wrote *Small Is Beautiful* must have had this canoe in mind. She is functional, simple, and good-looking. If I could have only one boat for the rest of my life, it would be a Wee Lassie.

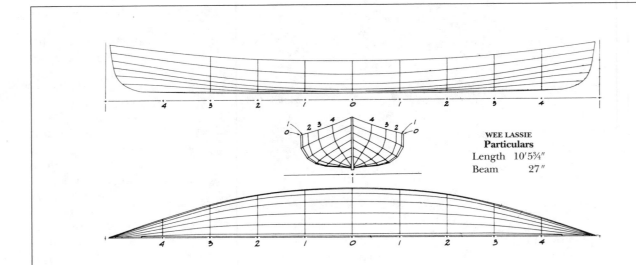

WEE LASSIE
Particulars
Length   10'5¾"
Beam   27"

MATERIALS
2 sheets ½" x 4' x 8' particleboard, for strongback and molds
2 planks 1" x 4" x 10' and two sawhorses, for strongback
Approx. 50 strips ¼" x ¾" x 12' Western red cedar, for the hull
1 piece 1" x 6" x 12' spruce, for inner stems and paddle
1 piece 1" x 6" x 12' mahogany or cherry, for rails, seat frames, and thwart
10 yards 4-oz fiberglass cloth, 50" wide
1 gallon epoxy and hardener
1 quart spar varnish, for ultraviolet protection
Approx. 90' of cane, for seat

Miscellaneous nails, glue, staples, throwaway brushes and pads, spreaders, and roller covers

TOOLS
Table saw (or the use of one), to rip strips, rails, etc.
Sabersaw or bandsaw, for cutting out molds
Staple gun, for holding strips in place while glue dries
6" random-orbit sander, for finish-sanding hull, etc.
Block plane (sharp)
Chisel (sharp)
Razor knife and extra blades
C-clamps (the more the better)
Spring clamps (the more the better)

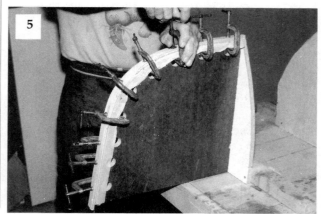

1

First cut out the largest mold shape from the pattern sheet. Lay out one side on the plywood, then flip it and mark the other side. Because the stem patterns overlay the mold patterns, trace these before the paper gets all cut up. Being careful to keep the patterns square with the plywood, trace the patterns for all of the molds. If you prefer doing your own lofting, simply pick up the shapes from the floor.

2

Cut out the molds with a sabersaw.

3

Build a simple strongback with 1 by 4s and inexpensive particleboard. Use 2 by 2s for cleats. Mark an accurate centerline on the strongback. Drill holes in the stem molds to make room for the clamps that will hold the inner stem laminate. If you prefer doing your own lofting, simply pick up the shapes from the floor.

4

Cover the edges of the molds with masking tape to keep the strips from bonding to the plywood molds. Be especially careful on the stem molds. Notice the definite notch at the sheerline, where you will begin laying on the strips.

5

Laminate four pieces of 1/16-inch by 5/8-inch spruce on each stem mold. Leave these clamped overnight. Before stripping the boat, remove the rough stems and bevel their sides so the strips will lay fair and have good gluing surfaces.

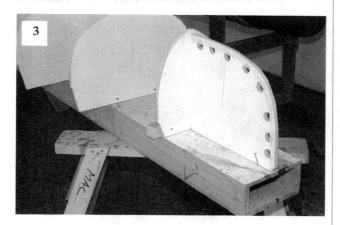

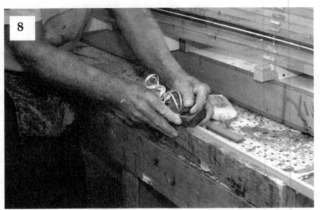

6

After beveling re-clamp the inner stems to the molds. Now you are ready to start stripping.

7

The first two strips are laid on, starting at the sheer-line and working toward the keel line. The strips are edge glued to each other, and glued to the inner stems. Check often to see that everything is aligned and fair.

8

A notched 2 by 4 holds the strips temporarily while you run glue or plane a slight bevel on them. I plane a bevel on the strips where needed, rather than using systems that involve using a shaper or other expensive equipment to interlock the strips. I think keeping it simple is important.

9

Use a 1 ¼-inch No. 18 headed nail, available in any hardware store, to fasten the strips to the molds. They have more holding power than a ½-inch staple. Some strips on the Wee Lassie require a fair amount of pressure to hold in place. The thin nail leaves only one hole, which is easy to fill with a toothpick after the nail is pulled. I use little blocks of cedar (about ⅛ inch by ⅜ inch by 1 inch) under the nail-head to facilitate pulling the nails later.

10

Use ¼-inch staples in between the molds to keep the strips tight and even with each other. Apply enough glue to get a good squeeze-out, then be sure you clean up the excess before it hardens. I keep my stapler lubricated with light oil to keep the glue from sticking to it.

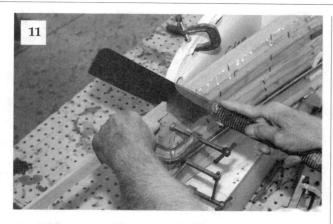

11

Keep your strips cut flush at the inner stem as you go up with the strips. I use a Japanese Dosuki saw that cuts on the pull stroke, and has very fine teeth, for this and any other handsaw jobs on the boat. One cut with this saw through a finished joint, and you have a perfect fit.

12

This is the way the hull should look when you are about half done with stripping. At this point, beveling becomes important. A sharp block plane and a little care will produce a good job. Keep the joints between the strips as tight as possible.

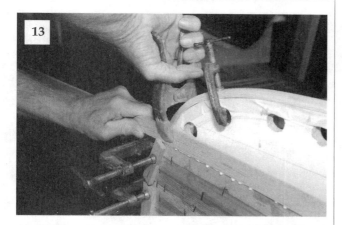

13

As the bends become tighter, use clamps to help hold the strips at the stems, until the glue sets. You have four or five difficult strips on a Wee Lassie, then the pressure eases off.

14

A short stealer strip is needed near the heel of the stem. This is the most difficult area to strip on the whole boat.

15

This photo shows how I handle the transition from stem to keel line. By running a center keel strip, you can control the fairness of the keel area. Without it, butting strip to strip, you can end up with a very unfair keel line. Cutting the strips into the keel strip takes time and care. I do as much of it as I can with the table saw, and the rest with the Dosuki saw, right on the boat.

16

After trimming the strips flush with the inner stem, I laminate thin (¹⁄₁₆-inch) strips of mahogany or cherry to make an outer stem. I use the same thin nails I used to hold the strips to the molds. Clamps and shock cord will help. Let this set up overnight.

17

Use a tack puller to loosen the nails and staples. A pair of nippers will pull the nails out, and the staples usually just pop out with the tack puller.

18

I use a Makita sander/polisher, with a 7-inch disc, at slow speed to rough-sand the hull. I use 24-grit to start. Wear a dust mask, and be careful to keep the disc as flat to the work as possible; you don't want to gouge or dig into the wood. Basically all you want to do at this stage is knock off the high corners of the strips. Slow and easy is the ticket.

19

After rough-sanding the hull, break toothpicks in half and fill all the nail holes. I tap the toothpicks in with a hammer, and then break them off. Epoxy will fill the tiny staple holes.

20

No matter how good you are with the disc sander, board-sanding is the best way to make sure that the hull is fair. The abrasive paper that auto body shops use on air files is just right for this. The process is good exercise, and it doesn't create the dust that power-sanding does.

21

After board-sanding, finish with a dual-action sander. I have a Porter Cable variable-speed with a contour disc that does fine. Start with 40-grit, and follow up with 80-grit stick-on discs. Be sure you wear a face mask.

22

After you are satisfied with the sanding, give the bare wood a coat of epoxy. Let this dry, and sand it lightly — just enough to rough it up; don't sand through to the bare wood. Cut fiberglass cloth to length and drape it over the clean hull. I smooth all the wrinkles out by hand before I wet out the cloth.

23

Begin wetting out the cloth in the center of one side. Make sure you wear gloves. I work the epoxy over the cloth with a spreader, available at any auto paint store. Work from the center toward the ends, and from the keel down. Don't try for a finished appearance; simply get the epoxy spread as quickly and evenly as possible.

24

When the cloth is completely wet out, I use my gloved hands to work out any wrinkles. Using scissors, trim the cloth at both stems. Don't try to wrap it around the stems or rails; that won't work. The following morning, sand lightly, and cut some strips of cloth on the bias. Recoat the entire exterior with epoxy, and wrap both stems with at least two layers of bias-cut strips. When the epoxy has cured, repeat this whole operation. After the last coat sets up, pop the boat loose from the molds. Lift up on one end, then the other. If you have used masking tape on the molds, the hull should pull loose easily.

25

Now, use the disc sander on the interior. The main purpose here is to eliminate any sharp edges on the strips that could leave voids under the cloth. When you have finished sanding, vacuum the hull, and you are ready to coat the interior with fiberglass and epoxy, proceeding as you did on the exterior.

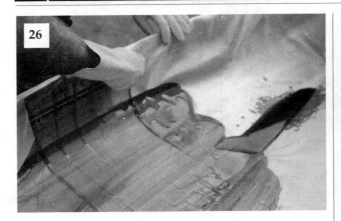

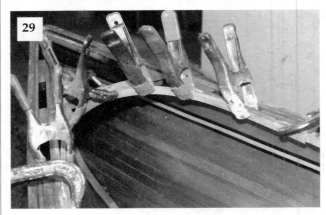

26

Drape the cloth inside the hull, and smooth it out as best you can. Pour the epoxy along the keel line, and work it up both sides and toward the ends. You are trying for a good, even wet-out, without drips or puddles. Work out any bubbles with your gloved hands. You want the texture of the cloth to just show through, but you don't want any white (resin-starved) areas. Let the epoxy set up.

27

Epoxy and clamp the outer rails in place. Let them set up overnight. Epoxy 3-inch-long blocks of the rail material, spaced 4 inches apart, flush with the top of the sheer strip. The following day, clamp the inner rails in place. When placing the blocks, take care to center one block on each side 43 inches back from the stem, so that there will be solid wood where the thwart goes in place.

28

Notch the thwart to lock into the rail. Run two 1 ½-inch No. 8 flat-head wood screws in through the rails to secure the thwart.

29

Laminate the deck supports out of thin strips.

30

The deck itself is stripped and 'glassed. Use your imagination — all kinds of designs and inlays are possible. Seal the bottom of the deck with epoxy.

31

Use a router with a ½-inch-round bit on the rails, deck, and thwart. If you have no router, a plane will do. Follow up with a dual-action sander. Prepare and 'glass the decks the same as you did the hull. Make sure the underside of the deck is well sealed with epoxy.

32

This is a detail of the finished thwart and rails.

33

The seat support is epoxied in place along the centerline. Two screws hold the caned seat to the support. I do not anchor the ends of the seat frame, as this sets up stress when someone really heavy drops into the boat.

34

Now sand everything in preparation for varnishing. I use about three coats of a good spar varnish to protect the epoxy from ultraviolet rays.

The author developed his canoe from the lines of J. Henry Rushton's Wee Lassie, shown in the drawings accompanying this chapter. The original Rushton boat rests at, and plans can be obtained from, The Adirondack Museum, Blue Mountain Lake, NY 12812. Full-scale mold and stem patterns for McCarthy's modified Wee Lassie are available for $20 from Feather Canoes, 3080 N. Washington Blvd., Unit 19N, Sarasota, FL 34234.

Bagging the Gull

by Jim Brown, with John Marples and Dick Newick
Drawings and Photographs by John Marples

The newly launched Gull, built the Constant Camber way.

Gull is a sophisticated skiff. John Marples has designed her to meet multiple requirements, including rowing, sailing, towing, and cartopping. She is pleasing but humble, being distinguished by features she does not have, like frames. But also, there are no chines, flats, or re-curves in her; she harbors no surprises for the water or the eye. Her bottom's not too bilgy; she's just stiff enough to carry a low-slung sail and perhaps a little outboard. She has enough stability, maybe, to keep her on her feet in case a bloke should blunder into the bow alone. It is this lack of buxomness, rare for hard-service dinghies, that lets her really move: with these slackish bilges, and two rowing positions for balancing the load fore and aft, Gull will fairly "schoon" along before the blades.

Gull's construction, on the other hand exemplifies the state of a new art — streamlined cold molding with stock compound curves. She is built by the Constant Camber method, using a vacuum bag, but this does not imply the high costs and technical demands of ultramodern composite boatbuilding. Also avoided are the advanced skills and labor-intensiveness required by traditional methods.

To be sure, when anything is avoided, something interesting may be lost. But with Constant Camber, something interesting is also gained. The project requires a discovery stage, building a simple mold and learning how it works. After that, the new "CC" builder is often amazed at how quickly he can produce quality laminated panels, and how easily those panels become sleek, sturdy boats.

If you've done some wood-epoxy work before, and don't get bogged down with perfection, your first Gull

should consume about 40 hours' labor time; after repeat familiarity with the process, you should be able to reduce the time to 30 hours.

Yet the attractiveness of this method is not just for ease of construction. Just as appealing is the single, sophisticated structure that an individual can create on his own. He can also re-create it, in numbers, and in various configurations, all with a minimum investment of money, tools, and time.

Several more designs, measuring from 10 feet to 14 feet in length, can be built from Gull's mold. These variations can range from a 10-foot "one-man model" trimaran to a big, barge-like pram. Constant Camber design is not addressed in this chapter, but it too is an interesting discipline. Working in triumvirate, the authors have, designed CC vessels varying from less than 10 feet long to over 60 feet. We have successfully transferred this technology to neophyte backyard builders, to skilled Filipino furniture makers, to Polynesian fishermen, and to African tribesmen — trainees with whom we could not speak. Even professional yacht builders have picked up the skill!

In this chapter on Gull we are disclosing, with some trepidation, recent developments in CC geometry that make the method appear applicable to series production, in wood, of single-hulled craft. Can such boats be produced at a profit?

Of course, much depends on the market, but we feel the best chance for CC may rest with small entrepreneurs, who can serve a diverse market with "short runs" of an easily customized product. This is where the technology appears to offer unique capabilities. and where we would prefer that it finds its yachting niche, if indeed there is one.

If the reader would contemplate a dabbling in this new art, Gull is a good place to start. She's a serious boat, rugged enough to withstand serious service, yet she is lithe. Her construction is simple enough for any artisan to achieve pleasing results, from scratch, or from "store-bought" CC panels. Concurrently, this project can put the builder well up on the learning curve of a skill that few others possess. If you sell your prototype Gull, you can keep your mold. Working as a licensed manufac-

turer (see note, page 90), you can produce and sell raw panels or finished boats. Compared to conventional cold molding, labor savings are probably sufficient to give these boats a leg-up in the marketplace — and, we hope to help put the small boatshop in business.

Your start-up investment in equipment and materials for the first boat should be somewhere around $500 (1985 prices).

Construction is described below in three phases: Mold Construction, Panel Making, and Boat Assembly from Panels.

PHASE I
MOLD CONSTRUCTION
Framing the Mold

Because most of the parts for this mold are alike, its framework is a lot simpler to build than the setup and framing for a conventional hull. (This hull doesn't have any permanent framing.) Two sidewalls, of the same shape, and 10 station formers, identical to each other, are made from sheet plywood or particleboard to the dimensions in the plans. (See mold construction diagrams.) One half of one sidewall is lofted, and then stacked with the other three halves so that all four pieces are cut at once. After the halves are butt-joined, eyeball and fair the big radius carefully while both sidewalls are clamped together, then cut the notches to receive the formers.

The station formers are made the same way, by clamping a stack of rectangular blanks together and cutting them on a sharp bandsaw (or cutting them individually with a sabersaw and then clamping them in a stack and fairing all the curves together). Be sure to draw the Reference (REF) line and the Prime Meridian (PM) line on the curved edges of the stack, before unclamping. After unclamping, draw a REF line on the faces of all formers.

Snug fits in the notches are nice, but not absolutely necessary, because the formers and sidewalls all are glued and nailed together, right away. But first, attach the 2 by 4 stiffeners to the straight edges of the sidewalls.

To assemble the mold, position the sidewalls with their stiffeners and butt straps facing each other. Slip the formers into their notches, and drive a toenail at each notch.

Note:
On September 18, 1984, James W. Brown was issued a U.S. patent (No. 4,471,710) for the Constant Camber boatbuilding method. Jim has been kind enough to share the details of this patented process. We must remind you, however, that builders of Constant Camber panels, whether for one boat or a series of boats, must pay a royalty to the patent holder in return for a license to build. This is only fair, since a considerable amount of time and expense has gone into the development of the Constant Camber process. The royalty in the case of the Gull is $10, and for other boats is calculated on the square footage of the panels. The procedure for getting your license is quite simple. For details, contact Kamberwood International Services, Inc., P.O. Box 550, North, Virginia 23128.

Right here is where the basic fairing takes place. Actually, it is self-fairing. Adjust each former in its notch so that the REF line comes exactly even with the top curve of the sidewall— presto! The formers have to describe a pervasive, fair, Constant-Cambered surface. Such a surface —and here's the whole point—can be cold molded with all-identical shapes. We will see that this feature opens the way to several others, which accumulate toward expediency in a kind of geometric progression.

Check the entire mold framework for squareness and fairness, then smear filled epoxy glue into the notched joints. The bottom edges of the sidewalls don't have to be level, but they should be parallel and straight, and the tops of all the formers should describe a fair curve everywhere. Check this fairness with a full-length batten laid over the PM lines on the formers, and see that the batten describes a straight, vertical plane down through the length of the model. Check this and make any adjustments before the glue sets.

Planking the Mold

Now, "strip plank" the mold surface with ½-inch-thick strips of clear, workable wood. Notice that the strips are of two widths, ½ inch wide on the "tight-curve" side of the mold, and 1 inch wide on the "easy-curve" side. This division between the two strip sizes becomes a visible indicator of the PM position, which we will be using later in lofting panel layouts. It's not a bad idea to "paint" the corners of the first small strip-plank with a fat felt-tipped marker to permanently locate the PM, even on the underside of the mold — you'll see why later.

Glue and nail the strips at each former. Sand the resulting mold surface fair and smooth, after planing down any high spots. Before concerning yourself with any low spots in your mold, mix a loose batch of epoxy putty and smear it thoroughly into the gaps and cracks between the strips with a squeegee to seal up the entire surface. Remember, we're going to be using vacuum on this mold, so the thing is going to have to be airtight. Fill the cracks all the way through as best you can.

Now, if there are any serious low spots in your mold

surface (they are very visible at night with a flashlight), apply another batch of epoxy in these lows, extended with a sandable filler, and fair the surface a second time. We're not after perfection here, only a mold surface that will produce nice, fair panels, ones that will themselves be receiving a light sanding to remove imperfections. If your mold comes out really rough, or if it starts giving trouble after a long production run, you can always cover it with a layer of veneer. When you're almost but not quite satisfied with its surface, push on by applying three thin coats of epoxy resin, for a final seal. With three really thin coats, there won't be any sags to sand and fair again. Your surface is now ready.

But there's another side to this mold business, the underside. It, too, should be made absolutely airtight. When you're making panels, staples will be driven into the mold from the top side, especially around the edges, to temporarily hold each plank in position. Some of these staples will enter the cracks between the strips, and if the mold isn't sealed from underneath, you will have a vacuum leak — no great catastrophe, because it usually can be located by its hissing sound and patched with a dab of mastic. But to avoid the nasty job of chasing leaks underneath the mold, turn the whole thing over right now and seal up its underside. You can extend the epoxy with fillers, so it doesn't take as much of it; work it around the formers and into the cracks with a squeegee.

For readers with mold-building experience who might not think of this tool as a mold, you're right. It is not really a "mold" in the contemporary sense of the word, as in "polished female mold" for a production run of all-identical fiberglass boats. This is actually a strip-planked, male "plug," which, because of its same-all-over curvature, is relatively a cinch to make. The "parts" that come off this plug, the CC panels, are not pre-finished as in fiberglass molding, but they are wonderfully fair and easy to finish individually. This is because most of the finish sanding and epoxy coating is done before these parts are assembled into a hull. You are working "on the flat," with them, and gravity is on your side. The sur-

Strip-planked CC mold for single-hulled boats from 10-feet to 14-feet long, complete with wheels for rolling out into the sun to accelerate the cure.

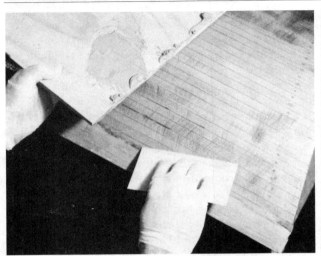

Epoxy putty is spread by squeegee into cracks in the strip-planked mold; results must be airtight.

Dum-Dum weatherstripping seals around the vacuum bag.

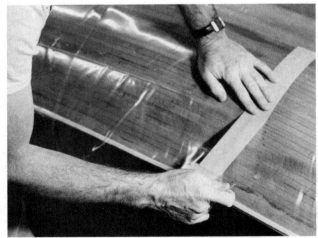

Tailoring the 4-mil polyethylene "parting film" to fit the mold. It keeps the panel from sticking to the mold, and covers the Dum-Dum until it is needed. The fabled "vacuum bag" is just another sheet of polyethylene — but not tailored.

faces are completely accessible with a power sander, and uninterrupted by structural nooks and crannies.

Best of all, this mold is not locked into producing a single hull size or shape. As we will see, it is the panel's perimeter layout that determines the hull's size and shape, allowing many variations from a single "mold." That's a real advantage to a manufacturer; he's not confined to making identical mass-production models.

Vacuum Bagging Explained

Remembering our own aversion to getting into vacuum bagging, and seeing that same hesitation even in master craftsmen, we have aimed these words to give you confidence.

Vacuum, as a shop process, is no big deal. To prove it to yourself, especially now that you have a vacuum mold, read through these simple steps until you get the idea, then dive in and make yourself a panel. The vacuum pump and accessories are inexpensive and uncomplicated, the warm-up experiments are engaging, and we promise that your ego will not altogether disappear, even on the first try.

Start by removing any epoxy residue, then wash the mold with plenty of plain water — just swish it down with a sopping-wet towel, rinse out, wring out, and wipe dry. The greasy film likes water, and will "jump right off," but if you leave it on the mold, or on the boat, nothing else will stick to it, not even more epoxy.

After the mold is bone dry, apply the "vacuum tape." There are fancy products used in the industry that go by this name, but for our purposes we can use something like Mortite, a hardware-store item that comes in a roll like cord but feels like modeling clay. It is widely used for household weatherstripping and caulking. You might find an equivalent at the auto-parts store, known generically as Dum-Dum, which is what we'll call the stuff hereafter. From either source, it's cheap. If you can't find Mortite or Dum-Dum, ask for weatherstripping at a mobile home supply store, or look for "hydraulic pump sealant," or commercial "vacuum tape." Whatever you use, it must have the right tackiness to stick to both the mold and the poly-film. Use whatever works. Lay a double bead of it all around the perimeter of your mold and press it down.

Then cover the entire mold with a layer of common, four-mil polyfilm, also a hardware-store item. Pull the film tight along the PM axis and allow it to hang about 6 inches beyond the Dum-Dum all around, like an apron. Press it into the Dum-Dum so it doesn't slide around.

The flat-sheet polyfilm will, when applied to the compound-curved mold, develop pleats, which have to be tailored to make the polyfilm fit. Cut darts in the film every 2 feet or so, starting up near the PM and going down all the way to the edges. Allow the film to overlap at the darts, and tape it back together with wide cellophane tape. Most of the wrinkles will disappear, but not all of them. No matter; the main purpose of this first layer of film is to keep the panels from getting glued to the mold; epoxy won't stick to polyfilm. It also serves another important function — protecting the Dum-Dum from dust accumulation so it doesn't lose its stickiness.

The bag itself? Well, that's just another layer of polyfilm, but this one is not tailored like the first. Remove the first one for now, and drape the second one over the mold and pull the pleats up into as few, large gathers as possible, and then press the rest of it down to the Dum-Dum. The large gathers that stand up must now be sealed with Dum-Dum. Open the gathers and insert a single bead all the way from the fold at the top of the gather to the bottom, joining with the Dum-Dum on the edge of the mold. Squash it thoroughly from the outside; you can see any gaps right through the polyfilm.

This method is preferred to cutting and taping darts for this layer, because the tape may leak. The first layer you made doesn't have to be airtight; it's just a parting film, but it shouldn't have any big gathers in it that could bunch up underneath the veneer. The second film, the bag, is the one that really gets sealed down to the Dum-Dum on the mold. When you handle this bag, try to preserve the gathers in their sealed condition. Now you have two complete polyfilm "garments" for your mold, one tailored and one gathered.

Here's how they will be used: After you have laid up a bunch of gluey veneer on the mold, on top of the first layer of film, the protruding apron of that first "garment" is folded up onto the veneer and held there with patches of masking tape — just to hold it up out of the way. The idea is to expose the Dum-Dum to the top layer of film, which is the fabled "vacuum bag." This bag is then applied over the top of everything, sandwiching the gluey veneer between the "bag" and the mold, with a Dum-Dum seal all around the edges. At this point we're going to suck the air out!

If you want to get professional, you can put in an "airway" by tailoring a smaller garment for your mold, this one made of plastic window screen. Cut it small, to fit well inside the Dum-Dum. It goes just underneath the bag, but don't let it contact the panel directly or you'll have a screened-in boat. To prevent this, throw in still another layer of polyfilm — we call this the "underwear" — just to cover up however much of the panel is still exposed after the first film is folded up around the edges of the panel. So, between the folded-up first film, the airway, and the underwear, your panel is well buried before the bag finally covers everything. That's good; all that padding will protect the bag from being punctured by the sharp edges of the panel.

The purpose of the airway is to provide a route for the air to escape from between all these layers of stuff.

The vacuum bag likes to rest on its own custom wall rack, to minimize damage from handling. Gathers and wrinkles in the bag remain filled with Dum-Dum.

To achieve a vacuum seal, simply press the bag into the Dum-Dum, and fill the wrinkles with Dum-Dum. Note the window-screen airway under the bag.

Old "fridge" compressor, scavenged for free, proudly pulls 15-inch Hg vacuum — more than enough. Note where the vacuum tube leads into the bag; Dum-Dum has been packed around here to seal.

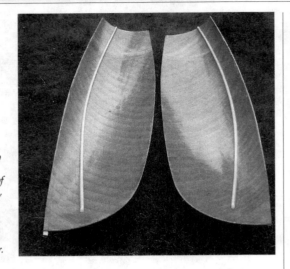

The two molded halves of the hull, before they were joined together.

It is not strictly necessary in this small-sized mold, and can be dispensed with if you're not interested in sophisticated vacuum technique. But if the mold of the bag should develop a leak, the airway screen provides a lateral escape pathway all over, and will "bleed off" the leak to the pump, thus avoiding a local loss of squeezing pressure on your glue joints.

As a consequence of sucking out all the air, the panel-to-be gets squashed down, absolutely smack-plastered, against the mold by atmospheric pressure. All we have to do is keep the air out for about three hours while the glue sets. The squeezing gives us very tight glue joints in the panel without using much glue, and without having to pepper the poor thing with thousands of staples, then go to all the work of pulling out those staples afterwards and filling the holes, as in conventional cold molding.

So now let's get on with the job and put two layers of film on the mold. The first layer is tailored, and adhered to the Dum-Dum. The second layer, the bag itself, has its pleats sealed with Dum-Dum and then is carefully set aside, preferably on its own, long, custom wall rack, where it can live by itself, rolled up lengthwise into a long sausage to minimize the chance of damage from handling.

Vacuum Pump

Before making a dry run at vacuum bagging, let's look at the vacuum pump itself. There is a variety of sources for pumps that suck air, from those you can build yourself to off-the-shelf models you can buy. At the expensive end, a vane pump of about one-sixth horsepower would be great for serious production work on this size mold. Such vacuum pumps are available from industrial supply houses like W.W. Granger or a Gast distributor, and cost about $200 (1985 prices).

Somewhat less fancy, but suitable, are old milking machines and refrigerator compressors, which are sometimes available from commercial refrigeration repair shops. These old pumps usually sell for under $50, and can be tested with a vacuum gauge. (A simple gauge can be found at an auto-parts store. Buy at least one of them and install it in your system near the pump to help in detecting leaks.) Household refrigerators with usable pumps are often discarded, and are available free. The prototype Gull shown here was laid up using just such a unit, scavenged from an ancient fridge, and has since been used to make dozens of other panels.

Some paint-sprayer compressors can be reworked to become vacuum pumps; their piston rings must be installed in reverse order and upside down. An oiler may have to be installed at the intake of a piston-type pump — just a pipe cleaner, stuck in a sealed jar of compressor oil that's mounted in the line at the intake, will probably suffice; the pipe cleaner carries oil from this reservoir into the intake line like a wick.

For your vacuum pump, you could even use an old refrigerator "all standing." Leave the cooling line intact, but disconnect the vacuum line and run it via a flexible hose extension right to the mold. Re-wire the pump to a switch. Now you can store epoxy reserves inside the old box; fix the light so it stays on, and replace the bulb with one of larger wattage to keep the epoxy at a nice working temperature.

For laminating with these thin veneers, on this small mold, we do not need a "hard" vacuum or a lot of pump capacity. The only reason to buy a big pump is to keep up with a big leak if it should develop in the mold or the bag, and a big leak will get you into trouble eventually, anyway. So, any pump of any type that will pull a vacuum of 15 inches of mercury is plenty, but it must be reliable. If you go into production, you'll want a back-up unit, because if your only pump gets hot and crumps out in the middle of a three-hour squeeze, you may blow a panel, whose materials are worth a lot more than the time it would have taken to run your whole rig through a three-hour test.

Some vacuum pumps are noisy; it helps to locate them, or any other steadily running noisy equipment, for that matter, far away from the mold, even in another room, to facilitate listening for vacuum leaks. And some pumps discharge oil vapor, which you definitely do not want in the shop.

But these are easy things to handle. Consider the versatility and simplicity of this tool. To repeat, vacuum is no big deal, and you can use it for all sorts of operations — spar work, decorative overlays, sandwich coring — limited only by your own imagination and performed by nothing more than manipulated air. However, vacuum does ask of you a bit of finesse. Unlike air pressure, with which you can get hundreds or even thousands of pounds per square inch, with vacuum all you can get is 14 pounds. Leaks amount to a large percentage of the total suction available.

However, for laminating with epoxy, all we need is six or eight pounds per square inch. You can almost get that much with a vacuum cleaner!

PHASE II
MAKING PANELS
Veneer

The chronology of this project actually begins here. Order your veneer before beginning work on the mold. It may take time to find a source, and it takes time for shipping.

Lightweight woods are best for this project, with Western red cedar at the top of the list. We like to go all the way on materials, especially for "learning curve" projects, where the challenge of handling inferior stuff can throw the student for a loop. Therefore, we recommend you use a premium-grade veneer; plan to make four layers of 1/16-inch thickness, since we want this boat to be almost bomb-proof.

Four laminations give us a fabulous CC panel. Not the cheapest or the quickest to build, but the easiest to build, with the least difficulty in bending, the least "springback," and the best puncture-resistance. The extra time it takes to apply one more layer is, with Constant Camber, not much time at all, as the two center laminations can be done together.

The two laminations in the center of the panel are laid with their grain running the same way, but on the opposite diagonal from the inner and outer surface laminations. That means the two surface laminations run the same way, too, which they would not do if our four-lamination layup had each lamination alternating direction from the other. So, the double inner lamination produces what is called, a "balanced panel" — that is, a panel with the same amount of wood running on both axes, and both surface laminations running on the same axis. This is standard practice for marine-grade, flat-sheet plywood, except that most flat panels have an odd number of laminations. So does our four-lamination panel, if we consider the two center laminations as one!

Those two center laminations can be applied to the mold without the problems of trying to bend a single, thick layer over the curve of this mold. What's more, those two perform as a single layer, one that is twice as thick as each surface lamination, yielding, finally,

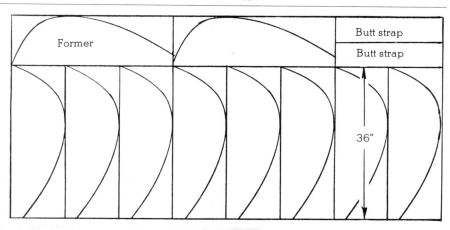

SUGGESTED LAYOUT FOR MOLD FORMERS AND SIDEWALLS
on 4 x 8' panels of 1/2" plywood or particle board.

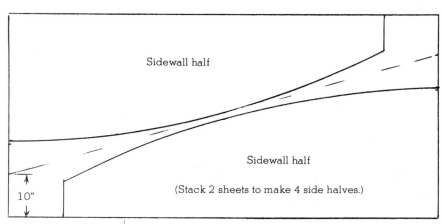

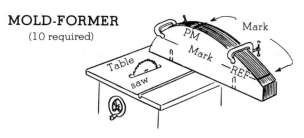

MOLD-FORMER
(10 required)

a balanced panel.

When this arrangement is applied to compound-curve panels, the physical properties that result are fantastic. The inherent strength of a balanced layup, when combined with the rigidity of the eggshell shape, gives a structure that is amazingly self-supporting. Gull weighs only about 80 pounds, but she is so stiff and puncture resistant that she needs absolutely nothing in the way of a skeleton to support her 1/4-inch-thick hull. Considering all three factors of weight, strength, and cost, this may well represent the most efficient method yet of permanently enclosing space. And with a renewable material! (We don't have to use premium wood on the larger structures.) That's why we think CC is interesting, and worthy of your attention.

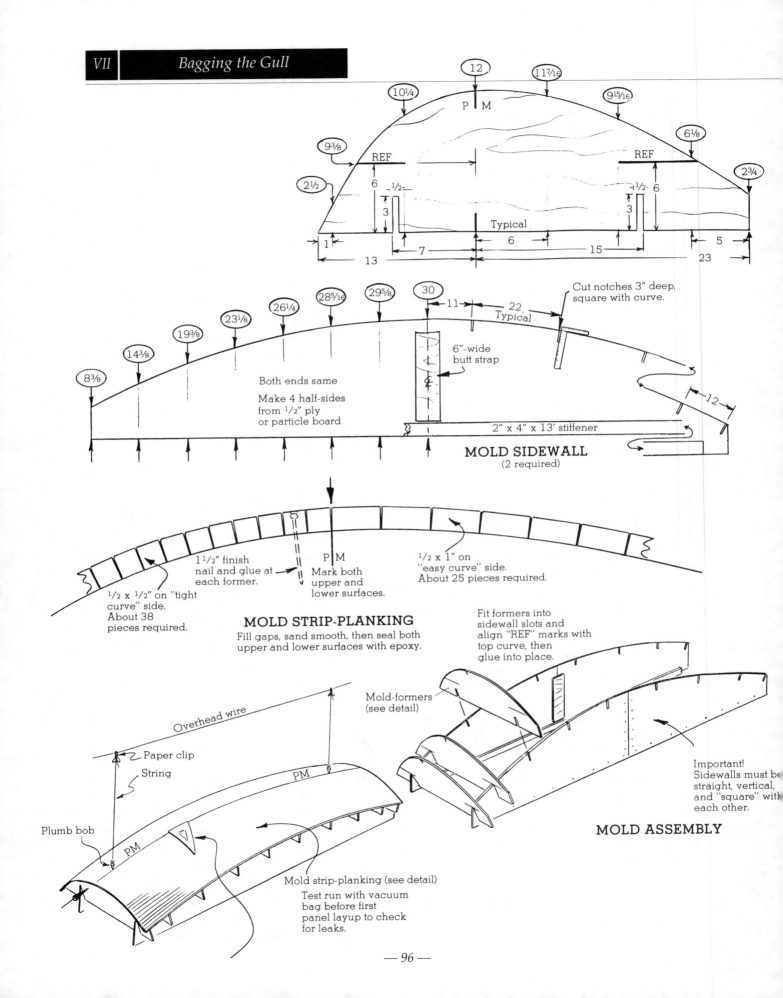

⑫

⑩¼   ⑪⁷⁄₁₆

⑨³⁄₈   ⑨¹⁵⁄₁₆   ⑥¹⁄₈

P M

REF   REF   ②³⁄₄

②½   6   6

½   ½

3   3

Typical

1   6

7   6   15   5

13   23

Cut notches 3" deep,
square with curve.

⑧³⁄₈   ⑭³⁄₈   ⑲³⁄₈   ㉓¹⁄₈   ㉖¼   ㉘⁵⁄₁₆   ㉙⁵⁄₈   ㉚

11   22
Typical

Both ends same

Make 4 half-sides
from ½" ply
or particle board

6"-wide
butt strap

2" x 4" x 13' stiffener   12

MOLD SIDEWALL
(2 required)

1½" finish
nail and glue at
each former.

P M
Mark both
upper and
lower surfaces.

½ x 1" on
"easy curve" side.
About 25 pieces required.

½ x ½" on "tight
curve" side.
About 38
pieces required.

MOLD STRIP-PLANKING

Fill gaps, sand smooth, then seal both
upper and lower surfaces with epoxy.

Fit formers into
sidewall slots and
align "REF" marks with
top curve, then
glue into place.

Overhead wire

Paper clip

String

PM

PM

Plumb bob

Mold-formers
(see detail)

Mold strip-planking (see detail)

Test run with vacuum
bag before first
panel layup to check
for leaks.

Important!
Sidewalls must be
straight, vertical,
and "square" with
each other.

MOLD ASSEMBLY

So much for plywood theory; it is included to explain why we recommend you place your order for about 500 square feet of ¹⁄₁₆-inch red cedar, plenty for a four-lamination Gull. That amount allows 40 percent for scrap, because this stuff is vulnerable to splitting in shipment and shop handling. If you try the Dean Company, of Gresham, Oregon, ask for short lengths; if they have them, they're cheaper.

Do you believe in Murphy's Law —that if anything can go wrong, it will? What if you make the classic blunder — inescapable at some point in your CC career — of forgetting to reverse the layup, and the layout, between panels? As in building two starboard panels. Or as in building one panel with its surface laminations running the wrong way — that is, not perpendicular to the stem. Or building the other panel with its "easy-curve" edge toward the sheer instead of toward the keel. Or perhaps you have cut the transom rake the wrong way. Come to think of it, we've probably made all those mistakes in the same boat.

Maybe you'd better order 750 square feet of veneer, just in case you have to make one and a half Gulls. If you don't build another boat, any extra veneer can probably be sold with your mold.

Cutting Planks

Your veneer will arrive in a bundle. Cut the bundle into 48-inch lengths. Then, using the spiling jig, cut 4-inch-wide strips from those lengths, 20 pieces at a time, making at least one edge straight and clean. Just use a straightedge for a template in the spiling jig; clamp the straightedge down on a stack of veneer and drive the Skilsaw through the stack, guiding it against the straight-edge. (We call these "semi-planks," because, even though they have one straight edge, they're not finished yet.)

Now comes the essence of Constant Camber. These stacks of semi-planks are "spiled" — that is, cut with one curved edge, using the spiling jig and spiling template. Notice in the drawings that the curve on the template, and therefore on the planks, too, is very slight, almost straight — but there must be a curve. You can also make planks with two curved edges if you wish, like a barrel stave, but one curved edge is enough on this small mold. Make your template according to plan, and then adjust its curved edge until the planks cut with this template will fit your mold with good edge contact. You'll find that it takes about five planks, cut with any one template adjustment, stapled lightly to your mold, to really observe the gaps between planks. And it is these gaps that will tell you how to adjust the template with a plane. Very slight adjustments are in order, until your planks fit with no more than a ¹⁄₁₆-inch gap.

Despite the theoretical perfection of CC, it is not possible to eliminate gaps entirely. Some planks respond differently to being bent over the mold, sometimes minutely distorting their profile. But the gaps between these small planks, when cut from a carefully adjusted template, will be on the order of ¹⁄₁₆ inch, and will all be pumped full of epoxy during "suckdown." Be careful to retain the same width on each end of your template.

It takes about 110 planks to make one panel, and instead of hand-carving 110 uniquely shaped pieces — each custom-fitted to its neighbor as in conventional cold molding — in CC we can chop them out 20 at a time, in cookie-cutter fashion. The reason they can be all the same shape is that the mold has about the same degree of curvature everywhere from end to end.

Notice that I didn't say the boat has the same sections everywhere; it doesn't. Our multihulls, with their long and very slender shapes, may have constant sections, but a monohull like Gull does not. Why? Because the panel layout gets "skewed" on the mold to give the hull a fine entry and a full exit, a feature made possible by the elliptical or "French-curve" cross-section of the mold.

Each panel, once free of the mold, gets "tortured" during assembly, as well. What results is a hull whose panels will no longer fit back on their building mold, but will fit the requirements of a wholesome, worthy vessel. There are limitations; we can't build all hull forms with these CC panels, but we can build a variety of good ones, both classic and contempory, all from the same mold. We've just begun to investigate the possibilities, and would welcome the participation of other designers as licensees.

Once your spiling jig is cutting good "cookies," it should take maybe half an hour to spile all 240 planks for Gull, which includes about 20 extra planks to be held in reserve for replacing any defective or damaged pieces. But here's a critical step: before removing each stack from the spiling jig, mark a bold line down the curved edge of the stack of planks at the Prime Meridian (PM) position. This mark is needed on every piece of veneer: it indicates which edge of the plank is curved. This line gets positioned approximately over the PM on the mold as a strike-up mark. To make sure no planks become reversed end-for-end during layup, try marking the "easy-curve" end of each stack with a squirt of spray paint.

The Layup Operation

The key to successful panel building is preparation. Arrange all the tools and materials you will need at the work table, preferably in open boxes, so that you can reach them easily while wearing sticky gloves. It will save time to pre-measure the exact amounts of resin and hardener before mixing them together. You'll need extra mixing sticks, gloves, and paper towels. An extra sta-

Here's what one panel's worth of identically shaped veneer planks and end kits look like. Note how the PM (Prime Meridian) has been marked as a vertical line on the stack of veneers; this is the reference in locating them on the mold.

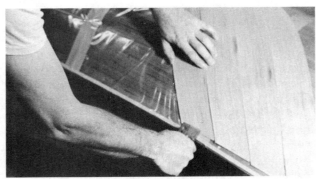

With vacuum bagging, stapling of veneers is almost eliminated, since it's the vacuum that does the squeezing. Stapling is at the extreme ends of the veneers — the part that gets trimmed off and thrown away as scrap. Here, a spring clamp holds one end of a veneer plank until the staples are driven.

ple gun is a good idea, since these tools are prone to malfunction at the wrong time.... something to do with epoxy in the gun (it's the easiest tool to forget to clean after "suckdown"). You'll need a screwdriver and a pair of pliers (for removing staples from errant planks), squeegees, Dum-Dum, masking tape, a knife, and mixing pots. You will also need a thermometer and a kitchen timer. Have the vacuum bag nearby, ready to go, along with the airway screen and its underwear.

The glue-spreading squeegee is a very simple tool, but it needs a bit of customizing. We cut notches in the edge of the plastic so that it spreads ridges of glue. The size and closeness of the notches determines the quantity of glue deposited. Start by cutting "V" notches in your squeegee every ¼ inch, but only about ⅛-inch deep. After your first panel, if it has a lot of glue squirting out of the joints of the top lamination, sand down the squeegee to reduce the depth of the notches so the squeegee spreads less glue. But beware, the squeegee will wear down with use, so watch out for too little, as well as too much, glue. You want just a trace appearing in all the top-lamination joints.

Lay the first layer of veneer on top of the first layer of polyfilm over the mold, dry (no glue). To avoid the possibility of a cumulative change in the diagonal

angle of the planks, start in the middle of the mold, locating your "origin plank" at about 45 degrees to the PM, and work toward one end at a time.

For your first panel, let's locate the bow at the "East" end of the mold, as in the drawings, so you can decide which diagonal to use for the origin plank. It runs Northwest-Southeast, right? Wrong! It runs from upper right to lower left, perpendicular to the stem. Check it out on the drawings and on the mold. "Origin-plank" marks on the edges of the mold will expedite the positioning of each layer.

Staple each strip of veneer into position carefully, so it lies on the mold evenly, with no edge-set, and a minimum of gap between it and its neighbor. Staple only at the ends of the planks, unless you need an extra staple in the middle to hold down a contrary plank; if so, just leave the staple in. If it comes through inside, it will be sanded off later — no problem. There's no need to try to get the planks absolutely flat; the vacuum bag will take care of that.

On this first layer, however, take time to select the best pieces, and get good edge-contact between the strips. If you want, you can use fancy veneers, alternating colors or even "book matching." This layer can be left bright on the interior of your hull, enhancing the beauty, and the price, of the boat. Or if it doesn't look good the first time, you can always paint inside.

Notice that not all the veneers are cut to the same length. Near the ends of each layer, there are shorter pieces at the corners. You can, however, cut those all at once, too. While fitting the corner pieces for the first layer, cut four identical pieces each time. Group these into four corner kits for use in subsequent layers. Of the four kits fitted at, say, the East end of your mold, use two of them for the West end, on the second and third layers. You'll need a total of eight kits per panel, two for each lamination. Mark the kits plainly.

This reversing of ends, and of veneer orientations, is necessary in order to produce our cross-laminated, four-lamination panels, whose two center laminations run the same direction — remember?

Get the system straight in your mind, and in your shop, on the first layer. You have time on the first layer, but all three succeeding layers must be completed within the working time of the glue. Therefore, the veneer for each layer should be inventoried in advance, complete with the correct corner kits for each pile, so that you don't have to think about which plank comes next, or which way it lies, when the glue is pushing you to move quickly. Once the glue is mixed, there's no getting up from the table.

Because all the planks are pre-cut, and we don't have to take the time to riddle every one of them with staples, we can laminate all four courses in one sitting. Unlike most cold molding, we don't wait for cure between layers, so the usual sanding between layers is not necessary. The amount of stapling is vastly reduced, and those staples that are used don't have to be pulled out — they get cut off with the scrap from around the edges of the panel.

Because with CC we have vacuum to do our squeezing for us, we only have to spread glue on one surface — the exposed surface of the veneer after it is fixed in place on the mold. This is an important efficiency boost: the task of handling glue is bad enough without having to handle hundreds of pieces of veneer that are dripping with the stuff.

So here's a tally of CC's expediencies: building a simple, inexpensive mold; "cookie-cutter" spiling; applying all four layers at once; vastly reduced stapling; one-side glue spreading; easy-access finish work; and best of all, no skeleton in the finished hull. All the work of establishing the shape does not become a permanent part of the boat and leave the shop with it, so construction can be easily repeated.

One more plus: enjoyment. From experience, we can say that this skill is a pleasure to learn, to perform, and, especially, to teach. Even after dozens of panels, there's something about the need for organization and judgment, the element of time, and the magic of vacuum that prevents the work from becoming one of those jobs like "putting in screws." Or worse, "pulling out staples."

About Glue

It is possible to cut planks and laminate half a Gull in about two hours. Admittedly, it's nice to have a helper for the second hour, especially on your first boat, because that last hour is a "given." That's all the fluid-time you can count on from a "room-temperature" epoxy, spread in a thin film but sandwiched between veneers, at room temperature. If you've never used epoxy, a few tips are in order:

The primary rules are, keep it off your skin, don't wash yourself with solvents, and ventilate the shop. But there's a lot more to be said about boatshop hygiene. We wear a cartridge respirator whenever we can smell anything noxious, from Awlgrip to Zolatone, including just plain paint and pine tar, and even the dust from aromatic wood such as Western red cedar. This precaution seems especially important for those who smoke. It's difficult to get a mask to fit tightly, however, if you have a thick beard.

Because we've worked around these materials for many years, some of us profess that long-term exposure to common boatshop chemicals, without adequate protection, has made us very sensitive to any noxious vapor. We've seen some good friends suffer severe dermatitis. Strong smells sometimes make us itch and feel badly; normal traffic fumes and even broiler smoke are unreasonably offensive, which is not reassuring. Now

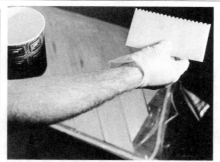
Glue is spread with a notched squeegee, the depth of the notches adjusted to achieve economical, yet complete, glue coverage.

The squeegee in use, leaving ridges of glue behind. Vacuum bagging is so effective in applying pressure that much less glue is needed than with more conventional stapling methods.

The second and third layers of veneer run parallel to each other and cross the first layer at about 90 degrees. Glue is spread over each layer after it is in place, except, of course, for the last (or outer) one.

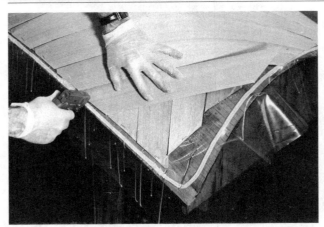

A "corner kit" of veneer planks is being installed at the panel's end.

that we know better, we splurge on thick rubber gloves, mechanic's hand soap, protective cream, mixing pots, paper towels, two-strap dust masks, exhaust fans, and charcoal-filter respirators.

In line with using first-quality veneer, we also recommend using a real "boatbuilder's epoxy," one that will cure quickly in thin films when exposed to the air, with minimum "sweat-out" residue. This is for the coating applications, where the residue, incidentally, should always be washed off with water. But for gluing, your resin may need to be slowed down. Depending on workroom temperature, at least one slower hardener will be necessary, to control the gel time. Several hardeners may be useful, for varying temperatures and applications; the more control, the better. In this panel-making application, you should test your glue/hardener combination to make sure it will provide at least an hour and a half of fluidity in an open-air, thin-film test. If the weather is hot, use a slower hardener in the glue, and try an early-morning session for the first panel layup, getting everything ready the night before.

When you're satisfied that you can repeat the layering operation without problems, mix a small batch of epoxy, just a few spoonfuls, as a sample. You may not necessarily need fillers (thickeners or extenders or fibers) in the resin unless the weather is hot or your epoxy is thin. Play with the stuff on some veneer scraps, spreading it with your notched squeegee and inclining the samples to test for sag. It is not a bad idea to add a few cotton microfibers and/or a dab of silica (wear your mask when mixing), particularly if your brand of glue is thin. Slightly thickened glue can be easier to spread until you get some practice, especially if you're shorthanded.

Write down the time you start mixing this sample, and close up your spreadings between two scraps of veneer, to insulate them as in the real panel. The glue generates heat, which accelerates the cure. Make about six samples, and watch them, starting in about three-quarters of an hour. Peel open one sample every 15

minutes to examine the glue. It should still be fluid in about an hour. When it looks like your glue is becoming too thick to flow under pressure, write down the time again. The difference between these two times is the limit of your glue at that temperature. It is wise to set a timer to 10 minutes less than that limit, and observe the thermometer, as you start mixing for each panel. If something goes awry during layup, the timer will tell you to stop laminating and get the bag on, which can be done at any point, to save what you've done. You can probably complete the panel later with another vacuum cycle. But we want it to work for you the first time, and it will, if you really get ready.

Therefore, now's the time to make a test of the whole system. Using scrap veneer and half a cupful of epoxy, make a small sample lamination on the mold, all four laminations, and put it "in the bag" — airway, underwear, and all. Pull a vacuum on your sample, and listen for leaks. If you want to make sure, turn the pump off for a moment so that you can really hear.

Let the pump run for three hours, and check to see if it gets too hot or loses vacuum. Then remove the sample and test for bond. Does the glue need more time? Even though it is still "green," you'll probably find it could do with less time.

Check to see that the test has not loosened the staples on your first, dry layer; the ends of the planks always should be down tight, to prevent them from popping up as you're applying the succeeding layers. Use ¼-inch staples for this project.

The Real Thing

From these trials, you now know about veneering and gluing and vacuuming. You are finally ready to cycle the mold with a real panel inside. Mix about a quart of epoxy, or slightly less, for the first glue line. Keep track of your usage, so that you don't mix too much for the next panel.

Now, a quart of epoxy, in one lump, is like a bomb. It'll get hot and set up quickly, causing smoke and even fire, unless you get it all out of the mixing pot right away. If the weather's warm, and you take the time to mix in fillers, don't dally! You must mix the epoxy with the hardener first, before adding the fillers, which takes time, so move that mixing stick! Scrape the sides of the pot and scour the corners and the bottom. Then add fillers, and whip again. As soon as it's ready, get it out of there. On the other hand, if it's cold, stir it well, and then wait for a minute or two to allow your mixture to "incubate" in the pot; a little time in a snug place starts those molecules crosslinking. Some resin-hardener formulations call for lots of incubation.

Pour the resin out directly on the first dry layer of veneer that's waiting on the mold; just dump it right down along the PM area. Get it all out of the mixing pot as soon as possible. Spread it quickly with the notched squeegee for an even coating. This is the moment you'll really want some help. Pull the glue downwards from the PM area, making strokes roughly parallel to the veneers; cross-seam spreading tends to pump the glue through the seams and out onto the inboard face of the panel. Spreading glue is the only messy part of the operation. It is over soon, but it takes practice to do it quickly and well, and some people seem to be a lot better at it than others. If you have trouble, try a shaggy paint roller — but that wastes glue and rollers.

Now cover the wet glue with another layer of dry veneer, beginning with its "origin plank" laid perpendicular to the first layer. Repeat the layering and spreading operation for a four-ply laminate, with the two center laminations laid at the same angle.

How much help can you muster? If you've got plenty, and four staple guns and squeegees, and rubber gloves for all (and a coxswain's megaphone for shouting orders), you can use the squad method. Two squads of two "players" each can work all laminations from the "origin" toward both ends at once. It helps to have a fifth person to do nothing but mix glue — and a "captain" to supervise the mayhem. But when you and your happy crew get to the end, don't forget to stop. Veneers for the next panel should be kept out of reach, and the last layer of wood on this panel should be left uncoated.

Don't be intimidated by these cautions. They are offered from the experience of working on big molds with large, willing crews who spoke only Swahili. By comparison, laying up just a small craft like Gull should be a genuine pleasure.

"Suckdown"

There. Your mold is "loaded," but this is no time to stand around! Fold the parting film up and "tack" it in place with masking tape, thus revealing the Dum-Dum. Throw on the underwear and lay down the vacuum tube, with the airway screen over the tube. Pack Dum-Dum around the vacuum tube where it passes into the bag. The portion of the tube that's inside the bag is perforated for vacuum pickup, so be sure all the holes are, in fact, inside the bag. Spread the bag over the whole works and push it down onto the Dum-Dum. The "gathers" should be already stuffed with Dum-Dum, but if you have any wrinkles in the bag at the Dum-Dum, they can cause leaks, so lift the wrinkles up enough to stuff them full of more Dum-Dum. Crank up the vacuum pump, and watch the "suckdown" begin.

As you saw with the test run, the bag will be drawn tightly against the panel, squeezing it against the mold like a transparent, all-over boa constrictor. Glue will come squishing out of all the seams and around the edges of the panel. Check to see that this is happening everywhere, and listen for the telltale hiss of any leaks. The bag may become punctured by sharp edges

protruding from the panel; holes can be quickly patched with Dum-Dum or tape — try tape first, because the plastic film won't respond to taping after Dum-Dum has been there.

Satisfied? Okay. Now let her "cook" for several hours, the actual time to be determined by the hardness of the resin remaining in your last mixing pot. Also, you can feel the glue's hardness through the bag; it only needs to be "cheese-hard" before you turn off the pump.

Pumps normally run hot, but yours shouldn't lose pulling power from start to finish. Check the gauge, and keep an eye on the bag every once in a while. If the gauge starts dropping and you can't find any leaks but the pump is hot, try aiming a fan, or a vacuum cleaner set on "blow," at the pump to cool it off — that might get you through making the panel. It's possible to lose vacuum from some happenstance that can be easily corrected, if you catch it in time.

Cure time can be shortened substantially with the addition of heat on the panel. Moving the mold out into the sunlight is the easiest way to increase the temperature. Even on a cold day, considerable radiant heat comes from the sun if it is shining. Otherwise, electric blankets or heat lamps will help, but be care-

"Suckdown!" This is the vacuum-bagging technique at work, gently and uniformly squeezing the four layers of veneer tightly together to form a cold-molded panel.

The first step after "unveiling" the cured panel is to establish a reference for marking its finished outline. This reference is called the Prime Meridian (PM) and is transferred to the panel from the mold (where it has been marked earlier) by means of a plumb bob suspended from an overhead wire.

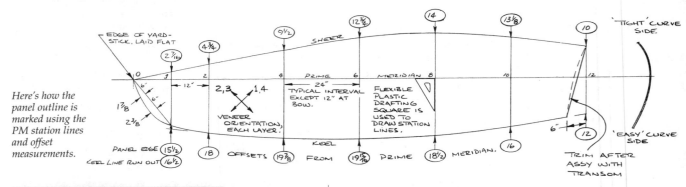

Here's how the panel outline is marked using the PM station lines and offset measurements.

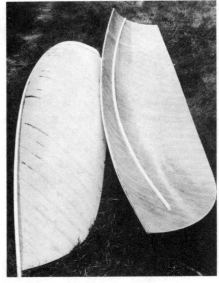

Once cut free of the mold, the panels are smoothed up inside, seat risers are added, and assembly begins.

ful not to melt the plastic or soften the Dum-Dum. A heater under the mold doesn't help much unless you place another garment, this one made of thick fiberglass insulation, over the top. Now you've got a tool!

If you can, allow the panel to sit on the mold overnight for a sure cure — unless, of course, you're in real production, where the right combination of epoxy, heat, and timing (and a host of other details not applicable to this project) will allow you to recycle the mold two or three times a day.

Unveiling this first panel is like Christmas morning — take off the wrapping, and enjoy. Then, roll up the bag and store it for the next time.

Clean up the top surface of the panel, and lay out and mark its perimeter shape, while it is still securely stapled to the mold. Make sure the parting film is covering and protecting the Dum-Dum. Be careful when sanding the panel; epoxy is harder than cedar, and a rasp or sanding block may prevent you from scouring out hollows between the hard spots.

Panel Layout

This step is equivalent to lofting, but it's pretty sim-

ple. Instead of describing the shapes of slices, or "sections," through the hull, we need only to determine the boundary, or perimeter shape, of our panel — i.e., where to trim its edges. Begin by leveling the mold; use a spirit level under the end formers (leveling lengthwise is not necessary). Erect an overhead plumb-bob line exactly over the PM, and locate the PM on your panel with the plumb bob about every 18 inches. Then draw a straight line down the panel with a batten to connect these PM points.

In our own shop, we locate the PM by drilling very small holes up through the mold — and the panel — at the PM, from underneath, patching the holes in the mold each time with Dum-Dum. But most people resist drilling holes in their boat, even though the holes get plugged easily during the finish operation, so the plumb-bob-established PM, described above, may be best for them. Getting underneath such a small mold is difficult as well, so you can choose between blocking up the mold for drilling locator holes or rigging the plumb bob, whichever suits your situation.

Then, after you've got the PM marked on the panel, use a large plastic draftsman's triangle and a bendable yardstick to mark station lines perpendicular to the PM, across the panel. Locate your station lines so that the given layout dimensions will fall within the limits of your panel.

At the same time, using the yardstick, you can mark the given offsets for the sheer and keel outlines on each station line, and drive a small nail at these points. Bend a limber batten along the nails (you may want help with this), adjust the batten carefully by eye for fairness, and draw the panel's final outline. The curve at the bow requires a very small, flexible batten. We like to mark our outlines with a fine felt-tipped pen, so that there's no pushing, as sometimes occurs with a pencil, to distort the batten. Any changes you make in the given offsets should be recorded for exact duplication on the second panel (see note, page 104).

When the outline is marked on this first (or any subsequent) panel, pry up its edges from the mold, using a flat pry-bar. Don't put your fingers under there to help lift; those staples are like needles, and bloodstains could ruin your clear interior finish. Instead, slip 4 by 4 blocks under the edge of the panel to hold it up, well clear of the mold. Sabersaw around the panel, just barely leaving the layout line. Discard the staple-riddled scraps, while wearing gloves, in a manner that makes it unnecessary for anyone to handle them individually again.

Sand smooth the interior surface of the finished panel. Apply three thin coats of epoxy, but leave the outer surface uncoated for now; it gets fiberglassed later.

Build and finish your second panel as above, starting from "The Layup Operation," only don't repeat the process exactly. On your second panel, be certain that the beginning layer of veneer is applied to the mold on the opposite diagonal to that layer on the first panel. Check twice. And when it comes time for layout, put the bow of the second panel at the other end of the mold.

Here's a final recap on how to figure these differences from port to starboard: On the second panel of a handed pair, reverse the angle of the first "origin plank," and put the bow at the other end of the mold, but keep the keel line on the same side of the mold — the "easy-cure" side. Make sure the "planks" of the inside and outside layers run perpendicular to the stem of that panel. In other words: between panels, you'll "somersault" the profile of the boat on the mold end-for-end inside-out (but not "capsized") — that is, you'll flip everything beamwise, bow-over-stern.

PHASE III
BUILDING THE BOAT

Now that you have your panels, building the boat can be an absolute joy. (As a matter of fact, if all you want is a boat, and you aren't interested in doing the work so far described, it makes a lot of sense to buy panels from someone who has a mold and wants to produce a run of panels to sell; then you can start here.) Relative to conventional boatbuilding, however, there are a few peculiarities, which are evident from the drawings and photos. For instance: The stringers that support the seats are installed before the hull halves are assembled; the actual joining of the halves is done with wire lacings; and there is no timber keel — just fiberglass and epoxy putty. In addition, there is a fair amount of "torturing" in this design, so you'll have the chance to see just how far you can go in modifying a CC hull away from the molded shape of its panels.

Most peculiar of all is that the joinery does not have to be first class, because all joints are glued and filleted with epoxy. In fact — and this is real heresy — you can build a stronger boat by fitting the wood joints loosely, then doing a good job with structural epoxy fillets.

Thorough epoxy coating of all parts during assembly serves to permanently seal the water out of joints (of which there are not many in a frame-less boat), especially if all end grain is meticulously presaturated with straight epoxy. "Juice," as it is called with nothing mixed in except the hardener, is also very good for sealing holes drilled in the wood before installing fasteners, like the rowlock screws of through-bolts. Bed everything in epoxy or a modern marine sealant. Soak the walls of the holes with it. Then, if the boat is used, and cared for by the user as if he built the thing himself, it'll probably last as long as you do.

If all this epoxy stuff sounds complicated, be reas-

Gull's cold-molded hull will be made from these Constant Camber port and starboard panels by joining them together along the keel as shown, then "torturing" them into the shape of a boat by bringing the stem portions of the panels together.

Once the panels are fastened together, the rails go on and the transom goes in. Knees, breasthook, seats, and oarlock pads complete Gull's construction.

Note:

If you go into production, you can cast a thin fiberglass template of one of your panels. After first double-coating a panel with epoxy, apply PVA mold release, and simply sheathe the panel with fiberglass laid over the PVA. Use two layers of light cloth and epoxy resin, with a layer of 2-inch fiberglass tape all around the edges. After cure, clean up the edges with a sander to achieve very fair curves, and then peel off the fiberglass; it is your template. Thereafter, you'll never need to lay out this panel outline again — at least for this design. The template is popped inside-out for use in marking both port and starboard panels as perfect mirror images. Remember to mark the PM on the template. You can also mark on it the position of everything else that gets fastened to the hull, like seats, stringers, bulkheads, trunk, footbraces, etc. Once you have a panel template, you can practically throw away the tape measure.

A full set (3 sheets) of working plans for the Gull is available from John R. Marples, 4530 S.E. Firmont Drive, Port Orchard, WA 98366. The price is $60.

sured. It is different, but far simpler than building the old-fashioned way. Once the panels are in hand, the actual boatbuilding is sufficiently simple to beg description in a word-saving "CC-gram" (see Telegram sidebar).

THE COMPANY WILL APPRECIATE SUGGESTIONS FROM ITS PATRONS CONCERNING ITS SERVICE

DOWN
EASTERN
UNION

CLASS OF SERVICE

This is a full-rate Telegram or Cablegram unless its deferred character is indicated by a suitable symbol above or preceding the address.

SYMBOLS

DL	= Day Letter
NM	= Night Message
NL	= Night Letter
LC	= Deferred Cable
NLT	= Cable Night Letter
	Ship Radiogram

FRED BROOKS
PRESIDENT

E.H. MORGAN
CHAIRMAN OF THE BOARD

R. SINGLETON WESTERFIELD III
FIRST VICE-PRESIDENT

Received at Naskeag Road, Brooklin, Maine

FROM: KAMBERWOOD INTERNATIONAL, BOX 550, NORTH, VA 23128

GREETINGS BB

   CUT TRANSOM EPOXYCOAT INBOARDONLY. PREPARE GUNWALES SEATSTRINGERS. BONDIN GUNWALES &SEATSTRINGERS W/SCREWS DRIVENTHRUPANEL. EPOXYCOAT SEATSTRINGER INPLACE STOP.
   ATTACH FIVEFOOT 2X4S ONTOPOF TWOSAWHORSES LEVELED FIVEFEETAPART. PLACEPANELS ONHORSES KEELSTOGETHER INVERTED. DRILLSMALLHOLES ATEACH STATIONLINE HALFINCH INFROM KEELEDGE. LACE PANELSTOGETHER 16OR20GAUGE COPPERWIRE. ADD HOLES&WIRES TWELVEINCHESAPARTKEEL THREEINCHESAPARTSTEM. TIGHTENWIRES ACHIEVE FAIRHULL NO SCALLOPS. STEM REQUIRESFORCE USE LONGWIRE ATSTEMHEAD SHORTERWIRES TOWARDKNUCKLE TIGHTENGRADUALLY SPREADSTRAIN EZYDUZIT WATCHOUT YOUARELOADING FIFTYPOUND MOUSETRAP GOMAN STOP.
   INSTALLTRANSOM W/WIRES&NAILS NOGLUEYET. PRESATURATE KEELEDGES &TRANSOMJOINT FOLLOW W/DUOKEISCHMUTZ CUREWELL. REMOVEALLWIRES PATCHHOLES SANDFAIR. APPLYTHREELAYERS NINEOUNCE GLASSTAPE TWOINCHESWIDE THREEINCHESWIDE &FOURINCHESWIDE INTHATORDER OVERKEELJOINT &TRANSOMJOINT INSIDE&OUT SANDFAIR STOP.
   REMOVESCREWS FROMSEATSTRINGERS REUSE TOINSTALL INWALES CURE. REMOVEALLSCREWS FILLALLHOLES. INSTALL&FILLET SKEG &FALSEWORK ATBOW SHAPETOSUIT. FIBERGLASS ALLOUTBOARD ONELAYER FOUROUNCECLOTH DOUBLEOVERKEEL. INSTALL ROTRESISTANT HARDWOOD KEELBAND STOP.
   BONDIN SEATS ROWLOCKPADS TRANSOMKNEES BREASTHOOK FOOTBRACES. EPOXYCOAT THREECOATS ALLRAWWOOD THENTHREECOATS ULTRAVIOLETFILTER VARNISH ALLBRIGHTWOOD. SAND&PAINT ALLOUTBOARDSURFACES STOP.
   OPTIONAL OARS SPARS SAILS RUDDER LEEBOARD NAMEBOARD FLOORBOARD FENDERRAIL FLAGSTAFF FIGUREHEAD STOPSTOPSTOP.
   BEGIN ASAP SAYHI AA REGARDS CC

The Sailing-Paddling Canoe Piccolo

by Robert H. Baker   Photographs by Gail Wills

Piccolo shows off her ability to carry two people in relative comfort. She's just as steady in a 20-knot breeze with the same two people aboard.

The Wonderful One-Person Boat, or more accurately, the Perfectly Respectable Two-Person Boat, started out as a very simple proposition. "What is needed," said Jon Wilson, the editor of *WoodenBoat* magazine, "is a 12-foot boat for one person, light enough to be easily carried, and very cartoppable, to be propelled with a double paddle."

So four of us sat down in *WoodenBoat*'s office on a cold rainy day in November to talk about it. The fellow in the easy chair pointed out that it is great good fun to go to sea with a friend; someone sitting on the floor thought it would be nice to steer her with foot pedals; and someone else wanted the beast to sail. Not bad for one 12-foot canoe-type thing. At least nobody wanted six berths, a head, and a galley.

I was just a little leery of trying to carry two large people safely in a normal 12-foot canoe hull, so I started from scratch. The principal dimensions were easy. I stretched her out to 12 feet 8 inches to give her more lift in the ends without making the deck line too full. Thirty inches beam is about all that can be managed comfortably with a double paddle, so that's what she has. The result is a very fine-lined, burdensome hull with some pretensions of sea-keeping ability. She has heavy stems to take banging on rocks and things, and since there is no centerboard, she has a relatively deep keel the length of her. The keel was given quite a bit of rocker to improve her turning ability.

The rig, since you could hardly expect to get up and run around the boat to handle it, had to have as few moving parts as possible, have everything lead to within easy reach of one person, and be short enough so that all the spars could be stowed comfortably inside the boat. Also, the rig had to be large enough to drive the boat, as I wanted her to really sail, not just look like she might.

The ketch rig seemed obvious from the start. You can get a reasonable amount of area in the two sails, spread out fore and aft to balance the deep ends and set low enough not to overpower her. The standing lug is ideal. All it requires is a halyard, a downhaul, and a sheet. Lead the halyard and sheet to jam cleats within reach of one person, and you're in business. Jam cleats are used so you can dump the whole mess in an emergency.

So what we came up with is a boat that weighs 51 pounds stripped, paddles easily, and sails very well. She will carry about 400 pounds in decent weather, will keep the sea out in bad weather with one aboard, and in general will do whatever is required of her. With her long keel, she will run straight in any combination of wind and wave, but will not be much interested in turning on her heel. But she isn't a dewdrop sailer, as she draws about 8 inches loaded. I certainly would not recommend her for whitewater work, but for poking around rivers and harbors, and along the coast in decent weather, she does very well.

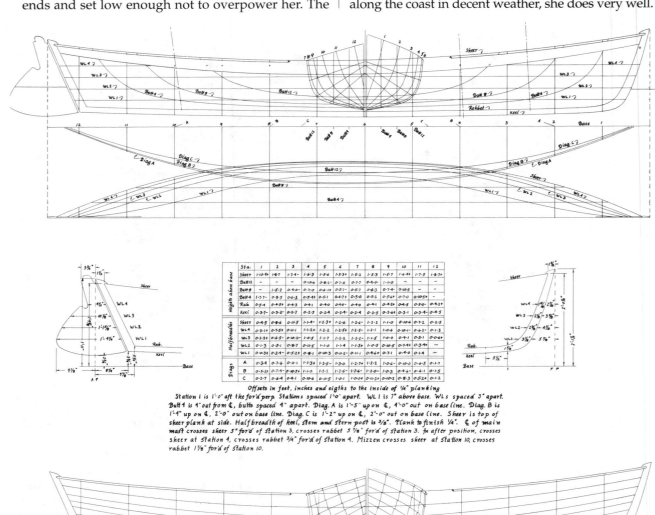

	Sta.	1	2	3	4	5	6	7	8	9	10	11	12
Heights above base	Sheer	1-10-4+	1-8-7	1-7-4-	1-6-3	1-5-6	1-5-3+	1-5-2	1-5-3	1-5-7	1-6-4+	1-7-5	1-8-7+
	Butt 2	-	-	-	0-10-6	0-8-2-	0-7-6	0-7-7	0-9-0-	1-1-0			
	Butt 8	-	1-6-2	0-9-0-	0-7-0	0-6-1+	0-5-7-	0-5-7	0-6-5	0-7-4-	0-10-5		
	Butt 4	1-7-7-	0-5-5	0-6-3	0-5-4+	0-5-1	0-4-7+	0-5-0	0-5-2	0-5-6+	0-7-0	0-10-5	
	Rab.	0-5-4	0-4-5+	0-4-3	0-4-1	0-4-0	0-4-0-	0-4-0	0-4-1	0-4-3+	0-4-5	0-5-0-	0-9-2+
	Keel	0-3-7-	0-3-2-	0-2-7	0-2-5	0-2-4	0-2-4-	0-2-5	0-2-6+	0-3-1	0-3-4-	0-4-5	
Half breadths	Sheer	0-4-5	0-8-6	0-11-5	1-1-4-	1-2-3+	1-2-6	1-2-6-	1-2-2	1-1-0	0-10-4	0-7-2	0-2-5
	WL4	0-3-1+	0-7-5+	0-11-1	1-1-2+	1-2-5	1-2-5+	1-2-1	1-0-6			0-6-2-	0-1-3
	WL3	0-1-3+	0-6-5-	0-10-2+	1-0-5	1-1-7	1-1-1	1-2-1	1-1-5	1-0-0	0-9-1	0-5-1	0-0-6+
	WL2	0-1-3	0-5-1	0-8-7	0-11-5	1-1-0	1-1-4	1-1-3+	1-0-5	0-10-5	0-7-4+	0-3-4+	
	WL1	0-0-3+	0-2-4-	0-5-2+	0-8-1	0-10-3	0-11-2-	0-11-1	0-9-6+	0-7-1	0-3-0	0-1-4	
Diags	A	0-3-4	0-7-6	0-11-1	1-1-3+	1-2-5-	1-3-0	1-2-7+	1-2-1	1-0-6-	0-10-0	0-6-3	0-1-7
	B	0-3-2-	0-7-4-	0-10-3+	1-1-0	1-2-2	1-2-6-	1-2-6	1-3-0-	1-0-3	0-9-6-	0-6-1	0-1-5
	C	0-2-7	0-6-4	0-9-1	0-10-6	0-11-5	1-0-1	1-0-0+	0-11-3-	0-10-2	0-8-3	0-5-2+	0-1-2

Offsets in feet, inches and eigths to the inside of 1/4" planking

Station 1 is 1'-0" aft the for'd perp. Stations spaced 1'-0" apart. WL1 is 7" above base. WLs spaced 3" apart. Butt 1 is 4" out from ℄, butts spaced 4" apart. Diag. A is 1'-5" up on ℄, 4'-0" out on base line. Diag. B is 1'-4" up on ℄, 2'-0" out on base line. Diag. C is 1'-2" up on ℄, 2'-0" out on base line. Sheer is top of sheer plank at side. Half breadth of keel, stem and stern post is 3/8". Plank to finish 1/4". ℄ of main mast crosses sheer 5" for'd of station 3, crosses rabbet 5 1/8" for'd of station 3. In after position, crosses sheer at station 4, crosses rabbet 3/4" for'd of station 4. Mizzen crosses sheer at station 10, crosses rabbet 1 1/8" for'd of station 10.

Scale in feet

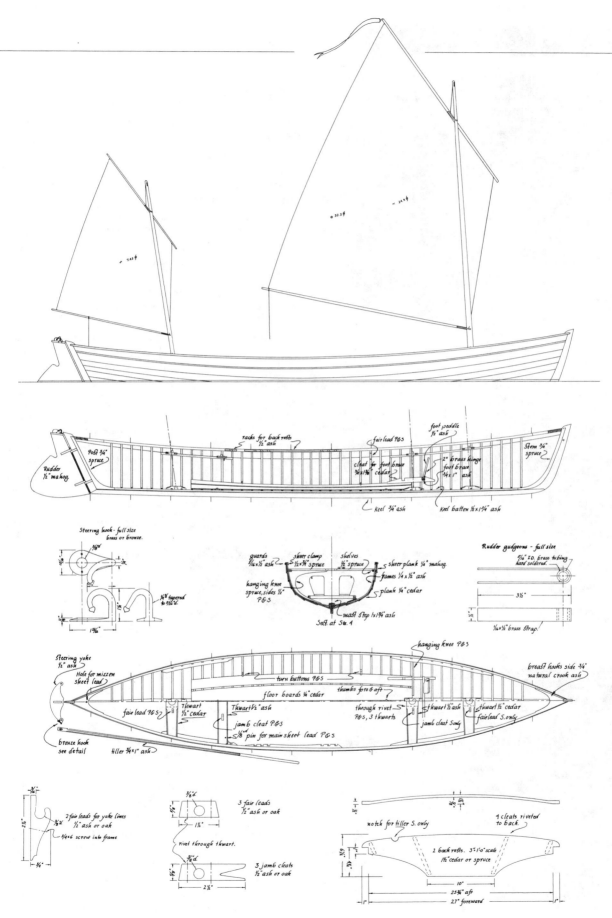

Steering hook - full size
brass or bronze.

Rudder gudgeons - full size
5/16" I.D. brass tubing
hard soldered.

3½"

1/16"×½" brass strap.

guards
3/16×½" ash
sheer clamp
½"×¾" spruce
shelves
½" spruce
sheer plank ¼" mahog.
hanging knee
spruce, sides ½"
P&S
frames ¼ x ½" ash
plank ¼" cedar
mast step 1×1¾" ash

Sect. at Sta. 1

racks for back rest
½" ash
fair lead P&S
foot peddle
½" ash
Post ¾"
spruce
Stem ¾"
spruce
cleat for foot brace
¾×1¾" cedar
2" brass hinge
foot brace
¾×1" ash
Rudder
½" mahog.
Keel ¾" ash
Keel batten ½×1¾" ash

Steering yoke
½" ash
Hole for mizzen
sheet lead
hanging knee P&S
breast hooks side ¾"
natural crook ash
turn buttons P&S
thumbs fore & aft
floor boards ¼" cedar
through rivet
P&S, 3 thwarts
thwart ½" ash
thwart ½" cedar
fair lead S. only
fair lead P&S
Thwart
½" cedar
Thwart½" ash
jamb cleat P&S
jamb cleat S only
1/8"∅ pin for main sheet lead P&S
bronze hook
see detail
tiller ¾×1" ash

2 fair leads for yoke lines
½" ash or oak
3/16"d.
¼×6 screw into frame

3/8"d.
3 fair leads
½" ash or oak
1½"
rivet through thwart.
3/8"d.
3 jamb cleats
½" ash or oak
2½"

notch for tiller S. only
4 cleats riveted
to back.
2 back rests. 3"=1'-0" scale
1½" cedar or spruce
10"
25¾" aft
27" foreward

Making the molds.

Setting her up.

Laminating the stem.

Lofting and Setup

Having committed the whole mess to paper, leaving out a few small details that were subject to change without notice, I got the okay from The Editors and commenced to build her. Since I had never designed or built a hull of this nature before, I rather expected a few surprises. The first came in lofting, as the long, easy lines of the hull don't leave much room for error. We found ourselves moving the battens by 32nds of an inch to make them come fair. Generally, if a batten doesn't run through an intersection just where it should, you can nudge it with your toe and set another nail. Not so here. The nudge will produce a hump or a hook without half trying. The point here is not to scare you before you start, but rather to be sure you loft the boat very carefully.

Take your time. The offsets are correct, I believe, as I picked them up from our own lofting. The lines are drawn to the inside of the planking, so you don't have to deduct anything, but the inner rabbet and the bearding line must be drawn to allow for $\frac{1}{4}$-inch planking. I took the angle of the plank to the keel at the midship section and used that as a constant angle for the back rabbet. So instead of a 90-degree angle, you have one a little shallower, which effectively leaves you a little more wood between the rabbets in the stems. This is not necessary, but every little bit helps here. Enough said about the lofting. It's perfectly straightforward as long as you're accurate.

Now that the boat is laid out on the floor, you begin to see that she is really a very small boat, but don't worry; you can fit into her.

In picking up patterns, the Mylar method seems to work very well here. Trace the pieces on Mylar and cut the patterns out with scissors. The Mylar is stiff enough to be drawn around. Molds are gotten out of pine planed on two sides for accuracy.

I built the boat upside down on a building horse that is used for everything in my shop. It consists of two pieces of 2-inch by 6-inch spruce, 16 feet long, separated by 4-inch by 4-inch posts set on the floor. It's tall enough to provide a comfortable working height. The molds then have a centerpiece that fits tightly down between the rails of the horse. On this, it is a relatively simple matter to square and true the molds. The ends of the molds can, of course, be carried to the floor in the usual way. There is no need to bevel the molds, as the strain on them is not great and the corners — edges — won't cut into the planking. Bear in mind that the molds forward of amidships are set on the after side of the station mark, and the molds aft are set on the forward side of the mark.

The Backbone

The stems, or the stem and the sternpost, are made of spruce to keep the weight down. If you have access to spruce knees, fine. Otherwise, the stems must be laminated. The laminations should follow the inner, rather than the outer, line of the stem. This allows for a little less bend, but will keep the plank fastenings from falling in the same line of grain. As the two ends have very nearly the same rake, one jig will do for both the stem and the sternpost, or you can make one thick one and saw it in half. One-eighth inch laminations are good. Epoxy does a grand job of sticking things together, but it sure can get messy!

While the stems are curing, get out the keel and the keel batten. Again, for the sake of saving weight, I used ash. One plank I used had a sweep to it that just matched the rocker, so the keel was sawn to shape, but the keel could have been sprung to shape just as easily. The grain in the keel batten should be as straight as possible, since ash tends to bend as it dries. To save a little more weight, taper the keel from ¾ inch at the rabbet to ½ inch at the bottom. The stem and sternpost are also tapered to a ½-inch face.

The keel and the keel batten are screwed together, using 1-inch No. 8 bronze screws, one at each end and one 2 inches forward of the station marks. That will keep them out of the way of the frame fastenings.

Clean up the stem and sternpost so they are sided ¾ inch, cut them to shape, and rabbet them. They are fastened to the keel with two screws and epoxy. When the epoxy has set up, you can clean up the rabbet where the stem meets the keel, and cut the back rabbet in the keel.

Set the backbone assembly into the molds, and check each mold to be sure everything is all right. The easiest way to keep the keel where it belongs is to wedge it down with posts from the ceiling. If, for some reason, you can't, use small angle brackets screwed to the keel batten and to the molds. It's hard to get the screws out after she's planked, so don't use the brackets if you don't have to.

With the molds set in place and the keel on them, run four or five light, springy ribbands over the

Joining the stem and the keel.

The backbone in place.

Checking for fairness.

molds to check the setup for fairness. Let the ribbands run naturally over the molds; hold them down with a single round-headed screw at each mold. Any unfairness will show up like a sore thumb, and the offending mold must be raised, lowered, shaved, or padded to rectify the situation. At this point, checking for fairness is more a matter of eye than of measure, although a few quick measurements can help you determine what's wrong.

So, with everything together and placed where you want it, you can start thinking about the planking.

Planking

Having been brought up with Eastern white cedar, I consider it the best stock there is. And, of course, the best of it comes from Massachusetts, Rhode Island, or Connecticut. The only trouble is that it is nearly impossible to find clear stock in any size, so I'll admit to a few alternatives:

The Eastern cedar from Carolina is a little brittle and in center cuts has a tendency to split right down the middle. Northern, or Maine, cedar is quite acceptable if you don't mind lots of knots. A knot at the edge of a plank — or worse, half a knot — can be disastrous. Western red cedar likes to split, and Port Orford and Alaskan cedar are both a bit heavy. However, all the cedars are quite usable. A nice piece of mahogany for the sheer plank sets off the line of the boat to advantage. Honduran is heavy — like oak — but Philippine will do well, as will a piece of Spanish cedar, if you can find it.

In the end, the planking stock you choose depends on personal preference and what you are used to. If you haunt the local mills long enough, you may find just what you want in your own backyard. Just remember that you are dealing with ¼-inch stock. If a plank or a species is going to be a bad actor, it will act twice as badly in very thin sizes. When push comes to shove, you could even plank with spruce from the local lumberyard.

Whatever you use, look for reasonably clear, tight stock, and you will be home free. All these planks can be gotten out in one length, so get stock 10 inches wide and 14 feet long, if possible.

In lining off the molds for the planks, please take a little extra time to get your plank lines visually correct. Avoid planks much over 4 inches wide as they will split easier than narrow ones. Also avoid any tendency toward downward hooks in the ends. You should have wider planks in the bottom and topside, and narrow ones at the turn of the bilge. Try to get one plank to run through the tightest part of the turn from end to end. Always bear in mind that the shape of the planks in a lapstrake hull can make or break the appearance of the finished boat.

If you wish, you can measure my planking diagram and go from there. Notice that my garboard and second plank are both 4 ½ inches wide when you include the ½-inch lap. This leaves 3 ½ inches unsupported, but I got away with it; you can, too, if you're careful. After the hull has been lined off to your satisfaction, you can start planking.

The garboards are the only plank that will require soaking. The twist at the ends is just too great to take a chance on, so fit the planks roughly and soak them thoroughly. I dropped ours in the river for the night. Clamp them up on the molds, and the stem and the sternpost, and go away to let them dry.

This is a good time to get out frame stock, which will be ¼-inch by ½-inch ash, not necessarily straight grained, but not with the grain running out badly either. Cut the frames on a table saw, plane them out by hand on the bench, and chamfer off the inside corners. The frames are installed in one length from gunwale to gunwale, so 6-foot stock is in order.

When you are sure the garboards have dried out, make the final fits, cut the bevel for the lap at the ends, and fasten them in place. The planking is so thin that the only acceptable lap is a dory lap. A ship lap won't do. Start the lap about 18 inches from the end of the plank. For fastenings, use ¾-inch No. 6 bronze screws in the stem and sternpost, and ⅝-inch copper tacks in the keel batten, about 2 inches apart. Always bore a hole the size of the fastening's shank in the planking. If you don't, the thin cedar will almost certainly split. I know from experience. Bore into the keel batten with a drill two sizes smaller and not quite the full depth of the tack.

Incidentally, I believe the planking for this boat should be really dry. Presumably, the boat will not be in the water long enough at any one time to do much swelling, but since this boat will most likely be on top of a car at highway speeds, she will dry out quickly. To keep her from opening up, use dry wood.

All right, the garboards are fastened, and it's time to bevel the laps for the next plank. Use a short piece of straight stock, place one end on the mark for the top of the next plank and plane the outboard face of each garboard until the piece lies flat. Do this at every mold and then connect the flats. Extreme care is required in beveling, but without it, the next plank cannot be spiled. The fastenings will pull the two planks together whether the bevels are perfect or not, but if the bevels are wrong, you will put a terrible strain on the planks. So go gently.

With the bevel cut on the garboards to your satisfaction, get out the second plank. I found from experience that the planking is so limber that putting it in a vise to plane the edges is less than satisfactory. Instead, clamp it flat on the bench top with the edge hanging out. Hold your plane — a small modelmaker's plane is ideal — in one hand and plane the edge true.

When clamping in the new plank, start amidships and work fore and aft. This will make the plank lie fair with no bulges. So, check the fit, cut the bevels at the ends, clamp it up again to check the fit of the bevel the whole length, make any corrections, and clamp it up again for fastening.

Whether or not to put flexible compound in the laps is up to you. If you feel there are bumps and humps in the joint, run in a very thin film of Boat Life or a similar compound. If you feel you've done a good job and everything is smooth and true, don't put anything in the joint.

Plank Fastening

Now you have to measure out the spacings for the fastenings and frames. The frames are to be 3 inches on center, which means there will be a frame on every station line and three in between. Mark frame locations out on the lap of the plank you've just clamped on. I used plank fastenings 1-inch apart, so there are two fastenings between frames. Mark those on the lap. The fastenings go in the center of the lap, but for safety, stagger the line of fastenings 1/8-inch apart. This will provide a space 3/16 inch from the edge of the plank to the first line of fastenings, 1/8-inch between, and 3/16 inch to the edge of the other plank. With all this marked on the lap, bore for the plank fastenings, but not for the frame fastenings. Here again, bore for the shank size of the 5/8-inch copper tacks.

The planks are clench nailed, or clench tacked, if you prefer. If you've never tried clench nailing, practice first on some scrap stock. The point of the tack should be placed diagonally across the grain, and as the tack is driven home, the point should turn up and in toward the main part of the plank, rather than down toward the edge. Don't try to set the head any more than flush with the surface of the plank. It's not necessary to go farther, and the hammer head can crush the plank.

After you have fastened in the first pair of planks above the garboard, get out and fit the next pair. When getting out planks for any

Setting the sheer batten.

The garboards clamped in place.

The garboard fastened.

Hanging the broadstrake.

Fastening the broadstrake.

Trying the third plank.

Patterns show the shape of the planks.

Planing the sheerstrake fair.

boat, I think it's a good idea to make the first plank for, say, the starboard side, the second for the port side, and alternate sides all the way up. This way, you can even out any small discrepancies in the molds and your plank lines will come out even. It's even more important in this canoe, where a little error makes a big difference. As you add planks, keep track of the plank lines to be sure both sides are going up evenly, especially at the ends where a difference really shows up.

Now, having fitted the next pair of planks to perfection, clamp then one at a time and mark them carefully for your fastenings. Remember that the frames must be kept parallel to the station lines or molds, or square to the keel, as you prefer to think of it. Remember to stagger the fastenings or run the risk of splitting the plank. Keep all this in mind as you go, and the line of fastenings will come out beautifully straight and even all the way up the side.

When you get to the plank below the sheer plank, stop a minute and consider something new. The sheer plank, whether it is spruce, cedar, or mahogany, will look very well with a nice ⅜-inch bead cut in the lower edge. When the bead is cut, though, there is very little wood left between the bead and the rest of the plank, so it is not safe to fasten through the bead. Therefore, to get good fastening room, you must increase the width of the lap from ½ inch to ⅞ inch, adding the equivalent of the ⅜-inch bead. Then you can fasten above the bead in safety.

Cutting the bead is no great problem, but it is a good idea to grind a little off the inside corner of the plane iron so it doesn't cut the groove too deeply. At the ends, where the plank is beveled, you will have to let the plane run out and cut the bead progressively less deeply by hand, or you will cut right through to the other side of the plank.

With the bead cut, you can hang and fasten the sheer plank, take off all the clamps, and stand back to admire your handiwork, but there are two more things to do before she can be taken off the molds. First, bore for all the frame fastenings, which will be 1-inch No. 13 nails, not tacks. They are larger by one drill size than the tacks, so bore accordingly. These holes must be in nice straight lines or the fastenings will come through the sides of the frames, or worse, clear of them.

One last thing. Fit stretchers inside the hull from

sheer to sheer at, or close to, stations 2, 4, 9, and 11. Now you can let go whatever is holding the keel down and wiggle her up off the molds. This will require one person lifting at each end. Set her in a padded cradle of some sort on a pair of sawhorses, and take a good look at what you've done.

Any fastening that isn't properly clenched can be taken care of now. Then she should be thoroughly sanded inside and given a good dose, on the inside only, of linseed oil cut in half with turpentine. The next project will be to fit the sheer clamps; let the oil soak in overnight so you don't get it all over you and your work.

The next step is to mark a centerline for the frames. Use a limber batten or a piece of broken bandsaw blade, bend it into the boat from one gunwale to the other, and draw a line through all the pre-drilled holes. This is one of the two places where a friend is a great help. Chances are the line won't pass nicely through all the holes, but as long as it comes close, you're in business. If it doesn't even come close to some holes, you will have to plug and re-drill them.

Planking complete.

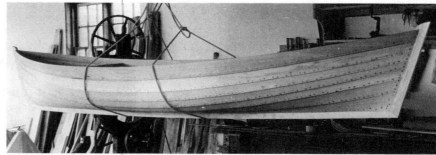
Off the molds.

Sheer Clamps

Now is the time for the sheer clamps. Some people call them "inwales," but that seems to me to be a cumbersome name. A sheer clamp is just what its name implies: it clamps everything together at the sheer. The Piccolo's clamp is a piece of ½-inch by ¾-inch spruce, long enough to go from the stem to the sternpost in one length. I went to the local lumberyard and picked through the piles of 2-inch by 6-inch framing stuff until I found a good clear one. Cut one end to fit nicely against the side of the stem, start bending and clamping at the bow, and work aft to the stern, making sure the clamp lies tightly against the sheer plank all the way. At the stern you can cut the clamp to length by eye and then plane it to fit tightly against the side of the post — so tightly that it wedges a bit.

When the sheer clamp is nicely fitted and all clamped in, mark the centerline of each frame on the underside of the sheer clamp, then take it out and cut the taper at each end for the breasthooks. Set the clamp aside and do the same for the other one on the other side of the boat. You can notch the clamp for the frame heads now or wait until later; it doesn't make much difference.

At this point, someone is sure to ask why I use a closed, or capped, gunwale rather than an open

Clenching the laps.

The boat and the molds.

one; that is, a gunwale with a lighter sheer clamp fastened on the inside of the frame heads and open between. I believe the closed gunwale makes a tighter, stronger, and better-looking job. However, if an open gunwale is your desire, you can make the clamp thinner — I suggest 5/16 inch by 3/4 inch — and deal with it accordingly. Obviously, neither type can be fitted until after the boat is framed, so let's get on with that.

Framing

Before you start framing, refer to the construction plan, and locate and lightly mark the position of the four shelves in the boat. These are fastened with rivets at every other frame, so mark these holes on the outside of the boat and do not put the frame fastenings into them until later.

Presumably you have already cut and planed the frame stock, and have made half a dozen extra frames for breakage. The night before you start framing, put the whole bundle of frames to soak, either in the bathtub or in any other container that is long enough. A 6-foot piece of plastic drain pipe capped at one end works well.

You can frame singlehanded, but that can be painful. You'll be a lot happier if you can find a friend to help. Though it doesn't take very long to write or read about framing, the job seems to go on interminably. Various people have helped me frame, and most have quit from boredom, so pick your friend with care.

In the morning get up steam in the box and have at it. The procedure is to bend in three or four frames, starting in the center of the boat, and then clamp and nail them. Then bend in three or four more, working alternately fore and aft. As each frame goes in, bore for and drive a 3/4-inch ring nail through it and into the keel. These nails should be staggered about 1/4 inch on each side of the centerline to keep the keel from splitting. The usual way to make a frame lie flat against the planking is to give it a good rap on the head to drive it down, but don't do it to these delicate ones or you'll start a crack somewhere.

The frame heads are cut off on an angle, 3/16 inch below the sheer out against the plank and 1/2 inch below it on the inside. Make a jig from a short length of scrap from the sheer clamp to mark them all evenly. The frames are cut this way to leave the most frame and take the least out of the notch in the sheer clamps. Having done this, notch the clamps to take the frame heads and bend the clamps one at a time into the boat. These are fastened with 1-inch copper nails driven from the inside at each frame, as well as a couple of nails beyond the frames at each end. Clench the nails up over the sheer plank so the guards will hide their ends.

Interior Structure

The breasthooks will go in next. Naturally grown crooks of apple, ash, or oak are best. The breasthooks are small, so you can saw them out of a rough limb with a small bandsaw or worry them out with a handsaw. Try to get both breasthooks out of the same crook, so the grain and color will match at the two ends. If you can't find a crook or don't want to cope with cutting one, the shape can be laminated, or as a last resort you can use straight-grained hardwood. But be aware that straight-grained stuff has very little strength when used as a knee and should be avoided if possible.

The breasthooks should be fitted to stand just a little above the top of the sheer clamps so they can be dressed off to a slight crown. They are fastened with a rivet through their ends and two bronze screws along each side.

Now with a small plane, well-sharpened and set close, clean up the tops of the sheer planks and plane the breasthooks to a slight crown. Bore a 3/8-inch hole in the after breasthook to make a fairlead for the mizzen sheet.

The guardrails come next. I made these of ash to save a little weight, but oak is perfectly good. Or, if your sheer plank is a light-colored wood, Honduras mahogany might look well. Try not to use a softwood, as the guards will chafe quickly. The guards are 5/16 inch by 1/2 inch, planed half round. Cut them to fit exactly and nail them in place with 3/4-inch ring nails. Where the guards feather out to nothing on the stem and sternpost, use a small 1/2-inch screw rather than a nail, which might cause the guards to split.

The shelves are spruce, 1/2-inch thick, molded 1 1/8 inches and sawn to shape. They fit in flush with the top of the second plank and are riveted through all at every other frame, starting at their ends. The after shelf, since it spans an even number of frames, requires two rivets in a row, and it doesn't make any difference which end of the clamps they are driven in.

The strength of the hull would probably be improved by making the shelf in one length from the bow to the stern, but such a shelf would also add to the weight of the boat and would certainly be a nasty thing to fit. I don't believe the added strength is worth the effort, but try if you like.

Of the four thwarts, the two in the ends are cedar and the middle two are ash. The three that are mast thwarts are 3 inches wide at the ends and swell out to 3 ½ inches in the middle. The fourth one, since it doesn't do much except hold the boat apart, is 3 inches all the way across. The ends of the thwarts are notched over the frames, and their undersides are relieved to fit down about ³/₁₆ inch over the shelves. The thwarts must be fitted with care, as they take the side thrust of the rig.

There are two fastenings at each end of each thwart driven down into the shelves. I used a combination of screws and bolts to be sure the thwarts won't come out. Three thwarts can be fastened now, but don't fasten the after mainmast thwart yet, as it is easier to fit the two hanging knees with the thwart removed.

The knees are ½-inch spruce laminated and fitted very carefully to the planking, jogged at the laps. Since the bend is very tight, I found the laminations had to be a skinny ¹/₁₆ inch or they would break. Here again, it is much easier to glue up a single, thick lamination (about 1 ¼ inches thick) and then saw it in half, instead of making two thin ones.

The knees are positioned on the forward side of the frames and tightly against them. Use one rivet on the lower end of each knee and a ¾-inch ring nail at each lap. Be careful here, as these fastenings are very close to the frame fastenings. With the knees fastened to the planking, the thwart is set down over them and fastened on each end to the shelves. Again, use one rivet through the end of the knee, with two or three screws through the thwart into the knee outboard of this.

The mast steps are ash, 1 inch by 1 ¾ inches by 6 inches. The holes for the masts are 1 inch in diameter, and the three steps are each notched over the frames to sit tightly on the keel. Two screws, each offset from the centerline at each end, hold them down. Be sure to cut a drain for the mast holes so they won't hold water.

Sweating the Details

From here on we'll be getting into the picky part of this little beast. These are finicky little details that are difficult to explain and time-consuming to do, but have patience — we're making progress and the end is in sight.

This is a good time to add the stembands, and to sand and oil the outside. The stembands are ½-inch half-oval brass. At the top of the stem and stern-posts, bend the brass over and flatten it as much as you can. Then, with a file, shape the flattened part to match the shape of the stem head. Bore and countersink for ½-inch No. 6 screws to be spaced about 8 inches apart. For the oil use either a linseed and turpentine mix if you intend to varnish, or one of the new penetrating oil finishes.

Marking the frame centerlines on the sheer clamp.

With three frames clamped in place, the clench nailing begins.

Sheer clamps are sprung in place, clamped, and clench nailed through the sheerstrake.

The spruce shelves notch over the frames against the top of the second plank down.

The Natural Crook Breasthooks are Handsome and Strong

*T*his sequence illustrates the process of cutting out a pair of breasthooks from a crook. First, the pattern is rough-traced so that a flat can be sawed along one side; this will allow a slab to be sawn off, leaving plenty of surface for the pattern. Next, the other side is slabbed off, leaving plenty of thickness from which to obtain two breasthooks. The two pieces can now be sawn to shape.

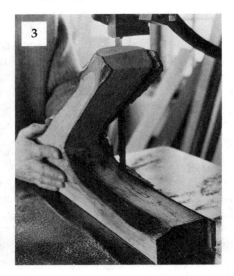

One word of caution about penetrating oil: When the can says "Use with adequate ventilation," it means just that! Penetrating oil can be pure misery in a closed-up space.

And so back to the inside. The floorboards are made as indicated; use leftover plank stock and pieces of broken frames. They can be clench nailed together with ⅝-inch tacks. The two pieces that carry the foot brace are ¾-inch by 1 ⅜-inch cedar or spruce, whatever you have. These are screwed on top of the floorboards, and must be notched over the frames and the partner knees. The foot brace is just a ¾-inch by 1-inch stick cut to ¾ inch square at the ends; it is dropped into the notches in these pieces. The floorboards are held down with two turnbuttons made of scrap frame stock.

This boat would be quite simple to finish out if only one person were to paddle her. But as soon as you introduce the second person, you are faced with making three adjustable positions for the back rests. The rack, for want of a better name, that holds the back rests is made of ½-inch ash and shaped as shown. Bear in mind that the width across the boat from the notch on one side to the corresponding notch on the other side has to be the same in all three positions. Therefore, the racks must taper with the beam of the boat. Fasten the racks with ¾-inch No. 6 screws.

Backrests are relatively simple. I curved them like a chair back to be a little more comfortable, but they could be made flat if you wish. Get them out of 1 ½-inch cedar or spruce and carve in the curvature. The result should be ⅜ inch thick.

Four hardwood cleats are riveted across the back; this should help prevent them from splitting. The forward backrest fits in either position in the forward rack, while the after one fits in just one position. The after rest, when standing vertically, will be against the thwart. Note that the backrests must tilt back fairly far, so relieve the top and bottom of the notches in the racks accordingly. Enough. If you get through that, you can get through anything.

Now you need three fairleads and three jam cleats. These are all of ½-inch by 1-inch ash. Rivet them through the thwarts, since

Fitting the mast step.

Hanging knees notch over the planking.

Thwarts, shelves, and knees tie the structure together.

Looking forward, showing the foot pedals in place.

Floorboard pairs are cleated together beneath, and held down with turnbuttons.

Backrests are sawn out of cedar, and four stiffeners are riveted to the after sides.

they take a fair amount of strain.

In addition to the two jam cleats on the after thwart, there are two pins for the mainsheet lead. These are ⅛-inch brass rod — brazing rod is good — about 2 inches long. Hammer a slight head on the pins and drive them into holes that are a whisker too small so they can't fall out,

Two fairleads must be made for the yoke lines. They are also ½-inch ash and are open so the lines can be dropped in. Make them according to the drawing and fasten them on the face of the frame, tightly against the clamp, with one ¾-inch No. 6 screw.

At this point, everything that is going into the boat is in, so you can apply whatever finish you desire inside and out and set her aside to dry while you make such accessories as the foot pedals.

Foot pedals are cut as shown out of ½-inch ash and fastened to the foot brace with 2-inch butt hinges. The bottom of each pedal is cut at a 45-degree angle so the pedal will tip aft as well as forward. The keyhole slot in the top outer corner is to take a knot in the end of the steering yoke lines; relieve the back of the round part so the knot will seat securely.

The rudder design is self-evident. It is made of ½-inch mahogany, oak, or ash — anything that is hard and strong. If you make it in two pieces, use two or three drifts of ⅛-inch brass rod and glue the two pieces together with epoxy. Taper the blade to ¼ inch at the after edge.

This canoe was billed originally as a complete do-it-yourself project, for which you had to buy nothing but basic materials. This is true as long as you know something about working metal. If you don't, then our billing is almost true.

The rudder hangers are fabricated of strap brass and brass tubing. I went to my friend Tony-the-Blacksmith for these, since he knows more about such things than I do. If you want to try to make them yourself, the four gudgeons are simple enough. But easy? I'm not so sure.

Each gudgeon consists of a ½-inch length of ⁵⁄₁₆-inch I.D. brass pipe or tubing and a length of ¹⁄₁₆-inch by ½-inch brass strap bent around and sweat-soldered to it. As there is no particular strain on the joint, soft solder will do, but hard solder will be better. Fit one pair carefully to the sternpost and one pair to the rudder. They are attached with two rivets each. Countersink the holes in the straps so the rivet heads can be filed off flush. The rudder is hung with a length of ¼-inch brass rod headed over on its upper end so it won't drop through, and long enough so the rudder will ride up when you go aground.

The rudder yoke is ½-inch oak or ash shaped pretty much to suit yourself as long as you stay within the overall dimensions. When you have the yoke shaped, ship the rudder and try the yoke to be sure it clears the rudderpost. The yoke is held in place with a ⅛-inch brass pin through the rudderhead.

Tony Millham also made a brass hook for the tiller. He did such a beautiful job that I hesitated to put it on the boat. You could very well put it on the mantelpiece to be admired. He made the hook with two pieces hard-soldered together. The plate is a piece of ⅛-inch stock cut to shape and draw-filed to remove excess stock where it is not needed for strength. The hook was drawn from a piece of ¼-inch rod, with a knob forged on the end; it was bent to shape. After it had been soldered to the plate and cleaned up, you couldn't find the joint.

You can make the hook the same way Tony did, but file the taper into the hook before it is bent. Hard soldering, I guess, is easy enough if you know what you are doing. Another method, of course, is to whittle a wooden pattern of the hook and have it cast at a foundry.

When you have the hook made, by whatever method, it is riveted onto one end of the yoke. This, by the way, is the weakest part of the boat. If you jam the tiller when you are getting it on or off, you stand a chance of cracking the yoke. The whole assembly is strong enough to do its intended job as long as you use a little care in getting the tiller on and off; so please be careful.

Speaking of tillers, this one works by being pushed or pulled. It is made of ash, ¾ inch by 1 inch and long enough to reach from the yoke to amidships in the boat. Taper it to ¾ inch square at the inboard end and round the last 18 inches for a comfortable handgrip. The hole for the hook is ⅜ inch, deeply countersunk on both sides so the tiller will swivel when dropped over the hook. I had a

The push-pull tiller can rest in the notch cut in the backrest.

Rudder and tiller rigged and ready. Note the mizzen sheet lead.

Tiller and yoke detail.

Halyard and downhaul detail.

With both sails rigged, the mainmast steps forward. With one, it steps aft.

piece of ash on hand with a gentle sweep to it, so I used that for the tiller. The sweep serves no useful purpose except to add to the overall appearance of the boat.

The first time we went sailing we found that the tiller, if left unattended, had a tendency to drop overboard and stream out behind the boat. Very embarrassing! So I cut a fairly deep round notch in the top of both backrests near their outboard ends. This notch retains the tiller very nicely. To make double sure the tiller stays put, a rope grommet is placed over it and is tied to a thwart.

So there is the hull, complete with all its fittings. Now we need spars.

The Rig

One of the features of this rig is that it enables one to reduce sail without working too hard at it. Therefore, both masts are designed to fit in any of the three mast thwarts, which allows three possible combinations of sail. As the mizzen mast would look ridiculous if it were the same diameter as the main, its large diameter is carried only to the height of the highest thwart, and then the diameter is reduced to an appropriate size. Out of the boat, the mizzen looks like a stretched-out tenpin, but in the boat it is fine.

All the spars can be gotten out of a 2-inch by 10-inch rough spruce staging plank 10 feet long. Go to the lumberyard and pick over their pile of staging planks until you find a decently clear one that measures a fat 2 inches thick.

Making the masts is straightforward, except for making the swelling at the foot of the mizzen. Please note that the holes for the halyards are bored at an angle to the centerline of the hull. This provides a fair lead to the yard, which is hung on the port side. With a gouge, relieve the lower side of the hole to make a nice round lead or "dumb sheave" for the halyard. Don't forget the small wooden jam cleat at the foot for the downhaul. This goes on the centerline and is fastened with a couple of small-diameter screws.

The yard and boom for each sail are the same diameter and very nearly the same length, so don't get them confused.

You have a couple of options for the jaws. I had some kinky apple branches around, so that's what I used. The jaws are only ⅜ inch thick, so the grain must follow the curve or they can be easily broken. A piece of oak with the right kink will do, but stay away from all softwoods. There is no great strain on the jaws in service, but banging around in the boat and on shore can do them in. The other alternative for the jaws is ½-inch brass half oval, which should be bent to shape a bit oversize and padded with leather or jute twine. Don't forget to bore a ¼-inch hole athwartships at each end of the yards and booms for lashing, and a ¼-inch hole through the boom jaws for the downhauls. Give the whole works two or three coats of paint or varnish and set all the spars out to dry.

Now you have built everything there is to build, and it's time to rig her. A good place to begin is with the steering yoke lines. These are ¼-inch spun Dacron, long enough to lead from the yoke to the foot pedals with a little to spare. They lead down through the yoke with a nice stopper knot on top. A Matthew Walker knot with a star-shaped leather washer underneath looks very well. You can, of course, burn the running ends, but a nicely done drum whipping looks better. The running ends lead forward under the two after thwarts, through the open fairleads, and finish with figure-eight knots on the fore side of the keyhole slots in the pedals. Since there are two positions for the foot brace, you need two knots. Adjust these so that, with tension on the lines, the pedals are leaning slightly forward. After you have used the pedals for a while, you can fine-tune them to your own taste.

I used ¼-inch spun Dacron for both halyards, as it stays limber wet or dry. The halyards are spliced to the yards just behind the jaws. If you used brass jaws, you may have to use small bee blocks to keep the halyards from working forward. They should be about 6 inches aft of the mast. The main halyard leads through the masthead hole, down to the thwart, aft through the fairlead, and through the hole in the jam cleat. Be sure the halyard is long enough so you can tie a stopper knot in its end and still get the yard down into the boat. Now rig the mizzen halyard, which comes down through the fairlead and forward to the jam cleat,

For downhauls use light stuff, 3/16 inch or so. These are spliced around the booms, through the holes in the jaws, and led through the hole in the jam cleat. The main sheet is more ¼-inch Dacron spliced around the boom and through the clew grommet. It leads around one of the pins in the after thwart and then to your hand; it must never be cleated, as that invites disaster. The mizzen sheet of 3/16-inch stuff is spliced around the boom directly above the hole, and goes forward through the fairlead at the foot of the mast to the jam cleat on the after thwart. This sail is so small that you can safely cleat it with no worry.

One last thing. The main needs a nicely made streamer, about 2 inches wide and 3 feet long, attached to the end of the yard,

I should throw in here a few quick thoughts on the paddle. The best length for this boat seems to be 8 feet 6 inches, although 8 feet will do very well. Since there just isn't room for you and 8 feet of paddle in the boat when sailing, a two-piece jointed paddle is a necessity. In the book *Sensible Cruising Designs* (International Marine Publishing Company, Camden, Maine), Mr. L.F. Herreshoff has a design for a very nice double paddle. Two-inch spruce staging plank would make a good one, but you will have to buy the ferrules for the joint.

So that's about it. Now find yourself a friend, pack a good picnic, and go see what the other side of the river looks like.

Building plans for Piccolo (plan #400-020) are available from The WoodenBoat Store, P.O. Box 78, Brooklin, Maine 04616. Call 1–800–273–SHIP (7447). The price is $36.

The Biscayne Bay 14

by Maynard Bray with Eric Dow
Construction photographs by Barbara Stacey Dow

The Biscayne Bay 14 is fast and maneuverable, and a pleasure to handle.

The Biscayne Bay 14 was designed years ago by Nathanael G. Herreshoff; her original plans are conserved at the Hart Nautical Collections of the Massachusetts Institute of Technology in Cambridge, Massachusetts. She is an unusually fine boat that can be built easily by careful woodworkers. Her light but strong hull and rig, combined with some outside ballast, make her perform better than most boats of her size. Some sailors, in fact, have likened her performance to that of a sports car. Her construction lends itself to sheet plywood, which results in a practical boat for daysailing and one that is easy to maintain.

Biscayne Bay 14 Particulars

LOA	14'5"	
Beam	5'0"	
Draft		
Board up	1'0"	
Board down	3'0"	
Fixed keel	2'0"	
Displacement (at DWL)	about 1,000 lbs	
Sail area	122 sq ft	

Frame spaces, 14".
Stem, oak or hackmatack, sided 1 ½".
Timbers, white oak, ¾" x ¾".
Floors, oak plank, ¾" thick.
Keel, oak, 1 ⅜" thick, top 1" above rabbet.
Lower stringers, oak, 1 ½" x ¹³⁄₁₆".
Upper stringers, oak, 1 ½" x ⅜".
Planking, Philippine mahogany, ½" thick.
Deck, Philippine mahogany, ½" thick; forward deck canvased.
Chafing strip, spruce, ⅞" x 1 ⅛".
Clamps, Douglas fir, 1 ¼" x 1 ¼".
Deck beams, oak or ash, ⅝" x 1 ¼".
Bulkhead, ⅜" plywood.
Hanging knees, ½" oak or butternut.
Stern, ⅞" oak.
Flooring, spruce slats, ⁹⁄₁₆" x 6", ½" apart.
Planking can be ¼" high-grade mahogany plywood.
Chafing strip can be Douglas-fir (Oregon pine) and should be tapered in both width and thickness as it nears the bow and stern.
Bulkhead can be cedar.
Stem can be mahogany.
Flooring can be cedar.
Iron keel shown; lead keel can be substituted if reconfigured for same weight.

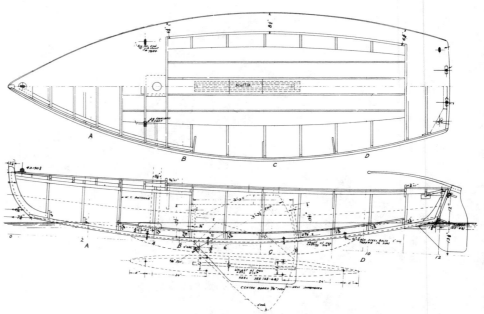

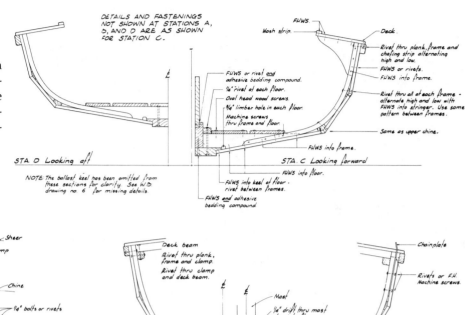

The Biscayne Bay's construction sections show ½-inch plank thickness, but ¼-inch plywood can be used. Floor-to-frame and knee-to-frame fastenings can be eliminated, as can the breasthook bolt.

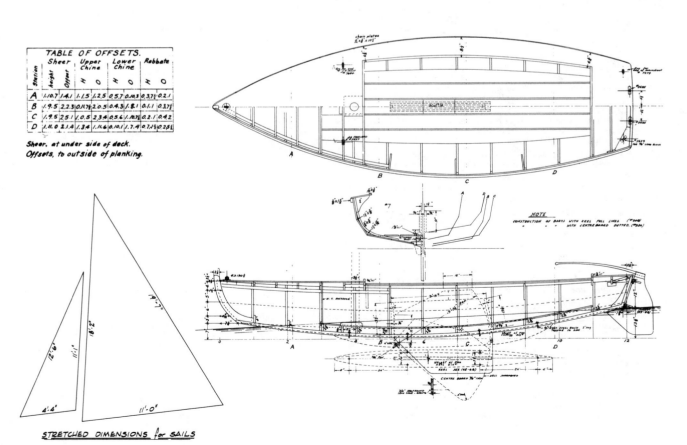

TABLE OF OFFSETS.								
	Sheer		Upper Chine		Lower Chine		Rabbate	
Station	Height	Offset	H	O	H	O	H	O
A	1.10.7	1.4.1	1.1.5	1.2.5	0.5.7	0.10.3	0.3.7½	0.2.1
B	1.9.5	2.2.3	0.11.7½	2.0.5	0.4.3	1.8.1	0.1.1	0.3.7½
C	1.9.5	2.5.1	1.0.5	2.3.4	0.5.6	1.10.7½	0.2.1	0.4.2
D	1.11.0	2.1.4	1.3.4	1.11.6	0.10.1	1.7.4	0.7.1½	0.2.5½

Sheer, at under side of deck.
Offsets, to outside of planking.

STRETCHED DIMENSIONS for SAILS

Spars and Rigging

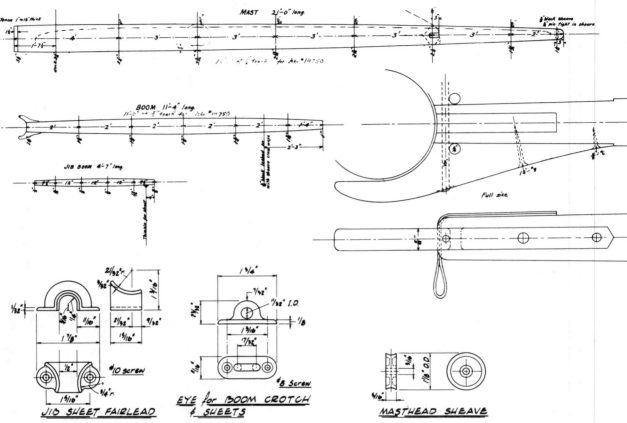

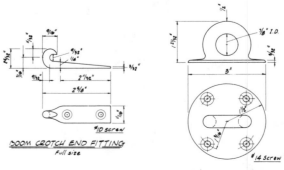

JIB SHEET FAIRLEAD

EYE for BOOM CROTCH & SHEETS

MASTHEAD SHEAVE

RIGGING LIST

SHROUDS · 2 required, 5/32" 7x7 stainless steel wire with a served, spliced eye around the mast at the upper end; lower end swaged or spliced around thimble. Length about 15' each.

FORESTAY · 1 required, 5/32" 7x7 stainless steel wire with a served, spliced eye around the mast at the upper end; lower end spliced around thimble which in turn is seized to hole in stemhead with light line. Length about 15½'.

MAIN SHEET · 1 required, 3/8" dacron dead-ended on aft deck to starboard with stopper knot, bowline, or splice through metal flange eye. Length about 25'.

JIB SHEET · 1 required, 1/4" dacron dead-ended on fore deck to starboard, same as main sheet. Length about 20'.

MAIN HALYARD · 1 required, 1/4" dacron attached to head of sail with bowline or snaphook. Length about 45' Hauling part belayed to cleat at forward end of cockpit.

JIB HALYARD · 1 required, 1/4" dacron rigged same as for main. Length about 35'.

CENTERBOARD PENDANT · 1 required for centerboard version; 1/4" or 3/8" dacron with lower end rove through vertical hole in aft upper edge of centerboard and held fast by a stopper knot contained in an intersecting athwartship hole. Upper end rove through a loose wooden stopper block and knotted for about 18" of centerboard travel. Centerboard is held in raised position by a metal pin through the trunk sides and the board near the aft end, thus eliminating the need for a pendant cleat.

LACE LINE FOR MAINSAIL LUFF · 1 required, lightly tarred hemp or 3/16" braided nylon rove through the sail grommets in the usual "forth and back" manner to enable easy raising and lowering

LACE LINE FOR FOOT OF MAIN AND JIB · 1/8" braided nylon rove through sail grommets and around boom and club. Tacks and clews of sails attached with seizing of the same stuff through holes in the ends of spars.

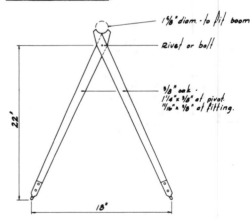

BOOM CROTCH DETAIL

BOOM CROTCH END FITTING
Full size

3" FLANGE EYE

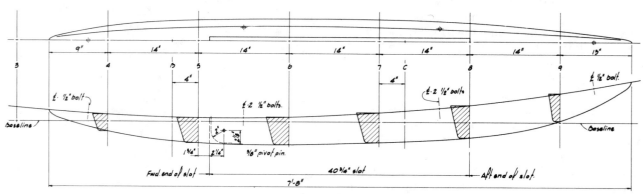

SHALLOW BALLAST KEEL

Table of Offsets for Iron Ballast Keel (C.B. Version)				
Station	Heights to base line		Widths from ₵	
	Bottom	Top	Bottom	Top
· 4	0·1·4 below		0·1·5+	0·2·2+
5	0·3·3 "	Same as underside of wood keel	0·2·1	0·3·2+
6	0·3·5 "		0·2·3	0·3·4
7	0·3·2 "		0·2·2	0·3·4
8	0·2·4 ·		0·1·6	0·3·0
9	0·0·2 above		0·1·1	0·1·6

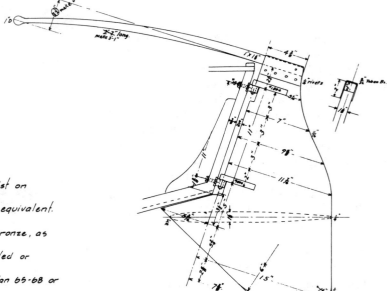

FITTING LIST

(This list may be used in lieu of the Casting List on HMCo. plan 76·145.)

3" flange eye, 1 required, bronze, as detailed or equivalent. (See Note 1.)

Eyes for sheets and boom crotch, 4 required, bronze, as detailed or equivalent.

Jib sheet fairlead, 1 required, bronze, as detailed or equivalent. (See Note 2.)

Rudder gudgeon, 2 required, bronze, as on HMCo. plan 65·68 or equivalent.

Rowlock, 1 required, bronze #1 or #2 size. (See Note 3.)

Rowlock socket, 2 required, bronze, top flange type to fit above rowlock.

Masthead sheave, 1 required, bronze, as detailed or equivalent. (See Note 4.)

Turnbuckle, 2 required, bronze, 1/4" size, either jaw and jaw or jaw and socket. (See Note 5.)

Main sheet lead block, 2 required, bronze, use 3/8" bullet block with eyestrap on deck and with seizing on boom.

Boom crotch end fitting, 2 required, bronze as detailed or equivalent.

Cleat for halyards and sheets, 4 required, bronze, oak or locust, about 4" long.

Note 1. Spartan Fig. #P·574 can be substituted. Attach flange eye with FHWS into breasthook; attach spliced end of painter to eye with cow knot for easy removal.

Note 2. Spartan Fig. #F·300 can be substituted.

Note 3. For sculling and steering in shallow water; may be used in either port or starboard socket.

Note 4. Can be eliminated by using a beehole in the mast, well lubricated with tallow.

Note 5. Merriman Part #3770·308 (1/4") can be substituted.

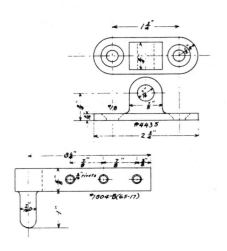

1

Start by drawing the boat, at full size, on a suitable lofting floor. A couple of sheets of white-painted ¼-inch plywood, laid end to end, can be used. The process of lofting and making the patterns and molds is standard boatbuilding stuff; information on how to do it is widely available. (See, for example, *How to Build a Wooden Boat*, by David C. "Bud" McIntosh, WoodenBoat Books.) Covering it here would only take space away from the specific instructions for this boat, so we will start by showing the results of these early stages. Here is a mold, one of the four that are required. It is made to conform to the inside of the planking and has been notched for the oak keel and the oak longitudinal stringers that back up the plank seams. These notches, as well as the reference lines (centerline and sheerline) — shown here being marked — are taken directly from the lofting.

2

Here the plywood stem pattern, which was lifted from the lofting, is being used to mark the 1 ½-inch oak board that will become the stem. If there's a sweep to the board's grain, have it run with the pattern's curved shape, but if the board has straight grain, like the one in the photograph, arrange the pattern as shown to avoid severe cross-grain. Saw carefully close to the line to minimize subsequent hand-shaping. Mark and chisel a rabbet in each side of the stem for the hull planking, but at this stage leave the rabbet uncut in the area where the stem will join the keel.

3

A plywood pattern is also made for the transom, and is shown here being used to mark the ⅞-inch mahogany from which the actual transom will be made. This pattern represents the transom's outside face, and because the inner face is larger, there must be a standing bevel cut on the six edges that represent the sides and bottom of the boat. An estimated bevel is good enough for now, as long as it is conservative and leaves some wood for shaving down after the boat has been set up. (The transom top can be rough-cut square to be dressed to its finished crown and bevel later.)

4

The keel timber is next; it can be marked without a pattern. Start by snapping a chalkline down the center of the 1 ⅜-inch piece of oak to be used for the keel. (The length of the keel timber should be 14 to 15 feet, and the width of the heartwood about 6 inches.) Firm up the chalkline with a pencil and a straightedge. The stations are then laid out square

across this centerline and spaced their true distance apart as picked up on a batten laid along the lofting profile, as shown.

5

Keel half-breadths at each station, picked up from the lofting on a tick strip, are then marked, after which a stiff batten is used to connect and fair the marks and give guidance for a continuous pencil line. Here Eric is sighting along the batten to check that it is fair before he marks it. The keel timber, of course, gets the same treatment on the other side of the centerline, after which it is ready for sawing to shape.

6

The keel was sawn out in two passes, the first being about an inch outside the lines. Although this centerline still sighted straight after the rough cutting (i.e., after the first pass), sometimes a timber will spring one way or the other as its edges are cut away. If this happens, it's nice to have enough wood still remaining for another layout based on a new centerline. After the edges have been brought to the marked line it's time for roughing in the rabbet, the first part of which is taking place in this photo. A ¾-inch-deep kerf is being made 1 inch in from the edge, the saw having been fitted with a guide that runs along the keel's outer edge.

7

With the blade set at the rabbet's shallowest angle (about 10 degrees) and to cut close to an inch in depth, the remaining keel rabbet cut is made on a table saw as shown. For this rough cutting, refer to the drawings and your lofting to get the rabbet depths, widths, angles, and their orientation correct. Take your time here and try some test pieces, lest you spoil the biggest single piece of wood in the boat. Assuming you're successful to this point, don't bother cleaning up the rabbet. That can be done after the boat has been set up and the stringers are in place.

8

Here is the keel after it has been steamed for an hour and a half and clamped over a bending jig. For springback allowance, the jig's verticals are at station locations but form a fair curve that is about 1 ½ inches greater than what will be needed. The longer the keel is left clamped to the jig, the less straightening there will be. Keep it clamped like this for three days.

9

The Biscayne Bay 14 is set up in the Herreshoff tradition on a "foundation" consisting of a perfectly straight fore-and-aft reference "strongback" and mold support pads that have been brought, by wedging as shown, to the strongback height at each station. Mold B is then set up on its station to be square with the strongback in both plan and elevation as well as centered over the boat's longitudinal centerline. Mold B is firmly fastened and braced in this position as shown to become a major strength member of the entire setup. The remaining three molds are then set up similarly, but without the diagonal bracing, since they will soon be tied to mold B by means of the keel.

10

With the stem permanently bolted to one end and the transom and transom knee to the other, the keel assembly is set into place over the molds. The upper face of the keel has stations marked on it, and the station B mark is first aligned with the forward edge of mold B and clamped. The other molds are then brought to their marks and also clamped; they, too, should now be square with the strongback. ("Upper" and "lower" used herein refer to the way things are when the boat is upright, not as she appears on the building jig.)

11

The stem's height as well as the curve of the keel forward of mold A is established by the 2-inch by 4-inch post shown here. Its height and bevel were taken from the lofting. With the aid of a spirit level Eric checks that the stem is plumb before clamping it in place against the triangular plywood brace.

12

Eric uses the level as he adjusts the transom to be horizontal. A short straightedge, clamped to the transom's outer face and aligned to the sheer marks, serves as a guide for the level, while a pair of posts to the shop floor holds the transom in position. Note that Eric has installed a 2-inch by 4-inch post halfway between the transom and mold D, similar to the one used near the stem and shown in the previous photo.

13

Besides having to be level, the transom also must be square with the boat's centerline. The usual check is by "horning" — that is, by checking that the port and starboard diagonal measurements from the keel to a transom corner are equal. Braces to mold D (shown in a subsequent photo) will hold the adjustment. You should check to see that the transom is level after horning, then recheck and adjust the horning. A temporary shore from the shop's overhead to the after end of the keel relieves most of the load on the transom support posts during transom alignment.

14

After the molds, stem, and transom are aligned, checked, and rechecked, the molds can be screwed to the keel as shown. As mentioned earlier, station marks on the keel establish the mold locations against the keel. Drywall screws are best for temporary fastening — they can be driven without the jarring impact of driving a nail, they can be removed at will and later reused, and, except for delicate pieces like the cleats shown here, can be driven without pre-drilling.

15

Now that the setup is aligned and secure it should be checked for fairness in the way of each plank by means of a batten, as shown here. The transom bevels can also be checked and dressed down as necessary at this stage. Fair lines are far more important than exact measurements; take the time to sight carefully and often, as Eric is doing here

16

Preparing the keel and stem for the lower stringers comes next. With a rabbet plane, start by tapering the keel width (outside the rabbet) to match the 1 ½-inch stem siding; then cut back the keel flanges as shown. The butt end of the stringer will fay partly against the side of the stem and partly against the edge of the keel, so the latter has to be chiseled flush with the stem, also as shown. Note that the guidelines for joining the stem rabbet with that of the keel have been drawn. Cutting will take place after the stringer is installed.

17

Rather than using the oak stringer itself, a softwood pattern is used, one that is of the same cross section and long enough to clamp over molds A and B. The object is for the centerline of the stringer to hit the bearding line at the intersection of the keel and the stem. This takes some fussing, so start shallow, work deeper, and check with the stringer pattern often. The photo shows about what the end of the stringer will look like, although the piece shown is the stringer pattern. After the pattern is fitted, its shape is transferred to the stringer itself, and after that piece is cut, a mirror-image stringer is cut for the other side of the boat. Stringer length is determined by fitting the after end and working forward, clamping to each mold along the way until a reference mark at or near the forward end can be made.

18

With its forward end steamed more or less to the required curve to assist in assembly, a single screw, assisted by 3M 5200 adhesive, is used to hold the stringer against the backbone. Later, all the stringers will be beveled so the planking can lie fair against them, and, of course, the rabbeting between keel and stem will be completed.

19

Inch-square cleats and drywall screws hold the stringers to the molds at each intersection while the hull is being planked. These screws will have to be removed before the boat can be lifted off the molds.

20

Neither a pattern nor steaming is necessary for the upper stringer, which is lighter and easier to fit than the lower. Here, Eric is sighting for fairness along a centerline marked on the stringer. Even if both the stringer and centerline prove to be a little unfair at this stage, the line can be adjusted so the "knuckle" between planks will form a fair and eye-sweet line. All stringers should receive the same examination and, if necessary, the same treatment.

21

The stringers now have to be beveled so the planking will fay snugly against them. Rough beveling can be done by eye using a smoothing plane and estimated by the shapes of the molds. For the finishing cuts, however, a straightedge (as shown) will be necessary. This is the time for the final dressing of the keel rabbet, using a rabbet plane. Oak grain changes direction often, so the trick is to go slowly and take shallow cuts with a sharp plane, reversing direction as necessary.

22

As a guide in beveling the middle plank, the stringers can be notched with a saw at 1-foot intervals, as shown. Saw only as far as the marked centerline on each stringer, then plane until the saw cuts disappear. Check with a straightedge, as in the preceding photo.

23

Unless you purchased plywood already scarfed to the required length, you will have to scarf it yourself. Scarfs should be about 2 inches in length for this ¼-inch plywood, and a stack of, say, four pieces can be beveled as though it were a single piece. Simply set each piece 2 inches back from the one under it, then go for it — first with a belt sander, then, more carefully, with a spokeshave and/or block plane. After the beveling comes the gluing. Apply a first coat of epoxy as a sealer, then a heavier second coat in a few minutes as the adhesive. Clamp as shown, using strongbacks, a spacer block under and another block over, waxed paper, and clamps (not shown) at the ends of each piece to keep them from sliding as pressure is applied.

24

The bottom panels each start with a 24-inch-wide, straight-sided piece that, through scarfing, has been made about 14 feet long. By tacking one of them in place as shown, you can rough-cut its outer curved edge by marking the underside along the lower stringer. Handling the panel is made easier by this first cutting; but, remember, it is a rough cut, so leave enough extra wood (about 3 inches) for subsequent fitting of the other edge against the keel.

25

This process, using a pencil compass, is called "scribing," a common boatbuilding technique that can be found fully described in almost any boat-building text. The idea is to mark for and then make a final cut that is a constant distance away from the object you want to fit against, that distance measured in the same direction you'll be sliding the piece. Since the edge being scribed here fits into a proper rabbet (at least, that is our fervent hope), the edge needs no bevel. Saw it near the line, then do the finishing with a sharp block plane. Tack the panel back in place, check it against the keel, and shave it a little here and there if you need to for a snug fit.

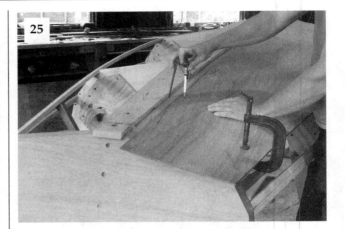

26

After fitting the lower edge to your satisfaction and tacking the panel in that position, you can mark along the stringer centerline for the upper, or outer, or opposite edge, as Eric is doing here. Rather than using a continuous pencil line, he's spotting at intervals and making a note of the marks that are opposite the molds and are to be given preference in establishing a fair line for cutting.

27

The line itself is established by a batten nailed as shown and made fair by sighting. Hold to the marks that come on the mold lines if you can. Remember that the line you draw represents the cut at the inside face of the panel, and that there has to be an outward-sloping bevel on this edge if there is not to be a gap showing on the outside of the hull where this plank meets the next one. In other words, these planks butt along the seam in a miter.

28

The amount of the bevel at any given point along the plank's edge depends on the angle of the knuckle in the boat's side at that point. A simple construction layout made right on the lofted stations is a quick way of figuring the edge bevel and of determining the additional wood needed to allow for it. Another way, which Eric used here, is to butt two plank scraps at the knuckle and measure the gap, then add half the gap to the first-drawn line. In this photo, Eric has picked up the gap allowance on a tick strip and is using the strip to lay out the cutting line. (The outer cut line equals the inner cut line plus beveling wood.)

29

Here, Eric is marking the outer line, the one he'll saw to and bevel from. He'll make a square cut, plane it fair and to the line he's marking, then bevel it down to the first (inner) line. If there's doubt, or if the beveled edge needs fine-tuning, you can check the bevel's angle from the lofting by means of a bevel gauge. Then check what you've done by putting the plank back on the boat, located exactly where you last marked it. Its outer edge should fall pretty much on the stringer's marked centerline, but, above all, it should be fair, for this is a line you and the whole world will forever see as the lower hull knuckle. (The stringer can be sprung in or out between molds to meet the fair plank edge.) When you're satisfied, mark and cut a mirror-image plank for the other side of the boat, and, likewise, check it for a good and fair fit.

30

Now for the second panel, shortly to become a plank. Clamp as shown, and mark from the inside. Trace or mark the lower edge to conform to the lower stringer's centerline, and leave some excess along the upper edge. Make sure here that the panel (or plank) lies firmly against the molds and stringers, just as it will when finished.

31

As an alternative, and much faster, means of making a precise square cut along the plank's edge, you can use a router with a laminate-trimming bit that bears against the accurately located marking batten. Beveling follows this operation. Next, fit the plank's hood (forward) end at the stem rabbet and check that the lower edge is fair and falls on the stringer centerline. After making a mirror image for the other side, you can lay this plank aside for the time being.

32

With the bottom panel back in position and tacked as before, bore for the permanent screw fastenings. These will be ¾-inch No. 8 flathead bronze wood screws, spaced about 5 inches apart. Be especially careful here at the transom to get the angle right so the screws won't poke out through the transom face. Don't drive the screws yet; just bore the holes for them.

33

After removing the panel and brushing away the residue made by the drill, spread the contact surfaces (but not the molds!) with 3M 5200 (or equivalent) adhesive, and reinstall the panel — permanently, with screws, this time. Start fastening amidships and work toward the ends. Don't bother with clamps.

34

Because the upper stringer is thinner than the lower one, it may have to be braced, as shown here, to take a fair curve from bow to stern. Use a stiff batten as a guide, and push the stringer out until contact is made.

35

The second plank can now be checked for fit against the bottom panel; when satisfactory, its upper edge can be accurately marked to the stringer centerline, faired, and beveled, as before. When the fit is okay and the mate for the other side has been marked, this plank can be permanently installed. Bore first, apply adhesive, and fasten as with the bottom panel.

36

Eric demonstrates another method of fitting the sheerstrake. Because the second, or middle, plank has been permanently fastened, the sheerstrake panel is nailed in place as shown and the shape of its lower edge is traced, roughly, from the inside.

37

After the sheerstrake has been rough-cut to that line, it is put back in place on the boat and its edge accurately marked by means of the scribing block and pencil, as shown. Mark the sheerstrake at intervals, then fair with a batten after it is off the boat. This line represents the plank edge's outside corner, so the edge gets an under bevel. Then the plank is once again put back on the molds, fine-tuned to fit along this edge and at the stem rabbet, then marked from the inside for a cut along the sheer using the marks made earlier on the stem, transom, and molds. Mark and cut the sheer, leaving a little extra wood (⅛ to ¼ inch) outside the faired line for adjustment that may be needed after the hull has been turned rightside up. Mark for a mirror-image sheerstrake; then hang this one as with the previous planks. (For structural balance, it is a good idea to keep up with the plank installation on the opposite side of the boat — that is, go port, starboard, port, starboard, etc.)

38

At this point your hull should be planked and about ready to be lifted off and turned over. First, however, cut off the protruding plank ends aft, if you haven't been keeping up with that operation, cut off the protruding lower end of the stem, and mark for beveling the stem to its specified face width of ½ inch.

39

You will have to do a bit of unscrewing at the stringer blocks, stem, and transom before the hull can be lifted free. The hull will have to be spread a little at the sheer as well in order to unlock the stringers from their notches in the molds.

40

The first task after the hull is right-side-up is to build and install the centerboard trunk. Although the 1 ⅜-inch thick oak bedlogs are the first pieces to be worked on, you should start by laying out the trunk on the profile of your full-sized lofting. From the lofting, the curves of the bottom and the top of the bedlogs can be picked up, using the nail-and-stomp, fair-and-mark-and-cut method. Fashion the bottom curve for one bedlog first, check and adjust the fit in the boat as Eric is doing here, then mark and cut the top to its correct curve by laying the piece back on the lofting with the bottom and ends on the marks. Make a second bedlog to match the first, dressing its edges by clamping both pieces together in a vise and treating the pair as a single piece while you plane away, making sure, of course, that you stay square with the faces as well while bringing the pair to the marked line.

41

There will be ¾-inch by ¾-inch rabbets to mark and cut along the tops of the bedlogs, into which will lay the ¾-inch mahogany trunk sides. Mark with a try-square and cut, as shown, on a table saw. You'll have to clean up the rabbets with a chisel, because the bedlogs are slightly curved and the saw has to be set for the depth at the ends.

42

In this photo, a trunk side's lower edge is being scribed with a pencil compass to fit the bedlog rabbet. After marking one of the sides as shown and marking the top as well, you can stack both side pieces together and saw and plane them as a unit. Fasten trunk sides and bedlogs together (5-inch spacing of holes) using this sequence: fit, clamp, mark, and drill, then disassemble, clean away the dust, spread the adhesive bedding, then reassemble and screw the pieces together. We recommend coating the back sides (the sides that face inward after the trunk is put together) with epoxy, since it will be difficult to do any painting in this narrow slot afterwards.

43

The posts are of 1-inch-square oak, giving a 1-inch-wide slot rather than the 1 ¼-inch slot shown on the Herreshoff drawing. (The narrower slot is more compatible with the ¾-inch mahogany plywood centerboard used for this boat.) The procedure is to fasten, by the method described above, one side of the trunk to the posts, then carefully align the other side and fasten it. Alignment is what's taking place here, with the aid of a try-square to assure that the bottoms of the bedlogs are aligned with each other.

Note that Eric has let the posts project a couple of inches below the bedlogs, as it is intended that they penetrate the keel thickness, to be sawn off flush with the outside of the keel later, after the trunk has been installed.

44

Be sure to plane off the lower corner of the raking after post as shown before you try to fit the trunk into the keel slot; otherwise it won't fit.

45

With the outline of the 1-inch-wide slot marked on the keel's upper face and a 1-inch-diameter starting hole bored through the keel at each end of the slot, the sawing can commence as shown. Cut carefully as close to the line as possible to minimize subsequent hand trimming. The square ends of the slot, however, will have to be formed afterwards by handsaw and chisel. Markings for the forward and after extremities of the slot were lifted from the lofting using the nearest station line (previously marked on both the lofting and the keel) as a reference. And, of course, the slot length must in any case match the distance between posts on the completed trunk.

46

Now put the trunk in place and mark the outline of the bedlogs on the keel. Remove the trunk and bore pilot holes out through the keel, put the trunk back in place (if the fit is tight, it will stay there of its own accord), and bore from underneath as shown for the 2 ½-inch screws that will fasten it there.

47

Again, remove the trunk, clean up the dust, and spread the contact area with adhesive bedding; a liberal slather is a good description. Put the trunk back for the final time, drive home those screws, wipe off the overspread and squeezed-out goop, and consider the trunk complete for the moment.

48

The floor timbers come next, but before you fit them, make sure that the hull has been shored up so it is level athwartships and has no twist. Start by making a half pattern for each floor timber as shown. Scribe each of the patterns to a close fit with the keel and planking. Eric used ⅛-inch plywood doorskin for pattern stock.

49

The height of the floor timbers is quite critical, since the floorboards should lie directly on them without shims. Take the height over the keel of each floor timber from the lofting, mark it at the pattern's centerline, then, using a level as shown, extend the line across the pattern. Cut a floor timber to this pattern, but leave it about ½ inch too high as a fitting allowance. Note that these patterns are for half a floor timber and have to be reversed to mark the other side.

50

After rough-cutting each floor timber to its pattern and snipping its ends to fit between the stringers, it should be set in place and pencil-scribed, as shown, for an exact fit against the hull. Marking both faces (with the floor timber held vertically) will give the final lines and correct bevel.

51

When the floor timber-to-hull fit is to your satisfaction, put the pattern back in place on the floor timber with hull edges aligned, and mark the floor timber's top edge for cutting. Here, the marking has been done and the excess wood is being sawn away.

52 (top of page 141)

In way of the centerboard trunk, where the spirit level is too long to fit, another method of transferring a level line can be used. Simply let the spirit level jam itself against the hull and the trunk side — level, of course — and use a try-square to mark a parallel line at the correct height. Floor timbers are fastened to the planking with adhesive bedding and screws in the usual pilot-hole-from-the-inside method, and to the keel with a pair of ¼-inch bolts or rivets, as shown on the plans. Don't forget to cut ¾-inch limber holes, as shown, so the bilgewater can drain to the pump rather than collect between floor timbers and do damage.

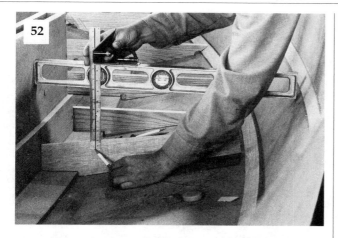

53

The 1-inch by 1 ⅜-inch oak stringers that stiffen the centerboard trunk come next, after all the floor timbers have been installed. The stringers will have to be sprung down against the tops of the floor timbers until fastened — use a post clamped to the trunk with a wedge under it, as shown here. The ends of the stringers are scooped out to match the 9/16-inch-thick floorboards. Bore through the stringer using a long bit so the drill motor doesn't fetch up against the trunk sides. Apply adhesive bedding between these pieces and the centerboard trunk just before the final installation. Fastenings are copper rivets or bronze bolts through the floor timbers and keel, as shown in the plans.

54

The guardrails of this boat are very much structural members in that they stiffen the hull and provide fastening wood for the deck. For that reason, they are extra stiff (⅞ inch by 1 ¼ inches), requiring that the hull be braced as shown while they are bent around and fastened. Braces are at each station (their lengths taken from the molds at sheer height) and are temporarily tacked in place. There will be some final fairing of the sheerstrakes to meet the guardrails, the latter serving as fairing battens and clamped in place as shown and adjusted to an "eye-sweet" curve before fastening.

55

Once the guardrails have been installed, the hull will be stiff enough so that the frames can be bent in, as is being done here. Remember, however, that throughout the right-side-up completion process, the hull should be shored level athwartships without twist. It's so easy to forget that, until the deck is on, the hull can be accidentally twisted out of shape even while it has ample strength in all other respects. The ¾-inch-square oak frames should be nosed off at their heels as shown in the plans and, as necessary forward and aft, beveled for a reasonable fit against the floor timbers before they are steamed and bent into place. Before the frames are bent in, a thin batten should be bent so the frame locations can be marked on the hull and pilot holes for fastenings bored. After bending, start fastening each frame at its heel and work toward the frame head with enough screws to hold good contact with the hull. Slitting the heels of the forward-most frames where the bend is tightest should eliminate breakage.

56

The tops of the steam-bent frames are secured by rivets that pass through the guardrail, into which their heads are counterbored and bunged. Rivets are also used at each stringer. Painting the hull interior should be done now, when all the bare wood is completely accessible; you'll notice that painting was complete when this photo was taken.

57

The sheerline you see after the boat is complete is the top outboard corner of the guardrail, and that line should be kept fair and eye-sweet at all costs, even though, according to the drawings, the official sheerline is at the top outboard corner of the sheerstrake. Furthermore, the top surface of the sheerstrake/guardrail has to be beveled (as is being checked here with the deckbeam mold) to conform to the crown (camber) of the deck, and the outboard face width of the guardrail should taper evenly toward the bow and the stern. Getting everything to come out looking right is quite a chore if one's approach is too analytical. Being guided by the above goals and adhering to the boatbuilder's creed of "What looks right, is right" is the best approach here.

58

This is a part of the guardrail tapering process: About ⅜ inch is planed off the thickness at the bow and the stern, this taper running in from the ends for about 3 feet.

59

The same deckbeam mold that was shown in photo 57 is used here for marking out the deckbeams. Note that the natural sweep of the oak plank is used to advantage, resulting in grain that will pretty much follow the curved shape of the beams. Mark and cut the beams a bit big to allow for a possible change in shape through springing, then check them against the beam mold and mark and cut a second time, if necessary.

60

The maststep is made of oak, sawn to its shape from a 2-inch-thick piece. The mortise is being cut here, the chiseling having been aided by the three 1-inch bored holes shown. Two transverse rivets through the step, one forward and one aft of the mortise, will be added to prevent splitting.

61

Here is the maststep installed. It has been carefully centered athwartships and fastened by ¼-inch drifts into the supporting floor timbers. In this photo the floorboards have been installed as well, a process that starts with the two parallel-sided pieces adjacent to the centerboard trunk. The floorboards are of ⁹⁄₁₆-inch by 6-inch cedar, with the outboard pieces tapered to look well and to rest on the floor timbers just clear of the steam-bent frame faces. The ⅜-inch gaps are being held at this stage by means of spacer blocks as shown. Although the floorboards will eventually be fastened with unbunged oval-head screws so they can be removed for maintaining the hull underneath them, that step won't be executed until the boat is nearly finished and the floorboards themselves have been sanded and painted.

62

Using the deckbeam mold and a try-square set for the 1¼-inch-high beams, marks are made on each frame for the sheer clamp, which runs from the stem aft as far as the fifth frame.

63

One of the 1¼-inch by 1¼-inch Douglas-fir sheer clamps is in position here, and bevels are being taken so that its top surface will fit the underside of each deckbeam. Mark the second clamp from the first, then level both clamps to the marks with a hand plane.

64

At the stem, the sheer clamps look like this. Note that short ¾-inch square spacers have been installed near the stem for the forward ends of the sheer clamps to lie against and fasten to.

65

Before the sheer clamps are installed, the frame pair against which the watertight bulkhead will lie has to be dressed off with a chisel, as shown. The bulkhead should seat well across about two-thirds of the frame's after face.

66

Rivets will hold the sheer clamps to the frames. Outboard, the plywood planking should be slightly counterbored so that, with filler, the rivet heads won't show. Make sure there is a wood-to-wood fit before riveting, since rivets, although they are neat, secure, and economical fastenings, have little drawing power. Note that some of the temporary spreaders are still in place holding the boat's specified beam; these will remain until the deckbeams take over that function.

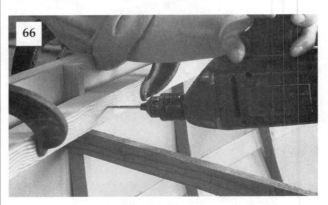

67

The breasthook lies on and is fastened to the sheer clamps with counterbored 2 ½-inch screws, as shown. Its top surface has been marked and planed to match the deckbeam mold. Be sure to slather the end-grain with adhesive bedding before the final installation. Yet to come is the ¼-inch bolt that runs out through the stem, counterbored, of course, to be flush with the stem face after bunging.

68

A pattern of many uses, the deckbeam mold is employed here to mark the transom's inner face for its final trimming. Remember (I'm sure you will) that this will be a beveled cut so that the deck will lie wood-to-wood over the transom's entire top edge.

69

A thin piece of scrap plywood laid on and marked as shown will become the pattern for the quarter knees, one knee a mirror image of the other.

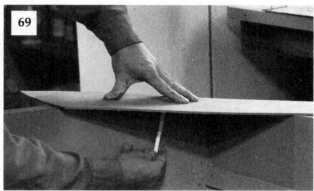

70

Here the bevels of the rough-sawn quarter knee's faying surfaces are picked up, the knee's basic shape having been sawn out according to the previously made pattern. The knees should be about an inch thick, and their grain should run on the diagonal. The ends should finish 1 ½ inches at the transom and ¾ inch at the sides to fit against the adjoining pieces.

71

The knees' faying surfaces are cut to the bevels on a bandsaw, using the pattern line as a guide. Since these knees will be hidden by the deck and will fasten from the outside, the knees' third edges need not be curved in the usual fashion. Fit and fasten the quarter knees, then make and install the filler piece that goes between them. The top surfaces of the transom, knees, and filler should be faired to match the beam mold.

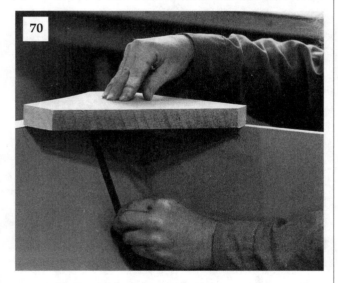

72

Now for the watertight bulkhead, which will keep the boat afloat in the event of a capsize. The vertical boards that make up the bulkhead are fastened to a deckbeam at the top (riveted to the sheer clamp in line with the frame) and an oak backing piece attached to the floor timber at the bottom. The outboard piece, being scribed to fit here, will fasten to the frame as well and notch around the sheer clamp as shown in subsequent photos.

73

Remember that this is supposed to be a watertight bulkhead, so bed the potential leak paths well. Here, Eric is slathering adhesive bedding on the after face of the frame prior to installing the starboard bulkhead piece. Remaining pieces will be added, each bedded against its neighbor, until the bulkhead is complete. Lower ends of bulkhead pieces terminate about ⅝-inch shy of the floor timber, allowing space for the floorboards to rest on the floor timber.

74

Because the sheer clamp doesn't run all the way to the stern, the aftermost deck beam is supported by notched ¾-inch cedar blocks that butt against the quarter knees and are fastened to the sheerstrakes. The notch in one of the supporting blocks is being marked here, directly from the beam. When shaped, the blocks will be screw-fastened from the outside as well as held secure by adhesive bedding, after which the beam can be set in place and riveted.

75

Pattern stock for one of the hanging knees that support the side decks is first fitted to the hull and tacked there, after which its top is marked by means of the beam mold as shown. Three pair of hanging knees are required, so there will be three patterns.

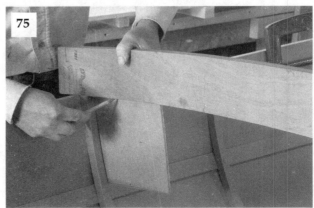

76

The hanging knees are of ½-inch oak shaped about as shown and fastened in the usual way of pre-drilling, bedding, and screwing from the outside.

77

In this photo, the remaining beams of the foredeck have been installed, each one riveted down through the sheer clamp, heads counterbored as shown elsewhere. Eric is boring for the screws that will fasten the 2-inch-thick mast partner. The mast hole has been carefully located using the maststep as a reference, taking into consideration the specified rake of the mast. The mast itself will be 3 ¼ inches in diameter at deck level, so the hole should be at least 3 ⅜ inches in diameter to give some clearance and allow for the turning of the deck canvas. The hole is cut with a sabersaw and made smooth with a rasp.

78

Above the sheer, the stem should be sided to about 1 inch. Here, Eric is rasping the sides of the stemhead smooth after it has been sawn to the desired thickness.

79

The last step before starting on the decking is to round off the top corner of the guardrails outboard of where the decking will land. The lower corner should be similarly radiused. (The marked line, ¼ inch in from the edge, is where the rounding starts.)

80

Cedar boards ½-inch thick become this boat's deck, and the first pieces to be fitted are those that make up the side decks. Eric has glue-scarfed two lengths end-to-end for the piece he's fitting here, since the side deck's outline has more curve than the stock he had on hand. After rough-cutting to the approximate shape, the outboard edge is marked on its underside, as is being done in the photo.

81

After its outboard edge has been sawn and planed to the line, the piece is placed back on the boat with its cut edge set inboard about ¼ inch, as shown, and the inboard edge marked with a fairing batten located at the cockpit opening. This piece of decking runs all the way aft to cover the transom, but can be allowed to run out at its forward end, more or less, as shown. Use this starboard side piece, after it has been cut to the finished shape, for marking a mirror-image piece for the boat's port side deck.

82

Before the side decks are fastened to the hull, chainplates of ⅛-inch bronze should be made up and installed, as shown on the drawings. Here is what one chain plate looks like as the holes for its four ¼-inch machine-screw fastenings are drilled out through the planking. The screw heads should be counterbored into the planking just enough to be filled flush and not show. The pre-bored chainplate unit, a bronze and oak sandwich that tucks behind the sheer clamp, should be aligned with the shroud angle in profile, and the projecting end of the chainplate itself should have an inward bend to match the shroud angle when viewed from forward or aft.

83

Both side decks have been installed in this photo, as have the chainplates that penetrate them. Pre-drill all the decking, then smear adhesive bedding where it meets the hull (i.e., the sheerstrake and guardrail), and fasten it with screws into the guardrails, deckbeams, and supporting knees.

84 (top of page 149)

Continue with the straight-sided pieces that will make up the foredeck, starting with the two center pieces, and working outboard as shown. Use the driest cedar you can find, and paint the underside before permanently fastening it down, in order to minimize the subsequent shrinking and swelling. Clamp or wedge the pieces tightly together, and use adhesive bedding between them to minimize movement at the seams. Continue by laying the stern

deck, using the same approach with wedge-shaped pieces, then putty over all the fastenings and plane and/or sand the entire top surface fair.

85

After the cockpit edges are planed flush with the beams and the outboard edges of the deck are radiused a little, you can begin painting. The forward deck is to be covered with canvas to ensure its watertightness, using the method of your choice. Our choice was to lay the 10-ounce canvas in white lead paste, then use a thinned coat of the same substance brushed on from above after the canvas was stretched and stapled in place. Epoxy can be used in much the same way as white lead, although it is more expensive. The side and after decks are simply painted and trimmed around the cockpit opening with the low coaming shown on the drawings. Toerails cover the raw edges of the foredeck canvas.

86

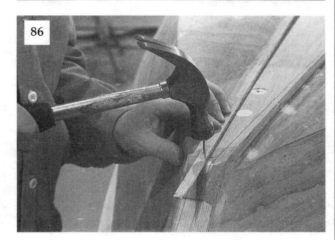

Now it's time to flip the boat upside down and finish the bottom. Fairing the boat's "chin" where the keel and stem join is done to a line marked from a batten, as shown. Bevel the sides of the keel to these lines, starting about 3 feet aft of the intersection and working the winding bevel to match the ½-inch face width of the stem. Besides using a chisel, rabbet plane, and spokeshave, you may find that a disc grinder is helpful in dealing with the oak's random grain. While the hull is inverted, saw the projecting ends of the centerboard trunk posts flush. (A bit below flush is even better to keep them from bearing against the lead ballast keel and jacking the trunk away from the hull.) Also, now is the time to plane the chines fair and eye-sweet, and to generally sand and smooth the rest of the hull. You can take this opportunity to get some paint on the bottom as well.

87

We're right-side up again, and Eric is marking the painted waterline, a slightly sheered line that begins at the "point" of the stem and ends aft at the top corner of the garboard. Shift the batten until it sights fair and lies about 3 inches below the top of the garboard amidships. Because the hull is already thin, being of plywood, the usual incised scribeline was omitted in favor of a pencil line and masking tape.

88

The forestay attaches directly to the stem through a hole bored crosswise, rather than at a chainplate, but for this simple scheme to work, the stemhead has to be strengthened with a rivet placed just above the bored hole, as shown. The rivet was made from a piece of ¼-inch bronze rod with a washer at each end. Here, the stemhead has already been cut to its final shape and its corners beveled to a finished appearance. Note how the deck rounds in to match the shape of the guardrails it sets on.

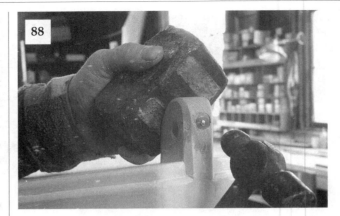

89

Three layers of ⅜-inch mahogany plywood glued together provide the material from which to build the rudder. Take the shape from the drawings and fair the curves, if you wish, as Eric is doing here, with an old bandsaw blade. Cut as accurately as you can to the marked line to save subsequent planing.

90

The rudder's trailing edge is tapered to ¼ inch, a process that is made easier because of the concentric outline of the plywood layers as they are sanded away. Guidelines indicating the start of the taper, however, marked so as to be alike on each side of the rudder blade, assure symmetry. Here, the exposed plywood end-grain is sealed against water absorption with brushed-on epoxy. The entire rudder, in fact, was so sealed.

91

This is how the pintles are installed on the leading edge of the rudder, let in to be flush and counterbored so the rivets can be peened flush or nearly so. The rudder/pintle configuration is such that the rudder cannot lift and detach itself from the boat during normal use. Only by swinging the rudder to 90 degrees (at which angle its forward, lower end clears the hull) can the rudder be unshipped.

92

The gudgeons are let in flush with the transom face, their location and spacing having been transferred from the completed rudder assembly; i.e., the rudder's protruding leading edge should just clear the keel. The gudgeons are well bedded and attached by means of machine screws.

93

The tiller can be of oak or ash, curved as shown on the drawings and carefully shaped to have an egg-shaped knob on its end, in the traditional Herreshoff manner. The neck diameter should be about ¾ inch and the knob about 1 inch, while the opposite end of the tiller should be sized about 1 ⅛ inches square to fit the rudderhead.

94

Mahogany plywood ¾-inch thick is used for the centerboard, which in this photo has been cut to shape and is having its after edge tapered for speed, as was done with the rudder. It, too, will be epoxy sealed before being painted. Use the drawing to get the centerboard's outline, and check that it will fit your centerboard trunk as well.

95

So it can be lowered with certainty, the centerboard is weighted at its after end with lead ballast, poured into a cavity cut through the centerboard as shown. The cavity has V-shaped edges that serve to hold the lead secure. A scrap piece of plywood temporarily screwed to the underside of the centerboard forms a bottom to the cavity and keeps the molten lead contained until it cools. Pour the lead proud of the top surface to allow for shrinkage; the excess, if any, can be planed flush.

96

As you will note from the drawings, this boat is to have a hollow mast, and, although it's a bit of a chore to build, its light weight will add to the boat's sail-carrying ability. Build it solid if you're lacking the time that these next steps require. We were curious, however, to learn about both the process and the end result, so here goes: Start by milling enough stock (spruce of some kind, preferably Sitka) to make two halves of the required 21-foot length, with allowance for scarfing and shaping of the ends. The 3 1/4-inch maximum diameter calls for about 1 7/8-inch by 3 3/4-inch rough-sawn dimensions. Here the 8-to-1 scarfs have been cut on a bandsaw and are being planed in stacked pairs.

97

Now scarf the pieces together as shown, using epoxy. Use at least six clamps for each scarf and take care to clamp the feather ends under tape-covered blocks, as shown. Also, sight along the entire length for straightness before walking away. Carefully plane the mating halves of the mast smooth to fit tightly against one another after the glue cures. Then place the two halves together, for marking, as if they were a solid stick.

98

Use the parting line as a centerline and set off the half-breadths (the diameters divided by 2) at the intervals indicated on the drawing; with a stiff batten, draw the mast outline on one face, symmetrical about the parting line. Separate the halves, and saw each one to the line, as is shown here. After planing one reference side smooth for bearing against the table saw's fence, saw the halves into quarters.

99

Here, the quarters are being planed smooth for a tight fit against each other when reassembled. If you haven't caught on to why we've quartered this mast, it's for ease in hollowing it, a process which is described in the following steps. At this stage, you should have the four quarters that will make up the finished mast dressed down to their finished dimensions, each one a perfect square at any place along its length.

100

Now for the hollowing of the quarters. Start by marking the specified wall thickness inward from what will be the outer surface of each quarter piece. The wall thickness diminishes with the mast diameter, so you'll have to mark points and fair them with a batten. (See, I told you that a hollow mast takes more time!) When finished, each quarter piece should have markings on two adjoining faces as shown in this photo. Go at the roughing-out process with a drawknife, as Eric is doing here, then plane carefully to the lines. Remember that the ends of the mast are left solid, so there will be a runout of the hollowing at the mast's head and heel.

101

Finish the hollowing with a round-bottomed plane, or planes, which more or less fit(s) the inside diameter. Notched support blocks, nailed at intervals along the bench, hold the quarter pieces steady for this operation. Note that, if sail track is to be used, the wall thickness along the after side of the mast should be greater. We chose a laced-on sail so we didn't need the extra thickness.

102

Here are the first two quarter pieces being glued together to form a half. The support blocks have been carefully leveled and trued, so there will be no twist or visible glue lines. Blocks and wedges hold lateral alignment and provide pressure at the glue line. Where wedging won't close the joint, use C-clamps. And if the mast-half won't stay in contact with the bed, force it to do so with more C-clamps placed in that direction. The second mast half, shown here as quarter pieces at left, gets assembled in exactly the same way as the first.

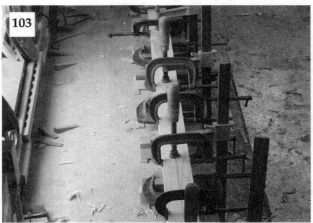

103

The two halves, their mating faces checked for fit, are then spread with glue and clamped as shown, using many clamps and with what will become the straight after side of the mast on the bottom in contact with the bed. From here on, the mast making proceeds as if the mast were solid; that is to say, after the glue cures, this tapered, four-section piece is planed to be square in section and have an even taper on all four sides, then marked and planed to eight sides, then made round in the usual way. Except for the almost invisible (we hope) glue lines, this mast and a solid one will look exactly alike; the difference is in the weight. Our mast weighed 16 ½ pounds when finished, considerably less than what a solid one would have weighed.

104

The booms are solid, and the main boom is fitted with wooden jaws, as shown on the plan and in this picture. The jaws are of oak and are let slightly into the sides of the boom so that the jaws appear to grow out of the boom.

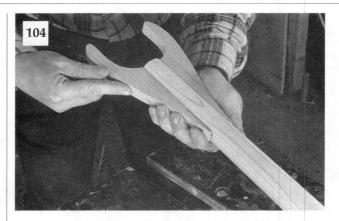

105

Both keel configurations shown on the drawing are of cast iron, which, presumably, was an economy move, since Herreshoff's custom was to use lead for outside ballast. Our boat is the centerboard version, and we decided on a lead rather than iron keel, since it would be easier to cast and install. Here is the wooden mold, its configuration modified to produce a lead keel of the same weight as the iron one (about 300 pounds) and a casting whose top surface is straight rather than curved to the shape of the hull. (If the depth of the keel is reduced by about 1 inch at station 4, by 1 ½ inch at station 5, by 1 ¾ inch at stations 6 and 7, by 2 inches at station 8, and by 1 ¾ inches at station 9 from what is shown on the plan, its weight in lead will remain about the same as the weight in iron.)

106

After the wooden mold has been broken away to expose the lead keel casting, the casting can be smoothed with a power plane, or a hand plane, for that matter, if you have the energy.

107

Although cast with a straight top surface, the keel can be bent to form afterwards simply by blocking it off the floor as shown and hitting it — fairly gently, working outward from the midpoint — with a maul. Make a pattern of the proper curve from your lofting or the boat itself and keep checking with it until you get the ballast keel hammered into a fair curve of about the right shape. The keelbolts will do the rest.

108

Here, the keelbolts have been bored (first, counterbore for their heads), and the hole for the centerboard pivot pin is bored. A slow-turning twist drill works well, cooled and lubricated with oil. Pull back frequently to empty the drill of lead shavings, which, if allowed to accumulate, will heat up and jam the drill. Note that the pin is located about a third of the way down from the top, a slight relocation from what is shown on the iron keel drawing — an adjustment made necessary because of the lead keel's reduced height.

109

Bolt holes are bored up through the boat's keel timber using the holes already made in the ballast keel for guides. The ballast keel is then lowered enough to allow it to be smeared with a liberal dose of roofing tar/bedding compound. Then, it is repositioned and bolted permanently to the boat.

110

After a few finishing touches, the Biscayne Bay 14 is ready to go. Not many daysailers are so easily trailered.

Building plans for the Biscayne Bay (plan #400-066) are available from The WoodenBoat Store, P.O. Box 78, Brooklin, Maine 04616. Call 1–800–273–SHIP (7447). The price is $75.

The Downeaster 18

by Graham Ero   Photographs by Anne Clark Ero

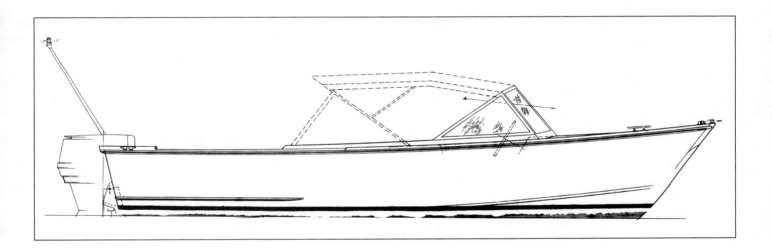

The prototype for Downeaster 18 was built in the mid-1980s, when *WoodenBoat* magazine was looking for an outboard runabout that would have traditional character, economy and durability of construction, and speed and comfort in a variety of sea conditions. The last criterion was particularly important, as the boat would be used on the coastal waters of Maine, which do not forgive the shortcomings of a poorly designed runabout. The boat would have to be easily driven, yet be able to negotiate both head and following seas with ease and agility. The desired boat would not be of the deep-forefoot type — so easily tending to gripe off course — and she would be of deep-V design, for speed and power underway.

The boat chosen was designed by Charles W. Wittholz and built by Graham Ero of Still Pond, Maryland. She does just what a runabout is supposed to do: go fast in safety and comfort. She really does carry a load (she's rated to carry eight people), and she handles quite easily. Because she has a somewhat narrow deep-V hull, she is not the stable platform one might expect, but that is the price one pays for the agility and power that is inherent in the form. She is lovely to see, at the mooring and underway; with a 75-hp outboard, she cruises easily at 30 mph.

Although fir plywood was specified by the designer, she was built with solid mahogany plywood, for added strength and durability. Materials costs ran about $5,000 in the mid-1980s, to which must be added engine and accessories. Compared with what is available in production outboard boats, the cost of the whole was a bargain. But fueling an outboard is not like sailing or rowing; the thrills have their cost.

— Editor

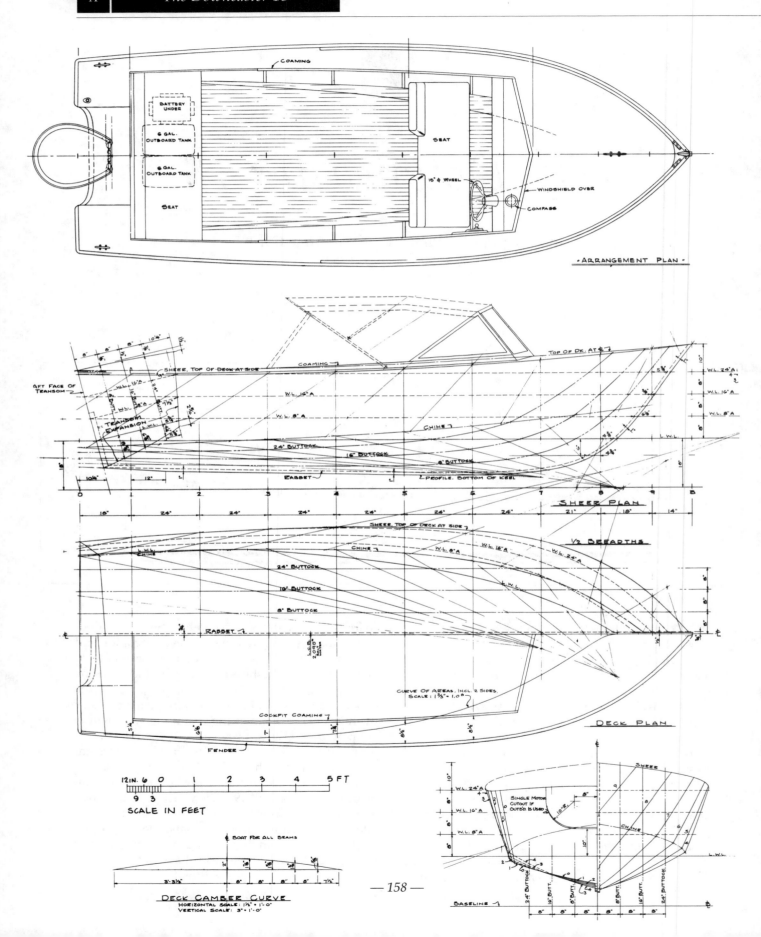

· ARRANGEMENT PLAN ·

SHEER PLAN

½ BREADTHS

DECK PLAN

12 IN. 6 0   1   2   3   4   5 FT
9 3
SCALE IN FEET

DECK CAMBER CURVE
HORIZONTAL SCALE: 1½" = 1'-0"
VERTICAL SCALE: 3" = 1'-0"

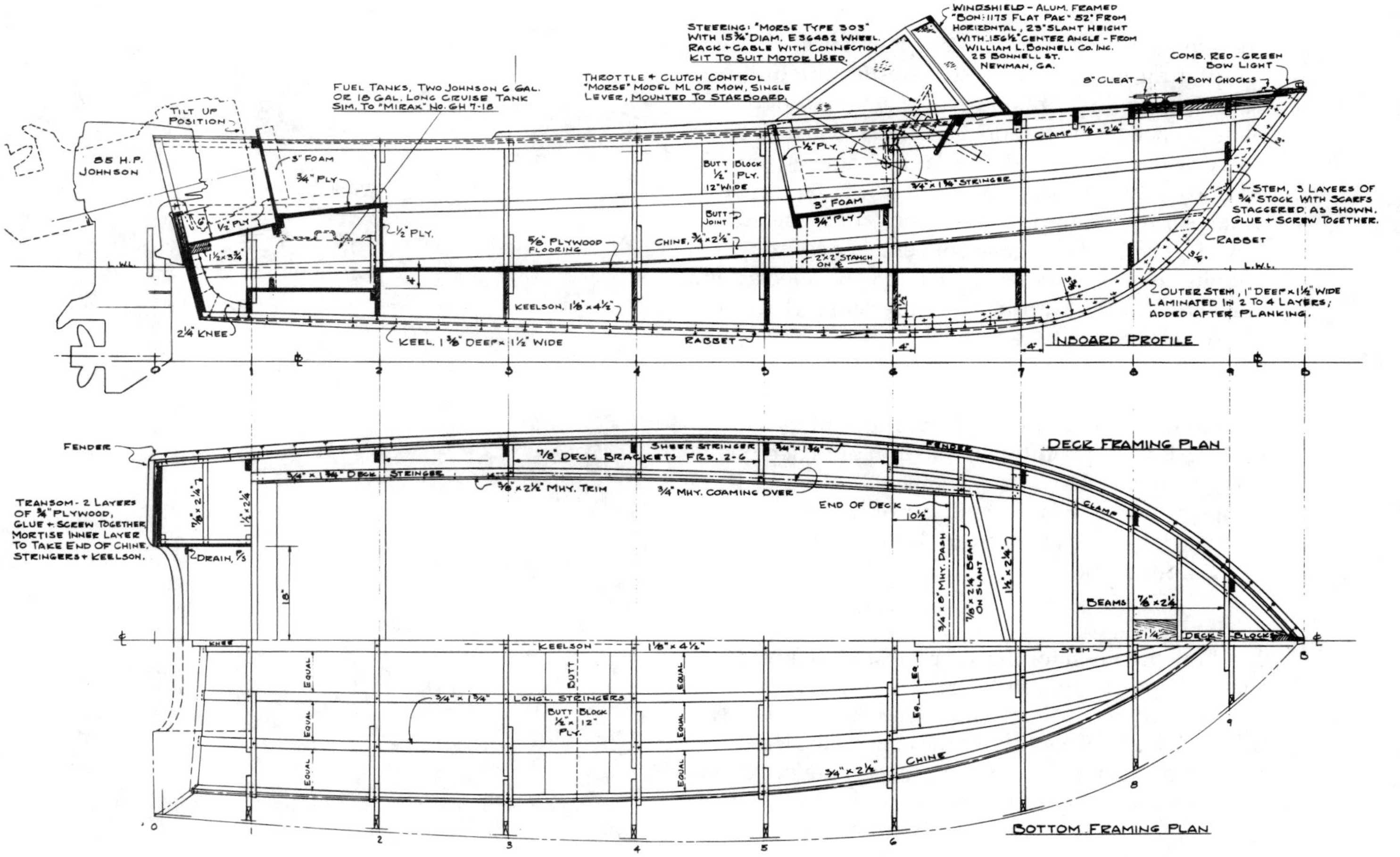

INBOARD PROFILE
WINDSHIELD - ALUM. FRAMED "BON: 1175 FLAT PAK" 52" FROM HORIZONTAL, 23" SLANT HEIGHT WITH 156½" CENTER ANGLE - FROM WILLIAM L. BONNELL CO. INC. 25 BONNELL ST. NEWMAN, GA.
STEERING: "MORSE TYPE 303" WITH 15¾" DIAM. E36482 WHEEL. RACK + CABLE WITH CONNECTION KIT TO SUIT MOTOR USED.
THROTTLE + CLUTCH CONTROL "MORSE" MODEL ML OR MOW, SINGLE LEVER, MOUNTED TO STARBOARD.
FUEL TANKS, TWO JOHNSON 6 GAL. OR 18 GAL. LONG CRUISE TANK SIM. TO "MIRAK" NO. GH 7-18
COMB. RED-GREEN BOW LIGHT
8" CLEAT
4" BOW CHOCKS
TILT UP POSITION
85 H.P. JOHNSON
3" FOAM
¾" PLY
½" PLY
½" PLY
1½ x 3¾
BUTT BLOCK ½" PLY. 12" WIDE
BUTT JOINT
⅝" PLYWOOD FLOORING
CHINE, ¾ x 2½
2"x2" STANCH ON ℄
¾ x 1¾ STRINGER
CLAMP ⅞ x 2¼
STEM, 3 LAYERS OF ¾" STOCK WITH SCARFS STAGGERED AS SHOWN. GLUE + SCREW TOGETHER.
RABBET
L.W.L.
OUTER STEM, 1" DEEP x 1½" WIDE LAMINATED IN 2 TO 4 LAYERS; ADDED AFTER PLANKING.
KEELSON, 1⅛ x 4½
2¼ KNEE
KEEL, 1⅜ DEEP x 1½" WIDE
RABBET
DECK FRAMING PLAN
FENDER
SHEER STRINGER ¾" x 1¾"
⅞" DECK BRACKETS FRS. 2-6
¾" x 1¾" DECK STRINGER
⅜" x 2½" MHY. TRIM
¾" MHY. COAMING OVER
END OF DECK
10½"
CLAMP
TRANSOM - 2 LAYERS OF ¾" PLYWOOD, GLUE + SCREW TOGETHER. MORTISE INNER LAYER TO TAKE END OF CHINE, STRINGERS + KEELSON.
DRAIN, ⅞
⅞ x 2¼
1½ x 2¼
18"
¾ x 8" MHY. DASH
⅞ x 2¼ BEAM ON SLANT
1½ x 2¼
BEAMS ⅞ x 2¼
DECK BLOCKS
STEM
KNEE
KEELSON 1⅛" x 4½"
BUTT
EQUAL
¾" x 1¾" LONG'L. STRINGERS
BUTT BLOCK ½" x 12" PLY.
¾" x 2½" CHINE
BOTTOM FRAMING PLAN

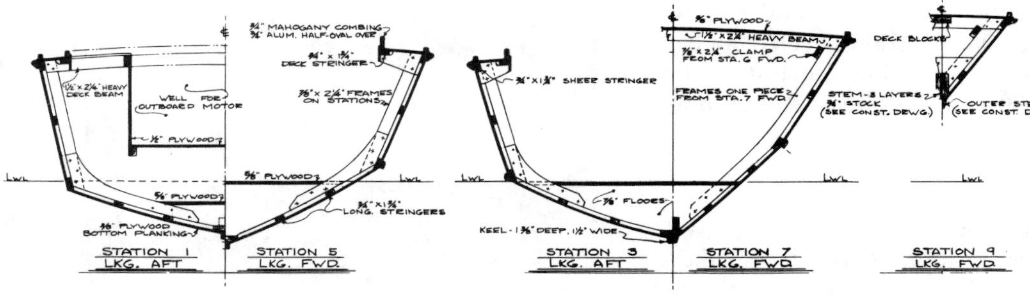

¾" MAHOGANY COMBING ¾" ALUM. HALF-OVAL OVER
¾" x 1¾" DECK STRINGER
1⅛ x 2¼ HEAVY DECK BEAM
WELL FOR OUTBOARD MOTOR
½" PLYWOOD
⅞ x 2¼ FRAMES ON STATIONS
⅝" PLYWOOD
⅝" PLYWOOD
⅜" PLYWOOD BOTTOM PLANKING
¾" x 1¾" LONG. STRINGERS
STATION 1 LKG. AFT
STATION 5 LKG. FWD.
⅜" PLYWOOD
1½" x 2¼" HEAVY BEAM
¾" x 1¾" SHEER STRINGER
⅞ x 2¼ CLAMP FROM STA. 6 FWD.
FRAMES ONE PIECE FROM STA. 7 FWD.
⅞" FLOORS
KEEL - 1⅜" DEEP, 1½" WIDE
STATION 3 LKG. AFT
STATION 7 LKG. FWD.
DECK BLOCKS
STEM - 3 LAYERS ¾" STOCK (SEE CONST. DRWG)
OUTER STEM (SEE CONST. DRWG)
STATION 9 LKG. FWD.
LWL

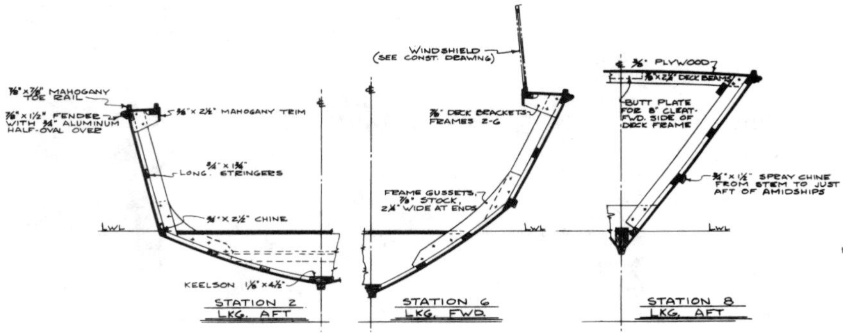

⅞" x ⅞" MAHOGANY TOE RAIL
⅞" x 1½" FENDER WITH ¾" ALUMINUM HALF-OVAL OVER
⅜" x 2½" MAHOGANY TRIM
¾" x 1¾" LONG'L STRINGERS
¾" x 2½" CHINE
KEELSON 1⅛" x 4½
STATION 2 LKG. AFT
WINDSHIELD (SEE CONST. DRAWING)
⅞" DECK BRACKETS FRAMES 2-6
FRAME GUSSETS, ⅞" STOCK, 2¼" WIDE AT ENDS
STATION 6 LKG. FWD.
⅜" PLYWOOD
⅞ x 2¼ DECK BEAMS
BUTT PLATE FOR 8" CLEAT- FWD. SIDE OF DECK FRAME
¾" x 1½" SPRAY CHINE FROM STEM TO JUST AFT OF AMIDSHIPS
STATION 8 LKG. AFT
LWL

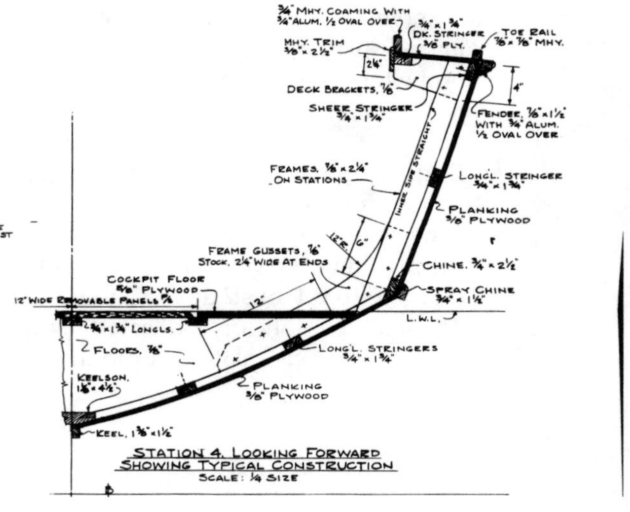

¾" MHY. COAMING WITH ¾" ALUM. ½ OVAL OVER
¾" x 1¾" DK. STRINGER
⅜ PLY.
TOE RAIL ⅞" x ⅞" MHY.
MHY. TRIM ⅜ x 2½"
2¼"
4"
DECK BRACKETS, ⅞
SHEER STRINGER ¾ x 1¾
FENDER, ⅞ x 1½ WITH ¾" ALUM. ½ OVAL OVER
INNER SIDE STRAIGHT
FRAMES, ⅞ x 2¼ ON STATIONS
LONG'L. STRINGER ¾ x 1¾
PLANKING ⅜" PLYWOOD
FRAME GUSSETS, ⅞ STOCK, 2¼ WIDE AT ENDS
CHINE, ¾ x 2½
SPRAY CHINE ¾ x 1½
COCKPIT FLOOR ⅝" PLYWOOD
12" WIDE REMOVABLE PANELS ⅝
L.W.L.
¾ x 1¾ LONGLS.
FLOORS, ⅞
LONG'L. STRINGERS ¾ x 1¾
KEELSON, 1⅛ x 4½
PLANKING ⅜" PLYWOOD
KEEL, 1⅜ x 1½
STATION 4, LOOKING FORWARD SHOWING TYPICAL CONSTRUCTION
SCALE: ¼ SIZE

1

Tools for "taking off" and making templates. Although templating involves an extra step in the building process, I begin by making a ½-inch plywood template of each frame station. Each can be corrected and faired with a plane, and then laid up against the lofted body plan to check for accuracy. Later, the templates serve as clamping jigs upon which each frame can be assembled — a great convenience assuring that any slips or misalignments can be easily detected and corrected as the framing members are glued and screwed together.

2

Taking off measurements from the lofting. Downeaster's lines were lofted full-size on plywood panels hung on the wall to conserve space. The ¾-inch lip or flange at the base is for support of the large square (not shown) that was used to draw the vertical lines of the lofting grid.

3

Marking plywood for the templates. Each frame template is begun by first striking a centerline and a waterline at 90 degrees to each other. A second baseline was arbitrarily established above the boat on the loft drawing to represent the bottom edge of each inverted template and, correspondingly, the top surface of the strongback upon which this template (and subsequently the frames) will rest while the boat is being built. By setting the plywood edge on the strongback surface, vertical alignment is assured and each template needs only to be plumbed and leveled on its station line. The additional waterlines and buttock lines are added to complete the grid for each frame template.

4

Connecting the dots; marking the outline. Next, the sheer and chine points are located from the lofted body plan. I also mark the rabbet line, and the intermediate points at the intersection of the buttocks and waterlines — all of which, when connected, depict the curve of the topsides and bottom.

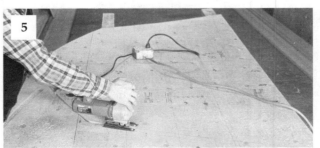

5

Deducting for planking and stringers; cutting the marked outline. Before cutting out the templates, it is necessary to reduce each one by the thickness of the planking (⅜ inch) plus the longitudinal stringers (¾ inch) to establish the actual outline of the frame. Then, all the dots are connected using a flexible batten, and each template is cut to this inner line.

6

Checking each template against the lofting. Each template is faired with a plane and then checked against the loft drawing. All frame templates should be exactly 1 ⅛ inches smaller than what is shown on the body plan.

7

Building a frame: layout for the inside edge. For frames No. 7 through No. 9, which are in one piece from keel to sheer, I allow enough width for the curved inside edge as shown on the plan. The remaining frame halves are made from two pieces joined with a gusset at the chine.

8

Building a frame: marking the outline from a full-sized template. The inside edge of the frames (except for the three forward ones) are straight. This means that once the slight curves along the frames' outside bottom and topside edges are planed in, the framing pieces are slightly thinner at each end than in the middle. To mark the frame stock for cutting, I simply lay the 2 ¾-inch-wide stock on the template edge so it is tangent at the middle, and mark to the template outline.

9

Building a frame: marking the shape of the inside edge. Once marked, the frames are ready for cutting.

10

Building a frame: sawing the inside edge. Frames No. 8 and No. 9 are almost straight, while frame No. 7 is cut to the slight convex curves of the bottom and top-side, as shown.

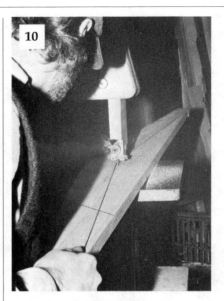

11

Building a frame: marking the heel. The heel of each half-frame is marked where it terminates in the bilge and is to be fastened to its floor timber.

12

Building a frame: marking the floor timbers. The floor timbers, which connect the half-frames at their heels, are marked to the template outline and carried up to the drawn waterline minus the thickness of the cock-pit sole. A centerline is marked on each floor timber for later reference.

13

Building a frame: clamping for fastening. After being sawn and planed to the marked outline, the floor tim-ber is positioned on the template with the half-frames clamped carefully to it. The frame assembly is kept flat by placing ¾-inch spacers at the sheer.

14

Building a frame: gluing. Cross spalls are temporarily fastened near the top edge of each frame assembly with drywall screws (corresponding to the new baseline described earlier). The half-frames are then glued and screwed to the floor timber. The screw holes are pre-drilled, then the half-frames are lifted off to receive the glue. When the half-frames are placed back into position, the screws find their proper locations, thus assuring a perfect alignment.

15

Building a frame: knees and side pieces. Knees (or gussets, as they are called in the plans) are required for the frames aft of No. 7, and are cut out alongside their inside edges to a curve that makes a smooth transition between the upper and lower members of the half-frame. The first gusset — flipped over — serves as a template for the corresponding one.

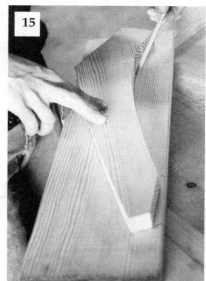

16

Setting the frames on the strongback; replacing the templates. I set up the templates on the strongback before building the frames so that, using battens, I can check the hull for fairness before starting to build the frames themselves. If anything appears wildly wrong with the templates, the problem can be identified and corrected without spoiling the valuable material of the frames or adding to the time that goes into making them. The templates are replaced by the actual frames as the frames are built.

17

Leveling and plumbing frames. Each frame is set into position on the strongback and clamped at the cross spall. Each cross spall has been stiffened by a second 2 by 4 screwed perpendicular to itself, creating a convenient means of clamping and fastening to the cross spall strongback.

18

Bracing the frames in place. Using cedar shims, a square, and a level, each frame is leveled, plumbed, and then held square to the strongback by longitudinal battens. A few diagonal braces between floor timbers and the strongback hold the frames plumb and give the framework extra stiffness to withstand the strain of the building process. Last of all, the portion of the frame projecting beyond the sheerline is trimmed, shimmed, and fastened to the floor of the shop to hold each frame assembly level athwartships.

19

"Taking off" the stem shape on Mylar. Using heavy, transparent, architectural drafting film, I trace the shape of the stem and forefoot from the loft drawing and create a pattern for marking these pieces on the wood from which they will be sawn.

20
Sawing a three-layer stem from the Mylar pattern. The stem is glued together in three layers of mahogany pieced together, joints staggered. Once the glue sets, the pattern is stapled to it, and the stem is cut out as shown.

21
Planing and sanding the stem. The sawn-out stem is planed, and sanded fair and smooth.

22
Beveling the frame edges for stringers. Using long, fairly stiff battens as guides, the frame edges are beveled so the longitudinal stringers and chines will lie in full contact against them.

23
Confirming the frame bevel. When working alone, it is often necessary to devise various "deadmen" to assist you. Here, a small, vertical batten, spacers, and C-clamps serve to contain the far end of the fairing batten used in beveling the frames.

24

Notching the frames for the stem. Frames No. 7, 8, and 9 must be notched to receive the stem. The locations of these notches are critical, yet difficult to judge. I recommend cutting gradually down to the measured marks, using the stem itself (and fairing battens sprung around the frames and laid against the stem) to check for a proper fit. I cut and fit until the sprung battens read fair and the stem is generally positioned according to the drawing.

25

Fitting a transom template. As with the frames, I first make a transom out of plywood scrap and 2 by 4s, then work it down until I get a good fit. The transom template allows me to cut and try until I'm satisfied it fits. If I get too much bevel or if I make some other mistake, it would cost but little to start over again.

26

Marking for the "real" transom. Once certain of the transom shape and all the edge bevels, I use this template for marking out the actual transom. I trace its shape onto the mahogany plywood and transfer the bevels from the template to the actual transom at 6-inch intervals.

27
Notching the "real" inner transom. The transom goes on in two layers. The inner layer is fitted into place and notched to receive the ends of the longitudinal stringers. This is a convenient method of construction, because it allows the keelson and stringers to run well past the transom and thus leave plenty of extra material for cutting and fitting their forward ends against the stem.

28
Sawing off the longitudinals. The longitudinal stringers, chines, and keel batten are sawn off only after they have been fitted, glued, and screwed to the stem and to each of the frames.

29
Fitting the keelson and the stem. The stem is notched to receive the keelson. The bottom edges of the floor timbers are also faired to receive this timber.

30
Joining the keelson and the stem. When the fitting and fairing are complete, the stem and keelson are clamped and fastened together with screws and bronze bolts. Bedding compound, instead of epoxy glue, was used here to facilitate repair if the forefoot is ever damaged.

31

Steaming the chines. Since the chines and longitudinal bottom stringers undergo a rather severe bend forward of frame No. 6, I temporarily fasten all of them to the boat at their after ends, and then steam their forward ends to make them limber enough to be pushed easily into place. This saves time, and I feel it yields better results than steaming them while off the boat and attempting to clamp their entire length in place before they cool. Either way, it's an easy matter to make the final fit against the stem after the chines cool.

32

Clamping the steam-softened chines into place. Various blocks are temporarily clamped to the frames to act as guides, ensuring proper and rapid placement of each longitudinal after steaming is complete and the steam tube has been removed.

33

Fitting the chines and the stringers to the stem. Once the chines and stringers have been clamped into position, steamed, and allowed to cool, they can be pulled out from the stem, planed to a good fit, and easily pushed back into place for fastening. Since at this stage there should be plenty of material projecting beyond the transom, you can cut away all you need (within reason) to make a good fit forward.

34

Stringers and chines ready for fastening. After fitting the longitudinals, I glue and clamp them overnight. After the glue sets, I drill and countersink each one for a couple of screws, which will add mechanical strength and back up the glue joint.

35

Putting the second transom layer in place. With all the longitudinals, the chines, and the keel glued and screwed in place, and with their ends sawn flush with the inner layer of the transom, the transom's outer layer can be marked directly from the inner one, sawn out, and installed.

36

Clamping the second transom layer in place. Using a plastic paint pan to hold the glue and a foam roller to spread it, the outer transom layer is glued into place. Screws are spaced at 5-inch intervals from the inside, countersunk, and bunged. Plenty of clamps ensure a tight fit all around the edges.

37

Fairing for the planking. Now the keelson must be beveled fair to receive the bottom planking panels. Once again a thin, straight batten is used as shown to check for fairness along the entire length of the boat, both sides.

38

Fairing for planking. A spacer block, equal in thickness to the longitudinals and spanning at least two frames, provides a fairly accurate scribing line for beveling the keelson. The batten, however, should always be at hand for guidance in the final stages of beveling.

39

Fairing for planking. The spacer block can also be used at the chine to prevent too much wood from being planed away during the beveling process. A batten placed athwartships, from the (beveled) keelson to the chine and over all the longitudinals, indicates the proper chine bevel, just as it did for the keelson throughout the length of the boat.

40

Fairing for planking. In the final step, the stem is faired to receive the planking panels, using vertical, diagonal, and longitudinal battens in much the same way as for the keelson and chines.

Note: Mahogany sheerstrakes, ⅝ inch thick, were fitted to this boat to add some charm and a bit of class. The naturally finished "real wood" made the boat look lower as well as more interesting and attractive. But separate sheerstrakes can be dispensed with, since they really serve no practical purpose. If you choose to go with plywood all the way, skip these first few steps relating to making and fitting sheerstrakes, and begin with step 52: installation of the side panels themselves.

41

In the profile, the sheerstrakes should be laid out about 6 inches wide, tapering a little toward the ends of the boat, particularly forward where the projected width should be about 4 ½ inches. The true widths, measured along the hull's surface, will, of course, be greater: how much depends on the flare. In Downeaster, the increase in the actual width over the projected width is about 1 inch at station 9, where the flare is greatest.

Install an extra batten to center at the sheerstrakes' lower edge, so both the sheerstrake and the side panel can be fastened to the batten. Always try to achieve an eye-sweet line after you establish the position of the batten at each station.

Since full-length sheerstrakes are impractical, they were installed in two pieces, butted together over a butt block at the fourth frame bay from the stem. The forward section of plank was clamped on the boat as shown, and marked from inside the boat to the line of the longitudinals.

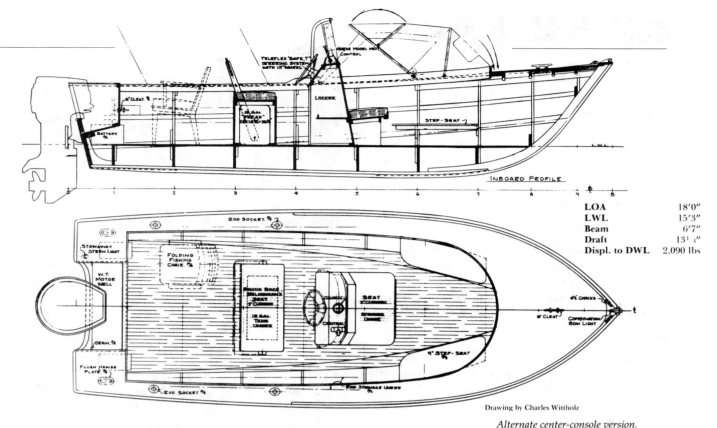

INBOARD PROFILE

LOA	18'0"
LWL	15'3"
Beam	6'7"
Draft	13¹⁄₄"
Displ. to DWL	2,090 lbs

Drawing by Charles Wittholz

Alternate center-console version.

FASTENING SCHEDULE

ITEMS	FASTENING SIZE & SPACING
Stem assembly	Glue and screw the three layers together with 2" No. 10 screws, as shown on the inboard profile
Transom assembly	Glue and screw the two layers of ³⁄₄" plywood together with 1¹⁄₄" No. 10 screws on 5" centers in rows 5" apart
Stem to keelson	Use ⁵⁄₁₆"-diam. bolt at frame 7 and at aft end of stem, plus three 2¹⁄₂" No. 14 screws (see inboard profile)
Stern knee to keelson and transom	Five ⁵⁄₁₆"-diam. throughbolts (three 3" long, one 4" long, and one 5" long)
Strongback to transom	Eight ³⁄₈"-diam. bolts, 5¹⁄₂" long, on 8" centers
Gussets to frames	Six 1¹⁄₂" No. 12 screws in each gusset, countersunk ¹⁄₈"
Deck brackets to frames	Two 1¹⁄₂" No. 12 screws at each frame
Deckbeams to frames	One 1¹⁄₂" No. 12 screw at each frame
Deckbeams to clamp (forward)	One ¹⁄₄"-diam. throughbolt at each frame
Keelson to floors	Two 3" No. 14 screws at each frame, 1–6
Stem to floors	One ⁵⁄₁₆"-diam. throughbolt at each frame, 7–9
Chines, sheer stringer, & longitudinal stringers to frames	One 2¹⁄₄" No. 14 screw into each frame, stem and transom
Bottom planking to stem, keelson, and transom	1¹⁄₄" No. 8 screws on 3" centers, staggered
Bottom planking to chines	1" No. 8 screws on 3" centers
Side planking to stem, chine, and transom	1" No. 8 screws on 3" centers, staggered
Bottom and side planking to longitudinal stringers	1" No. 8 screws on 4¹⁄₂" centers, staggered; or 1" No. 10 Anchorfast or equiv. ring shank nails on 4¹⁄₂" centers
Deck stringers to brackets	One 2" No. 12 screw at each bracket
Deck planking to sheer stringer, transom, and deck stringers	1" No. 8 screws on 3¹⁄₂" centers, or 1" No. 10 Anchorfast, or equiv. ring shank nails
Deck planking to beams and deck brackets	(same size as above on 4¹⁄₂" centers)
Keel to keelson	2" No. 12 screws on 8" centers
Outer stem to stem	1¹⁄₂" No. 12 screws on 6" centers
Coaming to deck longitudinals	2" No. 8 screws on 6" centers
Cockpit trim to deck longitudinals	1" No. 8 screws on 6" centers
Fender to hull	2" No. 12 screws on 6" centers
Spray chine to chine	1¹⁄₂" No. 12 screws on 6" centers
Motorwell to framing	1" No. 8 screws on 3¹⁄₂" centers
Cockpit floor to floors	1¹⁄₂" No. 8 screws on 6" centers

42

The plank was cut to shape on the bandsaw, and planed to the marked line. A compass plane made an easy job of fairing the concave edge.

43

The aft section of the sheerstrake is limber enough to be slightly edge-set if necessary to meet the sheer. Both sections are then clamped in place so the butt can be carefully cut and fitted.

44

Using a wooden block to prevent damage, the sheerstrake is driven into place so the lower edge centers on the longitudinal. It is important to leave at least ¾ inch extending beyond the actual sheer as extra wood for fairing after the boat is turned right-side up.

45

After the two sections of the sheerstrakes are ready for installation, an oak or ash butt block is fitted between the longitudinals to receive their ends. I made the butt block a full l inch thick to give it more holding strength, even though it stands proud of the longitudinals on the inside of the boat. Butt blocks of a softer wood, ¾ inch thick, would not have held the plank ends.

46

I left the sheerstrake clamped overnight before fastening it, to let it soften to the idea.

47

Since the rail areas are vulnerable to damage, the sheerstrakes are bedded and mechanically fastened without the use of glue. This will make future repairs easier. Fungicidal bedding compound is used here.

48

No.12 bronze screws 2 ½ inches long were used to fasten the sheerstrakes to the stem. Bending the forward ends of these mahogany planks was very difficult but did not require the use of steam as with the fir longitudinals (photo 31).

49

After the difficult forward section was completed, the long after plank was bedded and fastened into place, with care being taken to get a good fit of the butt joint.

50

Although the butt blocks did not lie fair with the longitudinals, the added thickness allowed the use of longer screws at the joint.

51

Since the sheerstrakes are thicker than the plywood planking, I didn't just saw them off flush with the stem. Instead, I cut a notch into the ends just wide enough to receive the false stem at the proper time. Alternatively, the sheerstrake thickness can be reduced to that of the plywood here at the stem, increasing to full thickness about 1 foot aft of the stem.

52

Planking panels were purchased in 20 foot lengths so the hull could be planked without joints. The panels were clamped onto the hull and marked for cutting from the inside at the lower edge of the sheerstrake and lower edge of the chine stringer. Both panels were marked this way, then cut to leave a little extra for fitting.

53
Some repeated trial-and-error planing and fitting will probably be necessary where the side panel joins the sheerstrake.

54
The panel is slowly worked down against the sheerstrake by marking the high points and planing until there's an edge-to-edge fit at all points.

55
With one panel fitted and ready to fasten, the excess length must be cut off at the stem to allow the other panel to pass by for fitting.

56
The side panels are so large that any change in their placement fore and aft can alter the fit dramatically. The spacer blocks allow the panel to be planed without unclamping its other edge or altering its position on the boat.

57

Once the fit is good, glue is applied to the longitudinals, and the panels are clamped to the boat for fastening. Along with various alignment markings, I pre-drilled some of the screws holes at random over the length of the panel so that the screws, when driven, would help the panel return to the exact position as before.

58

It is important to clamp the panel tightly into place before fastening.

59

When drilling for screws at the stem, stay close to the after edge of the stem (near the bearding line where the bevel dies out) so that the screw heads don't interfere when it comes time to saw off the panel to length.

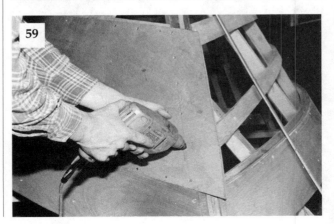

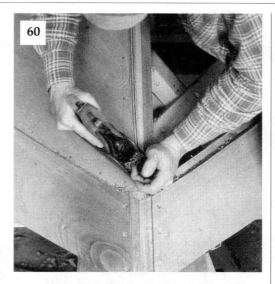

60

Here, the port panel is being planed flush with the stem. Note that the screws have been placed well back of the bearding line.

61

If a power drill is used to drive the screws, it should be a variable-speed type for proper control. Otherwise, the screws can be driven too deeply or stripped.

62

A bit brace, although a little slower than a power tool, provides the best control.

63

The next step is fitting the bottom panels. These are easy to rough-cut by simply laying one of the full 4-foot by 18-foot panels on the boat and clamping it down to follow the contours of the hull. Then, with a pencil, scribe the approximate shape. It is important, however, to leave a good deal of extra material all around, because the fitting of the bottom panels is more complicated than for the topside ones.

I started with the joint at the chine, and, once sure of a good fit there, I marked and cut at the keel. The fit of the chine is unusual and a bit difficult because the bottom miters against the side panel forward and overlaps it aft. Although this is the way most bottom panels are fitted, that reassurance doesn't make this task any easier. There is a lot of trial and error, fitting and planing, needed to produce a good fit. The extreme compound bend and curve near the bow makes this more difficult, and it takes a good deal of force to keep the panel in place. The panel must be bent into place many times while you slowly plane and fit this complicated joint.

From the transom forward to station 3 or 4, there is no problem; the bottom can overhang the side and be trimmed later. But beginning somewhere between stations 3 and 4, a transition to a miter begins. Around station 5 or 6, there should be a full miter that continues all the way to the stem. Actually, the miter becomes more of a butt between the panels as the stem is neared, and the angle between the bottom and the side panels becomes more of a straight line.

64

Here's a tip to aid in making a good fit: use 2 by 3s clamped along the keel with blocks on the ends to bear on the edge being fitted, as shown in the photograph.

65

After both sides are fit, the bottom panels are finally glued and screwed into place. Once set, the overhanging excess is trimmed off at the keel, stem, and transom, and then planed smooth.

66

The outer stem was easily laminated to the right shape using the boat, itself, as a form. Waxed paper protects the hull and keeps the stem from accidentally sticking to it.

67

Laminations of ¼ inch thickness are spread with glue and laid up one on top of another, then temporarily screwed down with drywall screws and with washers to prevent splitting. Clamps are used to keep the pieces aligned.

68

The outer keel (1 ½ inches by 1 ⅜ inches) attaches to the keelson and lies between the edges of the bottom panels. It is joined to the outer stem between stations 5 and 6 with a 2-foot-long, through-bolted scarf joint.

69

Hull turnover is not to be hurried. It should be a slow and careful process, accomplished with the help of friends. Smoothing, puttying, and painting the hull are most easily done beforehand.

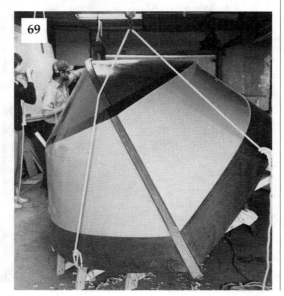

70

Deckbeams are fitted, leaving enough extra wood on the top edges for marking and cutting later. This is the time to dress down the boat's sheer so it is fair and eye-sweet.

71

Using a deck camber template, each beam is marked, removed, then cut on the bandsaw and reinstalled — permanently this time, using glue.

72

The sheer clamp is clamped firmly under the deck-beams and screwed into place for additional support. Then the final camber can be planed, leaving the beams fair and ready to receive the decking.

73

I installed a 1 ½-inch-thick foredeck stiffener, made from a piece that was cut off the transom. I notched both the stiffener and the deckbeam ¾ inch at each juncture to create flush joints the entire length of the foredeck. Once the joints have been glued with epoxy and screwed together, a very rigid structure is created.

74

The small side deckbeams are marked with the same camber template.

75

Any convenient radius will work for marking the beam ends; in this instance, the bottom of an oilcan was used.

76

The finished beams are clamped, glued, and screwed into place.

77

The transom cutout was checked several times against the plans before the cut was made. The upper edges were left square until the decks were laid.

78

Two athwartship beams support the outboard motor well, one beam fastened to the aftermost hull frame and the other attached to the inner face of the transom. For the well to be self-draining, its bottom is pitched downhill toward the stern.

79

Although a well outline is shown on the drawings, its dimensions may have to be varied a bit to accommodate your particular motor. Make sure the well is deep enough and long enough fore-and-aft so that the motor can be fully tilted and be turned from side to side. I cut the after deckbeam to bring the bulkhead (which also serves as the seat back) farther forward, thus enlarging the well.

80

The motorwell framing members were fastened using both glue and screws.

81

Fitting and assembly of the well itself begins with the side walls.

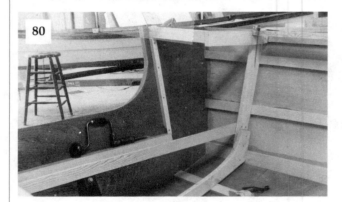

82
Where access is limited, such as in attaching the side walls to the well's bottom panel, bronze ring nails can be substituted for screws. Screws were used, however, in both support beams.

83
Downeaster's floorboards are laid out to produce two long center panels and a single forward panel that are removable, with the juncture between them falling under the forward seat where it is least conspicuous. Be sure all edges of the floorboard panels are well supported by framing members under them, as shown.

84
Running next to the hull, outboard of the two big, removable floorboard panels, are semipermanent panels that are notched around the frames and screwed down with oval-head screws. The center panels are tucked under the rear seat to hold them in position; at their forward ends, under the forward seat, finger holes assist in lifting them up for removal.

85
Screws work best in fastening the deck. A power screwdriver, while not a necessity, is certainly a great convenience.

86

Make very sure the deck framing is fair before you lay the deck itself. Note the carlins running along the inboard ends of the side-deck beams that give the decking continuous support.

87

After the deck is fitted and fastened, the overhanging edges should be planed flush with the carlins, deck-beams, and sheerstrakes. Put a small radius on the upper corners all around the deck edge if you plan to sheath the deck with Dynel.

88

Downeaster's deck was sheathed with two layers of Dynel and epoxy. Although such a sheathing is a builder's option, it adds significantly to the deck's durability. Start by rough-cutting the Dynel to size; stagger the joints in the layers so that one joint doesn't fall directly on top of another.

89

Position the first layer, and saturate it with epoxy poured into a paint tray and spread with a foam roller. Then add the second layer, carefully rolling out entrapped air so that both layers become fully saturated with epoxy. While wet, the Dynel can be slid around, to some extent, by pushing on it with the roller.

90

This shows the second layer of Dynel being placed on the foredeck. Dynel's loose weave allows it to conform with ease to almost any surface and bend around reasonably sharp corners without giving trouble. You should make certain, however, that the Dynel lies flat along turned-over edges to provide good landing for the coamings and guardrails. Generally speaking, creases in Dynel have to be flattened out (sometimes by ironing the cloth) before you lay it; sharp wrinkles or creases in the dry material usually carry through to the finished job, no matter how much epoxy you soak it with or how much you try to pull on the cloth while it's wet.

91

Trimming excess Dynel is easy if you do it at the right time in the epoxy-curing process — that is, when the cure is far enough along to prevent the Dynel from sliding, but not set up hard enough to make peeling away the unwanted excess difficult. Six hours of curing time worked well for me, although this varies with each situation.

92

For best appearance, the hardwood sprayrails should be tapered a bit toward each end; they can be screwed on any time after the hull has been turned upright. I used plain bedding compound, rather than the adhesive type, feeling that removal for possible later replacement would be easier if the sprayrails were not bonded to the hull.

93

Guardrails were similarly installed with screws and bedding compound. It is a good idea to give them an all-over coat of varnish before installation, particularly if they're to be finished bright, thus sealing the wood grain. Otherwise, there's a good chance that the bedding compound may dry prematurely and allow water to get behind the rails, where it can rot or discolor the wood.

94

A ready-to-install, aluminum-framed windshield — as shown on the drawings — can be purchased for Downeaster from one of several retail outlets, or you can build the windshield yourself from wood, as I did. If you decide on wood, start by fitting a two-piece baseplate as shown and fastening it to the deck as a starting point for the windshield.

95

The sills come next; they are screwed to the beveled forward edges of the base pieces.

96

The coamings are cut to fit against both sills and the outer ends of the base pieces. Contact surfaces of all these pieces should be varnished or sealed, then bedded — or, alternatively, they can be epoxy-glued into place.

97

Windshield posts consist of two layers, with the inner layer extending beyond the outer at the bottom for attaching to the sills. A variety of braces and clamps will be needed while fitting the posts to the boat. When viewed from ahead or astern, the sides of the windshield should angle inboard a little; that is, the posts should have tumblehome.

98

This shows what the after sides of the windshield sills and posts look like. A centerline knee, shown under the C-clamp, strengthens the unit.

99

The windshield headers are fitted to the trimmed-off outer layers of the posts and will be fastened to the posts' projecting inner layers in much the same way as at the bottom. Both headers and sills are mitered where they meet at the windshield's centerline.

100

Side braces come next, each one being fitted between the post and the coaming. A laminated mahogany knee was later installed at each top corner for added strength against wracking.

101

The dashboard was first fitted at its ends, then marked along its top edge and cut to match the deckline.

102

Trim strips along the inner edge of the deck will cover the turned-down Dynel. The angle of cut for the trim strip's forward end is being picked up here, using a bevel gauge.

103

The deck-edge trim strips should be clamped into place and checked for fit before being permanently installed. Since these strips are vulnerable to damage, I waited until more of the boat's interior work was completed before installing them permanently.

104

For any pieces, such as a forward seat beam, that don't fall on frame lines (and, therefore, can't be attached directly to frames), support cleats such as this one, are necessary.

105

You'll note here that only one of the seat beams requires a support cleat; the other conveniently lands on a frame and attaches directly to it. Four short fore-and-aft pieces, notched into the seat beams, complete the forward seat's support assembly.

106

The same assembly, looking to port.

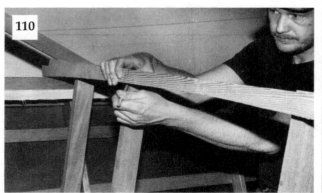

107

Four raking uprights support the seat back. They are attached to a beam as shown, and for a better appearance, I notched them for the seat bottom.

108

This shows the notch and the finished lower end of one of the uprights. Each upright was glued and screwed to the beam.

109

With all four uprights and the seat bottom in place, the unit is just about ready for the seat back.

110

The top edge of the seat back is cut to the same crown as the deckbeams and transom. You can use a leftover deckbeam as a pattern for cutting the uprights and as a guide for marking the seat back itself.

111

Moving now to the after part of the boat, the next task is to fit the seat back, which also forms the forward face of the motor well. Fuel tanks will rest on a small platform (the one I'm standing on) under the after seat.

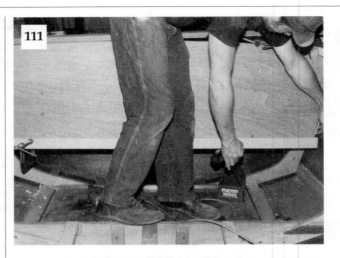

112

The bottom of the after seat is supported by a cleat across the back panel (shown being fitted in photo 111), and by a low bulkhead shown here. Conveniently, this bulkhead, with a support cleat across its upper edge, lands on a frame line.

113

Here is the after seat assembly, fitted and pretty much ready to accept the seat bottom. Note that the top of the seat back is crowned like the deck (and like the forward seat back, described earlier).

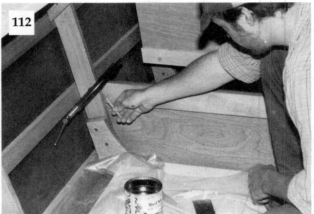

114

The after seat-bottom panel has to be removable for access to the fuel tanks under it.

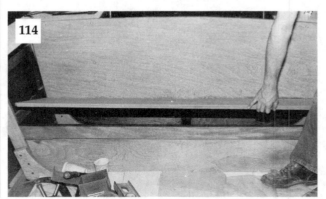

115

One of the last finishing touches is the installation of the toerails, which are shown on the drawings. You should have no trouble at all with them, except possibly at the bow where they originate. Here, you begin by fitting two short, wide pieces upon which the bow chocks will later mount. Make the miter joint along the centerline seam first, allowing for the deck crown so that the pieces will lay snugly against the deck as well as against each other.

116

Although there are several ways to shape and fit the pieces, I simply sawed a graceful curve along the inside edge as shown, and let that curve run out to scarf against the toerails. The matching scarf on the forward end of one of the toerails shows in this photo as well. The toerails, and the bow pieces just mentioned, should be hollowed a bit on their undersides for a tight fit to the deck at their lower corners. It is far easier to do most of the final shaping — along with applying a coat of whatever finish you'll be using — before installation, rather than afterwards.

This wraps up the building of the Downeaster, but here are a few words on finishes and their effect on maintenance:

I recommend that you seriously consider using an oil finish on Downeaster's interior, because with all of the frames, stringers, and other structural members, the interior of the boat will be the most difficult, by far, to maintain. With oil, such as Deks Olje #1, there will be no buildup or peeling of the layers. You will find recoating a relatively easy task, requiring only a light sanding beforehand. Keep paint confined to the less complex surfaces of the boat's exterior. Trim work, such as the seats, the sheerstrakes, the rails, and the windshield, can be oiled like the interior and receive the additional protection of the glossier Deks Olje #2, or an even glossier and more traditional marine varnish applied directly over the bare wood.

Building plans for the Downeaster (plan #400-071) are available from The WoodenBoat Store, P.O. Box 78, Brooklin, Maine 04616. Call 1-800-273-SHIP (7447). The price is $90.

Boatbuilding Books from WoodenBoat Publications

How to Build the Shellback Dinghy
by Eric Dow

Construct a beautiful dinghy following the step-by-step instructions of builder Eric Dow. The Shellback Dinghy is a modern classic with a traditional bow, a narrow rockered bottom, and a sweet transom that lifts well out of the water. Engineered with the amateur builder in mind, the Shellback has a practically frameless interior (there's a single laminated 'midship frame), which also makes her easy to clean and paint. The glued-lapstrake construction means she won't dry out when stored out of water for long periods of time.
Product #325-040
64 pp., illus., softcover
$15.00 ISBN 937822-27-2

How to Build the Haven 12 ½-Footer
by Maynard Bray

Developed by Joel White for a client who loved the Herreshoff 12½ but required a shallow draft, the Haven 12½ is a keel/centerboard variation of the original. This book will show you how to construct her using the same process used to build the original Herreshoffs in Bristol, Rhode Island. She's built upside down, with a mold for every frame. No lofting is required. Each step in this unique process is carefully explained and illustrated, which, with detailed construction plans (not included), provides a thorough guide for advanced amateurs.
Product #325-077
64 pp., illus., softcover
$15.00 ISBN 937822-13-2

Building the Nutshell Pram
by Maynard Bray

A step-by-step manual for the construction of this very popular Joel White design, for oar and sail. This revised instruction book is beneficial for anyone who wishes to build the pram from scratch using WoodenBoat's full-scale plans. Includes a listing of tools, materials, and fastenings, and more than 100 step-by-step photographs. Describes setting up, building, and fitting out the hull; constructing and installing the daggerboard trunk; making the rudder; rigging the pram for sail; and sailing techniques.
Product #325-035
32 pp., illus., softcover
$7.95 ISBN 937822-11-6

How to Build the Catspaw Dinghy:
A Boat for Oar and Sail
by the Editors of WoodenBoat

A detailed manual on the building of a superior rowing and sailing dinghy. A modified version of the famous Herreshoff Columbia model dinghy, this boat, which measures 12' 8", makes an excellent project for the boatbuilder with intermediate skills. It is fitted with a centerboard and a simple sprit rig, and is built carvel style over steam-bent frames. The boat can be built right out of this guide (although using the plans is recommended), which contains carefully illustrated step-by-step building instructions, and reduced lines, offsets, construction plan, and sail plan.
Product #325-010
32 pp., illus., softcover
$8.95 ISBN 937822-36-1

Forty Wooden Boats

by the Editors of WoodenBoat

Our study plans catalogs are best-sellers because they allow you to compare and contrast a variety of designs and building techniques along with providing vital statistics. Information includes beam, length, sail area, suggested engine, alternative construction methods, skill level needed (ranked by beginner, intermediate or advanced builder), level of detail provided in each plan, plus thought-provoking commentary.

Some of the 40 designs include L. Francis Herreshoff's ROZINANTE, Brewer's Mystic Sharpie, 5 kayaks built in a variety of methods (including a double-kayak), a canoe, 2 peapods (one of traditional plank-on-frame construction, the other glued-lap plywood), a catamaran, daysailers, a single and double rowing shell, skiffs, mahogany runabouts from the boards of Nelson Zimmer and Ken Bassett, and many more. The reader will find a tremendous amount of information at their fingertips at a very low price. These are the newest designs added to WoodenBoat's collection since the publication of *Fifty Wooden Boats* and *Thirty Wooden Boats*.

Product #325-062
96 pp., illus., softcover
$12.95 ISBN 937822-32-9

Fifty Wooden Boats

by the Editors of WoodenBoat

This popular book contains details usually found with study plans: hull dimensions, displacement, sail area, construction methods, and the degree of boatbuilding skill needed to complete each project. Along with the 50 designs—which range from a 7' 7" pram to a 41' 3" schooner— there are drawings that identify the parts of a wooden boat, a bibliography, a guide for the selection of various woods, and instructions by Weston Farmer on reading boat plans. Unlike most plans catalogs, *Fifty Wooden Boats* also contains lines that let you see the hulls' shapes.

Product #325-060
112 pp., illus., softcover
$12.95 ISBN 937822-07-8

Thirty Wooden Boats

by the Editors of WoodenBoat

More study plans selected by the Editors of *WoodenBoat*. This volume describes the designs that were added to our collection after the publication of *Fifty Wooden Boats*.

These 30 designs include: 6 powerboats, 6 daysailers, 11 cruising boats, 2 canoes, a kayak, and 4 small sailing/pulling boats. Also included is an article by designer Joel White on understanding boat plans.

Product #325-061
80 pp., illus., softcover
$12.95 ISBN 937822-15-9

The WoodenBoat Store
P.O. Box 78 • Brooklin, ME 04616-0078
Call Toll-Free U.S. & Canada: 1–800–273–SHIP (7447)